The Reluctant Traveller

Marjorie P. Dunn

Best wishes
Marjorie P. Dunn

The **Hallamshire** Press
1997

Cover picture: Detail from *The Town Old* by N. Whittock
Reproduced by kind permission of
Sheffield City Council Leisure Services Directorate (Arts and Museums).

© Marjorie P. Dunn 1997

Published by The Hallamshire Press
The Hallamshire Press is an Imprint of
Interleaf Productions Limited
Broom Hall
8–10 Broomhall Road
Sheffield S10 2DR
UK

Typeset by Interleaf Productions Limited
Printed in Great Britain by The Cromwell Press, Wiltshire

British Library Cataloguing in Publication Data
A catalogue record for this book is available from the British Library

ISBN 1 874718 51 2

Preface

*T*he *Reluctant Traveller*, whilst being a novel in its own right is also a sequel to *The T'alli Stone* and settles many questions left unanswered in that book.

This is John's story: The trials and tribulations of a man transported to Australia in 1817 for a crime he did not commit, his sojourn in North America, and eventual return to South Yorkshire 27 years later. Here, his enforced reappearance under an assumed name causes great upheaval in the lives of complete strangers and for the son who accompanies him. From the moment of his return, attired in the black frock-coat and stove-pipe hat of a distrusted and feared Mormon, he is haunted by the past. He strives to unravel the problems originating from his previous stay in Sheffield, but the effect on a well respected local family almost tears them apart with suspicion, love and prejudice. There are many interesting twists and surprises in this moving tale set in the Sheffield of the 1840s. It is also the story of a proud young woman who was willing to defy convention for her beliefs.

The Reluctant Traveller is a work of fiction, but some historical characters have been borrowed and given dialogue to suit the author's tale. Two books are recommended for further study of the beginning of the Australian wool producing industry and of North America's early cotton manufacturing.

John Macarthur by M.H. Ellis (Angus & Robertson 1955).

Industrial Genius Samuel Slater by Lewis S. Milner (Julian Messner 1968).

To Kurt and Heather

Acknowledgements

I am grateful to Sheffield Libraries and Information Services' Local Studies Library and Sheffield Archives for allowing use of research material, and also the Public Record Office, Kew, for allowing use of ship's log books for research. Grateful thanks also to Philip Marshall and to my husband Bob for their help.

Chapter 1

1844

The rattle of the bright yellow coaches of the Sheffield and Rotherham Railway drowned out all other sounds as the train slowed almost to a halt before approaching the Wicker Station. Adam Johnson reflected on the last and only other journey which he had made to Sheffield, some twenty six years before. Rows of tiny terraced houses now covered the once open fields where he had walked freely, and in the distance the old town looked even dirtier and gloomier than he remembered.

Adam fingered his rustic beard which half covered his bronzed face. It was a mature face showing all the signs of his arduous fifty years on earth, but his eyes were still clear and alert.

Everything about him had changed, not only his looks but his beliefs. The years had seen him grow stockier and he no longer walked with the jauntiness of youth, yet his carriage was that of a man of purpose. The hardships of convict labour had humbled him and scarred his body and soul. Even his name had changed, he rarely thought of himself as John Andrews the idealistic radical, the man who had sought refuge from injustice in this grubby town, which had later so cruelly despatched him to the other side of the world.

As a young man he had not wanted to come to Sheffield but the town had at least given him shelter from the Nottingham Constables who sought to curb his rebellious fervour. Then, he had arrived, ill, in the bitter cold of winter, on a jolting stage coach, grateful only for the chance to escape the damp of his uncle's cellar where he had been concealed. There were times when he had been happy in this town, and times of great tribulation but his greatest joy had come from Fanny. Poor Fanny, their dream shattered by circumstances beyond their control, yet in spite of the intervening years, his marriage and four children, he had never forgotten her. The endless hours of desolation on the New South Wales sheep station had almost destroyed him and the bitterness of his situation had eaten deep into his faith. The Mayor of Nottingham had failed him completely, forgetting the promise he had made to help clear his name, until in the end he had been forced to serve seven years of transportation for a crime which he had not committed.

He had not wanted to return to Sheffield but he had been ordered to come, or rather chosen, by the Elders of his Church. He was here in

England to convert souls to the Church which he had adopted and loved dearly. They had considered that his familiarity with Sheffield would be an advantage in his proselytizing, but he thought his past experiences in the town might prove otherwise. He would have preferred to labour in a place more deserving of the sacrifice he and his family at home had made, but he felt duty bound to come. However, he consoled himself with the knowledge that there were many souls in this iniquitous town in need of salvation, and also some who deserved the opportunity to find a better way of life in America.

The train finally slowed to a halt at the platform, and as the jolting carriages shook the passengers violently in their seats, Adam braced himself for the sudden stop. When all was finally still, he took hold of his carpetbag and prepared to meet his past. The tall young man travelling with him rose simultaneously and broke the silence between them.

'Father, at long last I feel that I will learn and understand something of the misery which you must have felt when you were forced to leave England.' Luke watched his father, noting the blank look on his face. 'Does it distress you?' he asked, unaware of the turmoil in Adam's heart and mind.

The youth's words had interrupted his gloomy thoughts, and he was glad to return to the present. Placing his hand reassuringly on his son's shoulder, he said, 'Those days are long behind me now, son! We are here to show people a new way of life and bring them to God. This is a test for me too, and a test of my faith! The Elders were not aware of the details of my past so I feel this is a proving ground, d' you see?' His voice was firm, belaying his own doubts. He noted with satisfaction that the youth gripped the leather-bound Bible closely with his free hand. He was proud of his son. It had been a long time before he himself had been tempted to read the Bible, but in the end it had been his salvation. That, together with his new identity and family were all that he lived for, it was his sole purpose for being here today, and was the source from which he drew his strength. 'We must find lodgings for the night before attempting to find our associates,' he stated, urging Luke along. 'There's an old coaching Inn by the Haymarket that had a good reputation, perhaps they will have room for us.' He led his son in the direction of the old *Tontine Inn* and was amazed as they passed through what was once the old Assembly Green to see the new development and building which had taken place over the years. Unfamiliar, ugly tenements and shops now lined the unusually wide street which led to the bridge over which he had often walked in his youth. This broad road reminded him of home, but once over the bridge, more nostalgic sights met his eyes, and he was appalled by the strength of feeling which rose in his breast after so many years. He fought down his panic, and although he knew that he was being foolish, refused to look towards the town gaol.

The *Tontine Inn* stood before him, deserted and shabby, and he caught the sleeve of a passer-by, 'Excuse me sir, can you spare me a moment?' he asked, raising his tall black hat from his head politely. 'What has happened to the old *Tontine Inn*?' He was aware of the curiosity in the other man's eyes and knew that his long black frock-coat and tall hat must make him a strange sight.

The man shook his head, 'The railway came and it wasn't long after that the *Tontine* became disused, in fact it is about to be pulled down'. Seeing the traveller's amazement, the man smiled, 'Been away long have you?'

The once-familiar accent in the man's voice brought memories flooding back to Adam. The man made to depart but Adam forced himself to speak. 'Remarkable! Things change so much,' he stated, recovering his composure. 'The place used to bustle with activity. I don't suppose you can recommend a respectable, low-priced place of accommodation can you?' then added, 'I would be most obliged.'

'There is a lodging house in Church Street, run by a Mrs Fisher. If she can't take you I'm sure she'll be able to recommend an alternative.' The man doffed his hat and renewed his journey. 'My thanks, and good day to you.' Adam called out after him.

They had no difficulty in locating the Fisher lodging house, where they found the proprietress friendly, the establishment clean and the charges acceptable, but the room into which she ushered Adam was small and overlooked the Parish Church. Adam was grateful that the night provided a dark screen, for beyond the window lay scenes which would have aroused poignant memories.

Mrs Fisher had no objections to providing a hot meal in spite of the lateness of the hour, for she never missed the opportunity to earn a little more money. She retired immediately to the kitchen leaving the two travellers to settle in. Although she was used to having strangers in her house, Mrs Fisher had an insatiable curiosity about each one. Today's guests were undoubtedly foreigners, with their strange attire and unusual manners, yet they spoke English like natives. Musing as she busied herself, she reflected that there were more foreigners coming to the town these days although few found their way to her establishment, preferring instead the hospitality of the Inns. No doubt, with a discreet question here and a gentle hint there, she would learn more throughout the evening for her method and charm usually proved quite fruitful.

In spite of Adam's resolve to keep the past to himself he found himself admitting to Mrs Fisher that he had indeed been to the town before, and from that moment on he found it difficult to satisfy her curiosity. The questions were harmless enough but she too had that same local accent which not only reminded him of Fanny, but disturbed his peace of mind. He had never told anyone of his affair with Fanny, not even the Church Elders, and perhaps that had been his biggest mistake. Guilt made him glance at his son; he was afraid that Luke might notice his unease, but Luke was content to satisfy his hunger and converse with Mrs Fisher.

As soon as it was possible, without being impolite, Adam left the table and sought sanctuary in his own room. Luke soon followed but sensing his father's weariness, he retired also, leaving Adam alone with his thoughts.

Sleep eluded Adam as he fought off an overwhelming desire to get up and walk the streets in search of peace. Each time he closed his eyes he was haunted by the past. He lay there praying for sleep to come until, in the end, he climbed down from the lumpy comfortless bed and walked to the window. That too was a mistake for there in the gloom he could see the tall spire of the church rising above the railings and beyond those he knew lay reminders of his past. He had consciously avoided looking towards the houses of York Street which they had passed on the way to Mrs Fisher's, although he had glanced keenly to where his former employer's shop had been on the High Street. Sadly, Webster's was no longer there; its original frontage had been altered considerably over the years and the present occupier was not even in the printing trade. There was no sign of a printers in the High Street now and he found himself wondering what had happened to the old firm.

Adam left the window and, bending his head wearily, sank to his knees in misery and sought his God.

'Oh, God!' he pleaded, 'Make me, Thy humble servant, strong enough not to disappoint Thee. Keep me mindful of Thy work and forgive me my weaknesses so that I may do all that Thou requirest of me, I pray, for I am merely flesh and blood and need Thy strength to sustain me. I am so far from my dear family and as a stranger in this alien place, let my mind think only of bringing souls into Thy Kingdom. In Jesus' name, Amen!'

He rose, seemingly calmed, and climbed back into bed. Tossing and turning he finally sank into a fitful sleep, but the face of Fanny came constantly to him, giving him no rest. In his restlessness he became entwined in the bed sheets and the more he twisted the more the sheet became ravelled around his neck, forming a noose. As it tightened the old nightmare came flooding back. He was John Andrews again.

Chapter 2
1818

The chains bit deeply into his neck as the man in front stumbled on the slippery, muddy road; John Andrews winced with pain. They were merely two of the many convicted men being marched on the long journey from York Gaol to the prison hulks lying in Langstone harbour, before their transportation to New South Wales.

The pain and humiliation of it all, his mind cried bitterly. He was nothing now, just a scrap of humanity without a future and fit only to be gawked at by mocking crowds of bystanders. These watched, grinning through their blackened or missing teeth as the prisoners marched by.

John drew the collar of his soiled shirt up under the rusty chain to where it had been before the man in front had slipped, almost choking him, and the coolness of the linen momentarily soothed the soreness of his neck. They had walked now for six days, passing Doncaster, the nearest point to Sheffield, and he thanked God that there was no chance that Fanny could have seen him in his plight. His clothes were becoming dirtier and more unkempt with each passing day and his body weary from the monotonous plodding of the march. His spirits were low as the cold winds brought heavy rains which numbed his limbs, making it difficult for him to co-ordinate his body movements. He was jerked constantly from both front and back by the other men in the crocodile, for if one man stumbled then every man in the line suffered from the snatching of the chains.

In the distance he saw the dark spire of a church, and the winding river which stretched out before him seemed to lead like a path up to its door. Normally he had no time for religion but today he would have willingly taken refuge within that Church. They had reached the outskirts of Derby.

The guard up ahead reined in. 'Halt!' he bellowed harshly at the weary line of men in his charge. 'Rest on the bank before we enter the town!'

Relieved at the opportunity to sit, John lowered himself down slowly onto the cold, muddy ground. His hands were numbed and blistered from supporting the heavy rusty chain and he rubbed them in the cool smooth mud in order to ease the pain.

As the clanking of chains ceased and silence settled over the men, John looked around him. This was his world, the river and the trees, not the hideous nightmare of the past months in gaol. A bird chirped merrily from a branch overhanging the water, reminding him of home. Was it possible that he might never see this peaceful countryside again? Would he never see his Fanny again, or the heather and valleys that he had grown to love? He thanked God that he had protected Fanny, by refusing to name her as the woman with him in the market place, at the time of his arrest. The wig which she had worn had concealed her identity well. Gervase had been right to warn him not to expose Fanny to the dangers surrounding his political activities, but he had not listened. She at least was safe.

Gervase Webster had been his friend as well as his employer, and had warned him yet again before the trial that a great deal of contrived evidence was stacked against him. All through the trial he had watched the reaction of the older man, waiting for signs of hope and encouragement, but he could tell from his friends deeply furrowed brow that things weren't going too well. He had been conspired against from the start in an act of revenge by the vicious overseer that he had denounced for cruelty against a child worker in the man's employ. At least his action had saved the life of the child who had been beaten and maimed by the overseer, yet from his own gaol the man had taken part revenge by having John beaten senseless in a dark alley one night. Months later someone had also instigated a plot to frame John, and although he had no proof he was sure that the overseer was behind this as well.

Nor was he convinced that this was the complete story, for the court had touched on his radical history and a letter which had been passed quietly to the Magistrate seemed to add the final straw to the prosecution. All hope finally died when the harsh sentence was pronounced. He had looked beseechingly across at Gervase, but his friend sat stunned, head bent and shoulders sagging, unable to face him across the courtroom.

He had simply been got rid of! They had taken the opportunity to rid England of one more rebel, one more man who did more than just sympathise with the down-trodden workers. For that, he had been sentenced to seven years banishment from those he loved.

As he waited, looking down in to the river, his mouth was dry and the flagon seemed to take for ever to come down the line of prisoners. New South Wales was reported to be hot and parched and here he was now, already longing for water. He took a mouthful and drank deeply before passing the vessel on. 'Thanks!' he muttered. He needed food too, not the slop served up by the guards but good solid victuals. 'Where are we now?' he ventured to ask, needing to talk and catching the eye of the passing guard.

'Derby!' came the short reply, 'Don't worry, you've a long way to go yet!' He regretted his sharpness. They were merely prisoners yet he was well aware of the consequences of getting too familiar, for most would take advantage of the slightest softening. Poor devils, they would be better off dead than going to the hulks! He rejoined the other guards who squatted round the wagon and promptly forgot his misgivings.

The longer John sat, huddled forlornly amidst the other prisoners on the wet bankside, the lonelier he became; he reached instinctively into the pocket of his jacket and withdrew the silver ornamented flute which no-one had attempted to confiscate at the time of his arrest.

Too late he remembered the risk he took in revealing that he carried something of value, for he was inviting envy and theft. He could hardly put the instrument back into his pocket now, someone had seen it; he raised the instrument defiantly to his lips and played softly. Complete exposure might possibly ensure safekeeping.

The gentle sound drifted out over the water and along the bankside, slowly and sadly echoing his mood. He was unaware of the stirring and interest amongst the bedraggled prisoners until a voice cut through the melody.

'Hey, you! Play something livelier, it's not a bloomin' funeral.'

Hitherto John had eyed his fellow travellers without feeling or emotion, so consumed had he been with self-pity and bitterness; now however he saw them for what they really were, simply men without hope. He let the music take on a lilting rhythm and the sound of humming broke out along the chain of weary men. Before long it seemed as if the men were sharing some desperate escape from their misery.

'Quiet, there!' a guard shouted, 'Quiet, I say!'

Ignoring the order, John continued to play, his spirits lifting as the men's voices rose higher, much to the irritation of the guard. For a few brief moments they forgot their ragged clothes and dirty bodies and joined in. The guard rose to shout again.

'Sit down, Henry. They'll never hear you! Besides, what harm does it do?' came the voice of the guard who had answered John's questions earlier. 'They'll make better time on the march if they're in better spirits, then we'll be rid of them that much quicker'.

'You'll be suggesting that I remove their chains next,' came the terse reply. 'I just hope you're right! I reckon that it doesn't pay to give concessions.' He fought to restrain his irritation and after five minutes stood up. 'Get them off their backsides and let's march them through the town!' he ordered. 'Blow that horn, and start them moving!'

John placed the flute reluctantly back into his pocket, and, conscious of having exposed his most precious possession to the eyes of a gang of thieves and ruffians, vowed to be cautious when sleeping and keep it close to his person.

At each resting place the men demanded that he played his flute; they cared not whether he was tired and weary when it was the only pleasure they were likely to have. In the evenings before they slept in their makeshift beds, in barns or the dark and dank cells of local prisons, they insisted on his playing. It satisfied him to play radical songs, much to

11

the displeasure of the guards, and it helped to while away the hours.

With a hundred and fifty miles already behind them, and an improvement in the weather conditions, John found that he was now more able to accept his fate. It was not that he was unaccustomed to walking for miles on end but the circumstances and his chains spoilt what previously had always been a pleasure. He whiled away the hours by studying the countryside through which they passed, endeavouring to name each leaf and flower that he saw, as he had done with Gervase and Fanny whilst walking on the moors around Sheffield. Then, they had done it to please her, and John now allowed himself the luxury of imagining that they were still by his side.

It was the towns which irked his sense of pride and frustrated him the most. He had long since abandoned his defiant cries to uncaring crowds, that he was innocent. Not one of them cared a hoot whether he was innocent or not, to them he was merely a diversion from life's humdrum monotony. His first protestations had brought jeers from the crowds and the prisoners had pulled sharply at the chains, wrenching at his neck. 'Stop making a soddin' spectacle of us!' one yelled. 'We're all bloody innocent, every goddam one of us! Shut your mouth or the guards won't like it!' he had then hissed at John.

The second time he had protested the other prisoners had all joined in, shouting, 'We're innocent!' The laughing crowds had loved this, much to the annoyance of the guards who stopped the crocodile and bullied the prisoners into sullen obedience. John had been prodded viciously with the butt of a musket and, as a result of the incident, the prisoners were deprived of their next ration of food, causing great resentment amongst them. They had even refused to talk to him and twice he had been deliberately kicked as he tried to sleep. In the end John acknowledged that no-one cared whether he was innocent or not, so for his own safety, he kept his own counsel. Only the flute had brought him respite and ease, and he knew that whilst he kept the prisoners amused he was safe.

For a few precious miles during the latter part of the journey they travelled by wagon, but this good fortune was short-lived when the vehicles were requisitioned to take female convicts to the port.

He could smell the sea long before it came into sight. This brought with it a feeling of exhilaration, as the salty tang temporarily offered relief from the stench of the sweating bodies around him. Perhaps, after all, things would not be quite as bad once they were at sea.

Breathing deeply of the fresh clean air, he trudged on. He had always dreamed that some day he might leave these shores for America, but the Americas were now beyond his reach and the prison hulks lay waiting out in the harbour. He was bitter as he viewed the row of ugly, dilapidated ships which were without sail, rigging or pride, moored against the mud banks exposed by the outgoing tide, for it was the manner of his leaving England which outraged him. John shivered suddenly, in spite of the warmth of the early evening air as he looked towards the rotting tombs that had once been proud vessels.

By the time evening was drawing to a close, they had reached the dock area where few people tarried on the almost deserted quay sides, yet from the taverns the bawdy voices of drinkers rang out in the still, evening air. Those outside were quite unconcerned at the familiar sight of marching convicts, and did no more than grimace at the sound of their clanking chains.

It appeared to John that he had no sooner reached the quay steps than a long-boat approached, into which he was forced, chains and all. Soon the enormous stinking hulk of a prison ship loomed over him, allowing him little time to appreciate his first, but short, sea journey. He was ill-prepared for the feeling of despair which struck deep into his mind as he stood on deck, for the ship was not only old and unseaworthy, it reeked of human neglect. Removal of the heavy iron collar and chains seriously affected his balance, and like the rest of the men he was forced to kneel on the deck until the giddiness ceased.

The guards ordered the convicts to take off their filthy stinking clothes, and then directed them to the washing tubs. The feel of the cold sea water on his tired, dusty limbs soothed him greatly, but he wasn't sure whether to be grateful for the wash, or resentful of the humiliating display he made before his companions. A set of grey convict trousers and shirt were thrust into his hands, but there was no towel with which to dry himself so he quickly covered himself with the rough, itchy clothes, which soon soaked up the water on his body.

John stood barefooted and apprehensive on the creaking boards of the deck, awaiting the fitting of ankle irons to which a chain was attached. He felt ensnared, like a rabbit. In panic he glanced around in those final moments before the chain was fitted, but it was no use, there was nowhere to escape to.

Finally, he was forced with everyone else down into the bowels of the hulk, and the stench which reached his nostrils made him gasp for air. The foul, fetid atmosphere enveloped him, causing waves of nausea to well up from the depths of his stomach. The ladders seemed never-ending as he climbed down through deck after deck, until deep-seated fears of the unknown beset him.

A harsh voice rang out from above, 'Get a move on, scum, or I'll shake you off the ladder. Find yourself a bunk and stay there.'

Endeavouring to co-ordinate the movement of his feet with the chain caused John to stumble and almost fall from the ladder. In his haste he trod

13

on the fingers of the man beneath him who bombarded him with a tirade of abuse. 'Stupid bastard—watch where you're putting your feet...' The rest of his words were lost to John as he struggled to regain his balance whilst muttering an apology.

At last the lowest deck was reached and he peered into the gloom, trying to get his bearings. There were feet kicking at him now as another prisoner attempted to reach the bottom, so John groped along the rough planks, feeling his way carefully. Slowly, with eyes becoming accustomed to the dark, he saw rows of cluttered cells, seemingly crammed with lifeless figures. 'No room!' yelled a voice as John tried to enter first one cell, then another. The slumped figures on the bunks made no attempt to greet him, finally John stretched out a hand to see if one of the bottom left-hand bunks was really empty.

'Not here, on top!' A feeble voice cried from the darkness.

Hoisting himself up onto the spare bunk, he found little room for his body. He was not a tall man, but the bunk was short even for him, and there was such little room above his head that he could not sit up in comfort. He lay there in his cramped position, hoping for a word of welcome or comfort from the other occupants, but none was uttered. Finally he called out in desperation, hoping that he could find answers to some of his questions. Again there was no reply until, after what seemed hours in the humid, putrid dungeon he tried once more to find another human soul willing to help him. 'When do we eat?' he ventured hesitatingly.

'We've eaten already—breakfast is at five!' The voice was not unfriendly when it came, but weary and final.

'When do we sail?' he dared to ask. He could make out the shaking head of the man in the bunk across the narrow divide.

'We don't!' At least the man was making an effort to speak. 'I've been here for months, just waiting for a ship to come. They only sail in spring and summer now, and time is going on. There is a ship in but you'll be lucky to sail in her. She's been there for days and nothing's moved yet. Each day we hope and pray for our turn to come—but it never does. Some men have been here for years.'

'Aw, shut it will you!' a voice called out of the darkness.

'Leave him alone!' another called out, 'He can probably give us some fresh news!'

The man opposite turned his body with seeming difficulty and said simply, 'They've all had a hard day out in the dockyards. Take no notice—let them rest.'

Hearing the sympathetic voice, John tried again, 'Do we have to wear these infernal chains all the time?' The man grunted in affirmation. 'God!' John sighed, 'I'm glad that walk is over.'

'Walking's nothing! It's working out there for hours on end until you're too tired to sleep, then coming back into this stinking hell-hole that breaks a man.' Suddenly the voice ceased, breaking into a chesty cough and John let the man be. When the coughing and gasping had subsided, the man continued, 'Where are you from?'

'I'm from Sheffield now, but I came from Nottingham originally.'

'Where's your home?'

'Saddleworth.'

'Oh!' He wanted to keep the man talking and dredged his mind for something to say. 'This place stinks!' he said with disgust. 'Is it always this bad?'

'It gets worse when they batten down the hatches, then when the privies overflow, you can't see what you're walking in and there's filth slopping everywhere.'

Nausea welled up from the pit of John's stomach but he fought it down because he had no idea in which direction the latrine lay. 'When do we go up top?' he begged feebly.

'You won't see daylight again 'til seven in the morning. You eat, sleep and maybe die down here.' The man's voice was weary, as if too tired to talk anymore.

Not wanting to lose what little human contact he had, John tried again. 'I'm John—John Andrews. What's your name?' He turned, but the cot was so small that he banged his head on the beam above. He then tried to stretch out his legs but found this impossible. He was trapped, unable to move more than a few inches, and unable to breathe for the foul stench. He could only imagine the tangy smell of the sea, for he could neither smell nor see it now! Within the hold he could hear men moaning, seemingly from habit more than need, and the constant clanking of their chains as they moved distressed John.

Suddenly, with great effort, the other man spoke again. 'My name is Wills, short for William.'

John knew that there were two other men within the cramped cell, which could not have been more than six foot square, but neither said a word. 'Who are the others?'

A grunt left the lips of one man but the other remained silent. Wills answered quietly. 'I shouldn't bother them—they live in a world of their own. Like Abe who was in your bed—he got as he couldn't take any more and pretty well stopped eating. The work out there finished him off.' There was little emotion in Wills' voice. 'It's a fact of life down in the hulks, you survive, or die, or go mad.'

Slowly at first, then more frequently, the ship began to move as the waves of the incoming tide hit the side and once more John's empty stomach heaved, whether from sickness or hunger he wasn't completely sure, 'Does it steady down soon?'

'Wait till there's bad weather and the water comes in, you'll wish you'd never heard of the sea.'

A loud sliding noise overhead drowned out Wills' voice, and all natural light disappeared. The heavy thud of bolts being drawn into place raised a groan within the hold. 'They're battening down the hatches now, and nobody goes up or comes down again 'til morning, no matter what,' Wills explained.

'You mean we're entombed in this godforsaken hole all night?' John could hardly believe his ears.

''Fraid so! You never get used to it, or the squeaking of rotten timbers, nor the patter of the rats which infest every corner. This ship isn't fit to hold anything, let alone people.' He was whispering now and John noticed that nobody else spoke.

'Where do you put your clothes? I'll have to take off this itchy shirt.' John whispered back.

'You don't!' replied the other man.

'What!' exclaimed John in horror, 'I can't sleep in this.'

'You take it off and that's the last you'll see of it, even if you put it under your head. This place is alive with thieves, or someone will swap it for a torn one. If you've anything valuable keep it concealed on your person or you'll lose it.' He turned away in an effort to get comfortable. 'Get some sleep, if you can, it's hard work in the daytime.'

'Thanks', said John gratefully. At least there was someone trying to help him, someone willing to talk, and he lay staring into the blackness endeavouring to make sense of his world. He no longer felt like a man, it was as though his mind, as well as his body, was imprisoned in a fragile shell, tossed to and fro on the dark, murky and engulfing water. He shivered. All night he battled to find a position in which his legs did not seize-up with cramp, all night he tried to ease the numbness which overtook his thighs and shoulders on the hard boards. His feet moved but the restraining chains did not and soon his ankles were chafed and sore. Many times during the night he felt like screaming into the blackness to prove to himself that it was not a dream.

He woke once with a feeling of terror as some insect or other crept across his flesh beneath the shirt, and he knew that it was not the only thing which shared his bed. He lay there afraid to open his mouth for fear that something would creep in, and with every slight itch from the coarse material he imagined some creature eating away at his flesh. This nightmare filtered through into his dreams, but he did not remain asleep long enough for his monsters to devour him. At one point in a dream he awoke bathed in sweat, thinking a giant rat was on the point of gnawing at his foot, only to find that the pressure of the chain against his toe had disturbed him.

At last the hatch slid back, waking him, and as the light shafted down into the hold his spirits rose considerably. Nothing, he decided, could ever be as bad again as the night which he had just spent. With difficulty he attempted to climb down from the bunk. Both his legs had to go in the same direction at once and because of the chain between his ankle irons he still could not do it. It was all he could do to lower both legs at once and allow his body to tumble after them to the floor. He narrowly missed banging his head on Wills' bunk as he went.

'You'll get the knack of it soon enough,' said Wills, 'and you'll learn not to rush at any task from now on!'

John realised that with four men manoeuvring within the tiny compartment it would not be long before they would get on his nerves, and he sought to escape the pressure by going to the privy. How it stank, and how he longed to go up on deck into the fresh air!

'What time is it?' mumbled one of the men who had remained uncommunicative the night before, as John returned to the cell.

'About six,' he mumbled, afraid to admit to having a watch in his possession.

'The boats come alongside about seven no matter what the weather. Where's the morning slop?' the other demanded.

Suddenly there was a movement along the gangway. A man approached their cell and thrust a bowl at each man in turn. It was tasteless, watered down gruel, the likes of which John had never eaten before. Wills watched him as he toyed with the spoon. 'Get it down you. There'll be nothing else, only a tack biscuit.'

The sharp tang of the salty morning air met John as he raised his head above the hatchway. He breathed in deeply. A blanket of low mist hung over the bay, causing the early morning to be cold and unfriendly as he followed the other convicts to the wash tubs. He had expected to see wide-open stretches of water, sunshine and freedom after the hateful night, but the clinging mist formed yet another prison. The salty washing-water felt sticky, dashing his hopes of rinsing from his mouth the vile taste of the slops which he had eaten. He had heeded Wills' warning and forced the 'food' down, in spite of the fact that it made him want to heave; he had been hungry, and still was.

Every task he performed became an arduous battle with his chains which restricted the simplest of movements and slowed him down. The shackling of his feet was in fact worse than the previous harnessing of his neck and tears of frustration and anger welled up in his eyes. He felt controlled, in both mind and body, by unseen powers and his will to survive was weakening.

Several long-boats drew up alongside the hulk and the prisoners were forced to climb down the precarious, rough wooden ladders fixed to the ship's side in order to descend into the smaller bobbing boats. Watching carefully as the more experienced prisoners climbed down first, John then tried to copy their movements, at the same time making sure that he stuck as closely as possible to Wills. But conversation for the pair was both difficult and tiresome, he had to be content in the knowledge that at least he had one friend on the hulk.

By noon of the first day he was already weary. His hands, which were unaccustomed to the heavy manual work of the dockyards, were bruised and blistered. The guards, one to every twenty men, watched the labouring gangs with relentless vigilance, clubs at the ready, missing nothing. They seemed to enjoy giving out punishment or shouting needlessly, to ensure the gruelling work never ceased. In the main they were callous men, uncaring and poorly paid, consumed by the power which they wielded over the convicts.

Even from a distance the sound of their chains could be heard as the exhausted men heaved the heavy ballast and stones. John became careless in his weariness and the chains more irksome, causing him to stumble frequently, and when finally he tripped and fell, he was too exhausted to lift himself up. Fortunately the noon break was signalled so he dragged himself up onto the nearest stone. He now had an hour to rest his tired, aching limbs, and to eat the offering which was his meal. The mist had lifted, allowing the heat of the day to add to his misery and discomfort. Not a word was spoken as the men devoured every morsel of their allowance of food, and John's only comfort was in looking forward to his evening reunion with Wills again, for they had been assigned to different gangs. It was only when John remembered the conditions in the stinking hold that his spirits plummeted once more, taking away all his anticipated pleasure. The afternoon became a painful nightmare.

The beauty of the setting sun was wasted on him for he could hardly stand, and the agony caused by walking was excruciating. His battered hands were bleeding and he could barely support the chains to his feet as he shuffled back to the long-boat. The need to lie down was overwhelming and no matter what he did, there was no relief. It would have taken little persuasion for him to jump into the sea and let his body sink into oblivion for all time. Dazed, he lowered his hand over the side and the salt water stung his raw hands so much that he nearly cried. By the time his boat reached the hulk he no longer cared for anything, not even the prospect of another revolting meal that would be his supper.

The stink from the hulk made him feel ill even before he had climbed through the hatchway, and he now lay in agony and despair on his bunk, understanding completely why the other men in his compartment had not wanted to talk to him the night before. He was almost relieved that the gang to which Wills had been assigned had not returned, for he was too exhausted to talk.

When eventually Wills returned it was some time before either man acknowledged the other. It was Wills who finally broke the long silence, as John strove to move and ease his aching limbs. 'Is it bad, lad?' he asked sympathetically, and waited for an answer which didn't come. 'It's hard, and tonight will be hell. By tomorrow it will be worse, but then as the days go by the pain will lessen.'

John groaned. 'I don't know which way to turn, every bone in my body aches. My hands are so sore too! There's not enough room up here to move and every time I do I catch myself on something!'

'I've been cooped up in this hell-hole for five months now', Wills said. 'At first it was the freezing wind that chilled me, now it's stinking hot. We're either freezing or sweltering, I'm not sure which is best. Look! In the morning, stick close to me, it won't make things any easier but at least we can talk together if we're in the same work party.'

A murmur of gratitude left John's lips but he felt no further desire to communicate with anyone and lapsed into silence. Wills let him be. He knew only too well what the lad was going through and there was nothing to be done about it. He rested his own weary limbs.

The night again seemed endless and when morning finally came, John's aching limbs refused to move. He rubbed the numbed muscles vigorously but this only served to aggravate the soreness of his hands, so he struggled to lower himself to the floor. His legs gave way then and he landed once more in a crumpled heap on the hard wooden boards. Tears of anger stung his eyes and the more he struggled the less progress he made.

'Shift yourself, you're in my way,' a man growled irritably at him. 'Come on, move!'

'Let him be,' Wills answered, calmly, 'You know what it's like at first. Have some pity on the lad!'

'He'll have to get over it when he gets up top. Nobody helped me!' The reply was sour, but John struggled to his feet and then sat on the bottom bunk. 'You can't sit on that either, it's my bed—yours is up on top.' It was a whining, persistent voice, disagreeable in every respect, it offered no encouragement to the suffering man. John was too weary to retaliate, accepting that the man was just protecting his only possession—his small bit of space. John had neither the will nor strength to argue, he simply allowed Wills to assist him to the privy.

How he later climbed out of the hatch he never knew. Wills had in fact pushed him up from behind, preventing him from falling back into the hold and then from falling forwards into the wash tub. He had helped him too, as he climbed down into the long-boat.

The day was long and arduous, and passed in a mental haze as John fought to keep up with the others. Every muscle seemed to resist the slightest movement, and tightening cramps gripped his calves as he bent to lift the heavy ballast. 'Keep going, lad!' Wills called out constantly, observing his struggles and fatigue, 'It's nearly noon.'

Wills had managed to get on the same gang as John, but there was a limit to the help he could give. Once, when he had gone to John's aid he had annoyed a nearby guard who had clubbed him viciously on the back, yelling, 'Get back to work, you scum! He'll survive without your wet-nursing, or I'll deal with him!'

Reluctantly Wills kept his distance for the rest of the day. Past experience had taught him that survival meant keeping on the right side of the guards. He touched his back where the club had landed, and winced. He wasn't even sure why he had befriended the lad, but life in the hulks was harsh, with no rewards, and loneliness was the greatest enemy. Nobody could be trusted, but this young man seemed oddly out of place with his educated voice, and Wills had not missed seeing his soft artistic hands on that first morning by the wash tubs, hands that were now blistered and torn. Wills was just an ordinary shepherd but he was familiar with the gentle folk on the estate where he had worked. What, he wondered, could have brought such a refined young man to the position he was now in?

The days passed slowly and the terrible stiffness in John's limbs gradually eased, despite the harshness of his daily toil. Only his conversations with Wills made life bearable and in spite of their different backgrounds these periods of companionship drew the men closer. Shepherding had given Wills a gentle patience, which luckily acted as a foil for John's occasional impetuosity.

On the sixth day, without warning, the men were mustered on deck in the early morning, and made to wash and tidy themselves up, in readiness for a visit from the Surgeon Superintendent of the transport ship *Speedwell* lying out in the harbour. Once the men were assembled in an orderly fashion, the Surgeon and his assistant proceeded to inspect them before conferring with an officer, who then started to read from the list of names before him.

'The following prisoners will be transferred to the transport ship within the hour...John Wells, Peter Wilks, Mathew Grimes, John Hind, William

Hall…' Thirty names in all, the rest were dismissed immediately for the dockyards.

John had not recognised Wills' name in the list, for his friend had never disclosed his full name, but 'John Andrews' was not called out. Bitter with disappointment, John found himself once more amongst the parties being taken in the long-boats. He had no opportunity to say farewell to Wills and the prospect of returning to the dismal, filthy hulk alone in the evening severely depressed him.

That evening the *Speedwell* remained at her mooring awaiting the turn of the tide. As John looked enviously towards the vessel he concluded that by morning he would be alone and friendless again. The long journey to Botany Bay with Wills would have been some compensation after the gruelling work of the yards. How he would miss Wills, with his steady, comforting ways and his words of encouragement! It was with a heavy heart that he took one last look at the ship which contained his friend before being forced below deck for the night. It could be months now before he was selected to go and the chances of his ever joining up with Wills again were extremely remote.

The *Speedwell* did not sail from Langstone Harbour that night, nor did it sail for another ten days, due mainly to lack of co-ordination between the Admiralty and the prison governor. Each morning John woke expecting to find the vessel gone, but on the tenth day the men were once more assembled on deck for medical inspection, raising his hopes afresh. His obsession with the presence of the other ship had incurred the displeasure of the guards on more than one occasion, as the numerous bruises on his back proved. It was highly unlikely, however, that he would be selected for shipment so soon and he listened with scant attention as the voice drawled on.

The list seemed endless, meaningless, as unfamiliar names were called out and John stared hopelessly out to sea. The Mayor of Nottingham had let him down. He had promised to help clear his name, but in the end he had taken no positive action, and John knew that once the shores of England were behind him, it would be too late. The Courts of England had dealt badly with him, but he knew in his heart that it was his association with the radical movement that had been his downfall. This had deprived him of everything that he loved and believed in. He tried not to think of Fanny now, and kept her in that corner of his mind which gave him solace in the depths of the night, when the sound of scampering rats and the touch of creeping things repulsed him. She had become his light in the darkness and all the more precious for the comfort she gave him. Her spirit of defiance and flashes of good humour he missed, just as he grieved for the warmth of her body against his.

'Peter Smith, George Sayers, John Andrews, John Walker...' Had he heard right, or was he dreaming? He moved forwards, hardly able to absorb the words. 'Get below and gather your belongings. Quick about it, you lot! Then get your allocated clothing and leave the old ones behind!'

John scrambled frantically amongst the men in an attempt to get below, half afraid that someone would call him back—but nobody did! He appeared to have made it!

Clutching at the meagre possessions he had been allowed to keep when arriving at the hulk, he realised just how few they were. His indentures, money, and all that he owned had been in Fanny's basket and would have been seized by the Militia. All that remained was his silver watch and flute, plus a mere five shillings and four pence as a safeguard for his future, and these he must constantly guard against theft. It was fortunate that only the flute had ever left the bag hung round his neck, so no-one knew they existed. When he washed, this bag was secreted in his trousers on the floor, and even these were trapped by his foot. Not even Wills knew he had this treasure.

He was issued with a woollen cap, which looked absurd, a Guernsey frock, two checked shirts, two pairs of raven duck trousers, a neckerchief, shoes and stockings. These were a great improvement on the itchy working clothes of the hulks.

'Selected prisoners on top deck! NOW!' bellowed the boatswain, as he went from deck to deck gathering up the prisoners who were due to sail. When finally all were mustered, they formed a ragged line. 'Right, you lot! When the blacksmith's ready you're to get a present,' the boatswain sneered, 'lovely new leg irons, compliments of His Majesty's Government!'

One by one they shuffled forward and John watched as the rusty anklets were removed, revealing bruised, angry weal's of flesh. Those prisoners, who had been on the hulks for months had thin, almost skeletal-like ankles, whereas John's were raw and bled frequently. With the anklets removed, his feet felt light, cold and naked, and he could see ulcers angry with pus. The blacksmith showed no signs of emotion as one man after another stood before him, their sores ready to receive yet another chafing iron bandage. Amongst this motley assortment of human beings John stood, humiliated by his prison clothing which was marked by a large letter 'A'. His spare clothing, marked 'B' was in a bundle beneath his arm, and by the means of these letters he was to alternate his weekly washing. At last he was ready to be transferred to the transport ship.

The *Speedwell* smelt cleaner than the hulk had done but, in spite of the freshly holystoned decks and scrubbed out holds, it was impossible to remove the smell of fetid bodies. He had never reconciled himself to the rancid smell of sweaty human flesh, much less when it was his own. In spite of this loathing, he could not suppress the buoyant feeling which ran through him at the thought of leaving the hulk, and meeting Wills again. Yet Wills was nowhere to be seen. Looking round the deck he sought to find his friend, but there were only groups of men lounging about and scrutinising each newcomer with more than idle curiosity. John felt exposed by their gaze, and he remembered Wills' warning to him to be on guard against old hands and their stealth. Their searching eyes seemed almost to fasten on his hidden possessions, and he knew that he must guard himself against such felons. Nor must he incur their displeasure in any way, so he was careful to remain as unobtrusive as possible in their presence.

'Is it you, John?' came an excited voice, 'I don't believe it!' Wills hurried over as fast as his chains would allow. 'I never dreamed we'd make it together—you don't know how lucky you are to have been on the hulks for such a short time!'

'Wills!' John exclaimed, spinning round. He would have embraced his companion had they been alone. 'God! I never thought I'd see you again. I thought you'd have sailed before this!'

'I thought we would—but we didn't!' There was no mistaking the joy in Wills' eyes. John had never seen him happy before. 'It's good to have a friend here,' Wills said with real pleasure in his voice.

'Let's try and stick together!'

Wills shook his head, 'I've already got my berth and the others near me are full. Unless we can bribe someone to move we've had it!'

The disappointment on John's face was obvious but there was nothing he could do to change the situation and John did not wish to draw attention, even to Wills, that he had anything of value on his person which could be used as a bribe. 'Then we must keep in touch and meet on deck.' John replied, and before he could say more, the officer on deck ordered the prisoners to go below.

For three days the *Speedwell* remained at anchor in the shelter of Langstone harbour whilst winds raged, tossing her about in the water like a cork. Three days in which John came to realise that he had another enemy—boredom. For an hour or two the first day he spent time studying the ship upon which his life would depend. A guard curtly answered his questions regarding her origins, revealing that the vessel had been built in Calcutta about ten years previously. As Botany Bay ships went, this square rigger was more seaworthy than most, and John sighed with relief at the news, hoping that it promised a safe journey.

By allowing the men up on deck by divisions the guards were able to control the number of men in their charge, and although they still observed carefully every movement, they permitted them to split up into groups.

John, however, preferred to remain alone, being unable to meet Wills who was allowed up at different times, and fell to observing the groups which huddled together. He had a mistrust of their camaraderie, such little time had passed for true companionship to develop and it was his opinion that they planned mischief of some sort. He was no fool however, and took great care not to alienate himself from them, nor to spend too much time in conversation with any of the guards.

In spite of his enjoyment of the fresh air, and his relief from hard labour, he found that the time spent hanging around, watching and waiting for signs that the ship would sail, badly disturbed him. He observed first one, then another relation of the prisoners coming aboard to tearfully part forever from their loved ones. He had no one! There had been insufficient time to inform his uncle, Gervase, or even Fanny of his despatch from the hulks, and the haste of this action seemed yet again to confirm that his conviction had been for political reasons rather than criminal ones. His Majesty's Government was banishing him as quickly as possible, but needlessly, for there was no longer any fear of an insurrection in the country. The feared uprising in June against poverty and starvation had collapsed even before it had begun, due mainly to the treachery of Government infiltrators in their midst. The good harvest which had followed pacified the poor of the nation, and they had become complacent about their prospects once more.

Dressed and shackled as he was, John found the absence of friends and relations welcome, for he was ashamed, and preferred to remain aloof from the emotional trauma of farewells. To his great relief then, quite suddenly, the *Speedwell* weighed anchor and sailed out into the vast ocean. Once the ship was under way, the hatches were removed, thus allowing the men up on deck again by divisions, in turn. John was unprepared for the overwhelming feeling of isolation and insignificance as he viewed the mighty ocean stretching out before him. The vessel heaved up and down with the swell, and he realised just how vulnerable they were. In spite of the sun's warmth on his body and the taste of salt on his lips, he shivered as he looked down into the rolling sea below, and wondered what perils lay hidden in its depths.

Later, the sight of Lizard Point in the far distance offered no hope, for what use now was his ability to swim, when his ankles were chained together. He would simply be dragged down by the weight into a watery grave, like his poor mother before him.

It had been as a result of her death that his uncle had forced him to learn to swim, by practising every day in the river which ran past the big house near Nottingham where they lived. His uncle had been afraid that his grief-stricken nephew would emulate his mother's suspected suicide.

Several times John had seen Wills from a distance, but their turns on deck rarely coincided, so John concentrated all his thoughts on finding ways to reach his friend. In the early days of the voyage most of the other men on the *Speedwell* lounged about, resting their sickly, abused bodies until they gradually sank into despondency. Their legs began to swell from insufficient exercise and it wasn't long before some became bored and irritable. The daily routine of scrubbing decks came as a relief to John after the hardships of the hulks, and he welcomed the opportunity to be useful, whereas others became resentful. At first, the weather was surprisingly pleasant, the sea calm, and even the food palatable. But as the vessel moved further south she was caught by the fresh winds from the west and the weather became stormy and wet. When the ship reached blue waters John's leg irons were struck off and the surgeon applied red oxide of mercury and bandages to his painful ulcers. One man fell from his bunk after a sudden motion of the ship, dislocating his shoulder, and John resolved not to wander about unnecessarily when the ship pitched to and fro.

The damp, cold, westerly gales persisted, they travelled on with sails well trimmed to the wind and, in spite of the weather, the ship's surgeon insisted that the side scuttles remain open night and day to allow fresh air to pass through the ship. Every day they were made to maintain the cleanliness of the lower decks until eventually the winds slackened and they were once more able to swab and sand the upper decks.

With three weeks sailing behind them, agreeable weather replaced the squalls and storms, and as they turned down into the North East Trade Winds so the quarrels in the berths increased. Soon, in the heat, even petty squabbles amongst the prisoners developed rapidly into violence and the stench of bodies and privies seemed to permeate everywhere. The guards increased their vigilance and became more ruthless as the restlessness grew amongst the transportees.

John tolerated the men who shared his berth but they were argumentative and coarse, appearing also to resent his need for solitude. In order to seem companionable he made every effort to conceal his dislike but they were not his type at all. Most of all he dreaded the nights when gangs of the worst of the prisoners riotously roamed the decks, annoying and beating those who were quiet and orderly. They thought nothing of rifling the ship's chests or cutting up other men's beds. He was delighted when one convict, as a result of his nightly rampage, was chained in irons to a ringbolt on deck for having beaten up another man.

The guards searched the lower decks regularly for knives and offensive weapons, and removed everything of value to the ship into a safe place, leaving the prisoners to get on with their quarrels. The name of Thomas Hallard became synonymous with trouble, and John kept well out of his way, as this notorious jail breaker constantly agitated and stirred up other prisoners to complain about their rations. There was very little to do to break the monotony and when, after the men had been woken at five each morning to bathe in the wash tubs and the decks had been scrubbed, the idle hands of the hardened criminals quickly turned to mischief.

By the end of the fourth week the Captain decided to act. He employed carpenters to partition off a part of the ship adjacent to the main hatchway and next to a large porthole, in which he incarcerated the marauding villains. Fear of mutiny amongst the convicts prevented the guards from relaxing their vigilance, and John could well understand why their contempt for the prisoners grew with each passing day.

An appalling lack of common sense and decency seemed to reign below deck and John shook his head in disbelief as men stole each other's clean clothes and mindlessly threw their own dirty things overboard. They blocked the privies with wood and clothing until the sickening sight and smell of human effluent turned his stomach. In the face of such stupidity and in spite of the twice weekly washing of clothing it wasn't long before sickness set in.

When tempers flared, John retreated into his own daydreams. He missed Wills' simplicity more than he had thought possible. It was at this point that he felt the strong desire to play his flute. No one knew that he had it, for none of the men who had marched with him were on board. Surely, if he used it openly and regularly, this might possibly provide its own safe keeping and be his salvation. He knew the seductive powers of the flute on emotionally starved men and women, and those who applauded would hardly appreciate its disappearance or tolerate its theft. Selecting the moment carefully, in the mid-afternoon when things were as mellow as they could be and the scrubbed decks were strewn with listless bodies, and when the sentries in their stifling scarlet uniforms stood awkwardly in fear of falling asleep on duty during the hottest part of the day, he set out to woo them all.

Slowly, and deliberately, he slipped the flute from his sleeve where he had temporarily concealed it, took a deep breath and gently played the first few notes. So soft was the music that at first no one stirred, then, as he played louder, eyes turned with wonderment in his direction, as they had done on the march to the hulks. He was pleased with himself but vowed that no radical song would pass his lips this time, for it would gain him nothing. If his music found him favour then so be it—it was time his luck changed.

A man called out across the deck, 'Can you play us a jig, Sorr? Something to cheer us up?' It was an Irish voice.

Happy to oblige, John played a tune with a lilt in it, and was pleased to hear humming in response. No one seemed to complain, although there was a constant wary eye cast over the deck by their over-dressed guards.

For a while boredom and sufferings were forgotten, yet all too soon a voice bellowed, 'Ration time. Get below!' then, 'You, with the flute, what's your name?' a guard demanded.

'Andrews, Sir!' answered John politely.

'Right, get below with the rest!' There was neither anger nor remonstration in his voice as the guard dismissed him, and John felt quite pleased with the afternoon's accomplishment.

Later, when the hatches were battened down and the stuffy, gloomy evening was well advanced, John noticed a youth of no more than fourteen years peering into the compartment, through its dimness. John raised his eyes questioningly at the watching boy. 'Do you want something, son?' he asked, not unkindly, and receiving no reply tried again. 'Is anything wrong?'

'No!' came the reluctant reply.

'Well, what is it then, has the cat got your tongue?' The boy reminded him of Tom Linley, the young lad Gervase had rescued from a wretched existence back home.

'Is it easy to play? That thing you blow at—can anyone do it?' His eyes were large and serious. It was obvious that it had taken him some time to pluck up his courage to approach, in spite of his deep curiosity.

It was strange, John reflected, just how like Tom he was, simple and enquiring, and how like Gervase he, John, now felt. That man had had the patience of Job where the youngster had been concerned and John had done nothing but mock the boy. 'Come here, I'll show you!' he offered, raising the flute to his pursed lips and blowing a sharp note. 'Like this— here, get hold of it like I do.' He stood behind the boy and held the instrument just as he had for Fanny when she had asked the same question. That had been the moment when he realised he loved her, when he had been so close to her and the perfume from her hair had wafted gently under his nose. He shook his head and threw his shoulders back to throw off the painful memory. 'Don't open your mouth so wide, just blow across the hole.' Taking the flute back again he said, 'I'll show you tomorrow on deck then we won't disturb the others.'

The boy nodded gratefully and slipped away into the gloom.

'What's your name boy?' John called after him.

'Joe, Sir!' came the reply, then he was gone.

'Play us a tune!' A voice demanded from somewhere along the deck.

From within his own compartment a voice hissed warningly, 'Don't encourage him, he fags for a fella!'

There was no time to digest this information fully before several voices called out from different directions, one rising higher than all the rest. 'Are you deaf? Get on with it man!'

For a full half hour a strange silence settled over his deck as the ill-assorted human cargo listened from their cramped berths. Suddenly, the stillness was interrupted by a loud rapping on the hatch above. 'That's enough down there, you lot—let's have some peace and quiet now or you'll be ironed all night.' This brought a response of cat calls and defiant whistling, for the men knew that the guards had more sense than to step down into the darkened holds. The hatch was struck more violently this time. 'Quiet down there, I said! If you're not, no-one comes up tomorrow!'

A hush fell over the deck as each man retreated into his private thoughts, but the die was cast, and each evening after dark when the hatches were battened down, John would play. For a while some men would whistle and sing, mostly out of tune, in their desire for distraction. Some even attempted wild prancings in the name of dancing, much to the amusement of their fellow prisoners and John did not object to the diversion. He earned a form of respect which gave him safety of a kind, and he wondered if this might in some way help him to reach Wills.

Young Joe took to hovering around when and wherever he could, but a brutish man kept a close eye on him constantly, and possessively allowed the lad little freedom. He had a strange hold over the boy and John sensed that Joe was always reluctant to go back to him.

When an opportunity finally came, John decided to ask, 'Why do you let him bully you? He's not your gaoler. Is he a relative?'

The boy lowered his eyes sheepishly and shook his head. 'No, but he protects me from the other men—he's kind to me if I do all that he asks of me!'

The resignation on the boy's face disturbed John. 'You don't owe him anything do you?'

'Perhaps I do!' Joe shrugged his shoulders. 'I met him on the hulks and he rescued me from another man who wasn't very kind to me.' The boy had lowered both his voice and his eyes in a manner which told John all he needed to know. Joe had sold himself to the man in exchange for protection. There was nothing that John could do to change things and although he recoiled at the knowledge, he knew interference would only have repercussions on Joe. He was a victim of a system which forced boys like him to become hardened criminals. There was no virtue in a hell-hole like this.

Chapter 3

The Speedwell was four weeks out now and the drinking water stale and tepid. Food was beginning to taste stored or rancid, and twice each day all were given a ration of lime juice and sugar to ward off the scurvy and other ills. John longed for tender fresh vegetables to replace the rice and peas which were now issued monotonously every day.

Slowly, one by one, there began complaints of headaches, constipation and loss of appetite and a constant stream of patients headed for the hospital, all seeking a comfortable bed and relief from the boredom of the voyage. Most returned grumbling and complaining yet again, leaving John to suspect the surgeon of being either uncaring or a wiser man than the prisoners had bargained for.

An old rascal in the adjacent compartment had almost driven them mad with endless complaints that his bladder refused to function, and that he was convinced it would burst before very long. He returned from the hospital quarters with a face more pained than when he went, and a temper very inflamed as well. 'Bastard!' he spat, 'Stuck a rotten catheter up it he has!'

John mused over the old lag's indignation, his suspicions about the Surgeon confirmed, for he had followed the old man only that day to the privy and knew that he had parted with ample water then.

Time hung even heavier on their hands now, with petty squabbling worsening all the while and becoming more violent with the oppressive heat. Those men fortunate enough to have the wit to fashion needles, toothpicks and other items from the bones of the Saturday salt beef or pork did so, whilst the less industrious gambled everything from a nail to their ration of wine. The mere sight of a sail in the distance broke the monotony for as long as it was visible, and on one occasion the performance of a pair of sporting dolphins almost brought tears of relief to John's eyes.

Suddenly, off the coast of Africa, they lost the North-East Trades and clouds rolled towards them from the west, causing such heavy seas that John had only heard about. They were repeatedly lifted and dropped violently down again. With every minute the sea became more violent, tossing the vessel from side to side until as she came out of each swell so did the contents of John's stomach. He felt that his end had surely come!

Torrential rain lashed the ship with unbelievable violence, adding to the pounding of the sea on her sides. The decks were constantly awash with sea-water which poured down through any crack it could find onto the men below. They felt trapped and in the hands of God as they were flung to and fro beneath locked and battened hatches. It was impossible for a person to think of anything other than survival as they floundered hour after hour in darkness, amidst sodden bedding and spilt privies. John had no desire to eat, for barely had the food entered his stomach than it was spewed forth again.

Lashing winds split and tore several sails before they finally eased, but the rain continued incessantly, preventing them from drying out their clothes and bedding. The deck, where John slept, was thankfully no longer awash with water, though much had found its way down to the lower decks causing John grave concern for Wills who was down there.

Soon, everyone was shivering and unable to warm themselves in their bedding as it was wringing wet. One by one, they started coughing and sneezing, and before long some were running high temperatures.

When, eventually, the rain ceased, the hatches were removed and the men released to take their bedding up onto the top deck to dry out. They clambered frantically out of the holds, greedy for freedom and the fresh air which some had despaired of ever enjoying again. The sickly pallor of the convict's faces after their ordeal was pitiful to see; bed-ticks and germs had multiplied, eager to strike at their human pray. John shivered with cold; his worries increasing when Wills did not apear on deck, but he was not allowed to go down into the lower holds to find him.

The guards had fared better than their charges because, having once battened the hatches down on the convicts, they had been able to confine themselves to their cabins, leaving the prisoners to fend for themselves. There was no joy, however, on the crowded deck, for everyone was equally weakened by sea-sickness and the lack of food. Coughing and delirious voices brought on by fever kept John awake at night but at least now, with the easing of the rough weather, the sea-sickness had ceased .

The task of scrubbing out the filthy holds to lessen the spread of disease began once the weather improved. An attempt was made at disinfecting the vessel by sprinkling vinegar here and there, though what good such a small amount of the liquid would do John could not imagine. He was battered and bruised from the tossing of the ship and only undiluted lemon juice was available to put on his sores to prevent infection.

He saw trouble ahead as the restlessness amongst the convicts increased daily, although he endeavoured to distance himself as much as possible from these outbreaks of squabbling and fighting, being appalled by the depravity of it all. His sleep was rudely disturbed one hot, stifling night, when an argument erupted between two men in an adjacent compartment and he knew that the dispute could only end in trouble. No amount of humouring placated them and it wasn't long before the abusive words turned to violence as they lunged at each other in the gloom.

Within minutes a heavy pounding on the battened hatches heralded the arrival of the guards. 'Stop that fighting down there, you barbaric lot!' a voice commanded, but the row continued. 'Stop it you ill-bred ruffians, or suffer the consequences!' The guard turned to his companion, 'Open up the hatch, quickly now.' The awful stench that rose from the open hold sickened the man and caused him to catch his breath. 'God, they stink!' he spat out in disgust.

The commotion from below increased as other prisoners now hurled abuse and missiles up at the guards.

'What do we do now?' asked the younger soldier. 'Do we have to go down?'

'Not damned likely! You'd never come out alive from amongst that lot.' He turned and shouted again into the hold, 'Quiet!'

'Sod off!' a voice screamed back in response.

'Sons of bitches!' another added, as further missiles flew into the air.

The guard stiffened. 'Who said that?' he demanded.

'Come and find out, you yellow-bellied flunkies!'

The fighting which had ceased whilst the prisoners hurled abuse at the guards resumed then, but this time the violence spread amongst the rest of the men. Sounds of destruction and splintering wood rent the air. Looking anxiously at each other, the guards cocked their muskets defensively and the older man fired a shot into the air. 'That damage will result in a lashing for the culprits and punishment tomorrow for everyone else,' he yelled. 'Send up the ring-leader before any more harm is done!'

'Come and get us then, you poxy-faced devils!' The fighting continued although to some it was now just a way of letting off steam.

On deck the anxious guards were unsure what to do next. 'Stop this rioting or we fire!' the older man roared.

'Try it then!' came the swift and challenging reply. 'Send the Captain down here—we'll cut his bloody throat!'

Both guards raised their muskets simultaneously and fired down into the hold and a scream rang out. There was an immediate silence, broken only by a moan of pain.

'One more spot of trouble and we'll fire again!' one soldier called down, as he violently hammered the hatch back into place before withdrawing, with no regard for the wounded man below.

Stunned by the realisation that they were trapped, and that the wounded man had been abandoned to his fate, John stumbled to his feet in the dark and ran to the hatch. 'You can't do this!' he yelled angrily, 'Someone's been hurt—open up the hatch! In God's name—aren't you human?' There was no reply from above and he called softly, fore and aft, 'Who's hurt—where are you?'

'He's here with friends,' grunted a voice, 'there's nothing we can do except stop the blood. He's got a musketball in his leg but those bastards wouldn't dare come down here in the dark anyway.'

Making his way back to his own compartment, John lay back in his bunk. He could see the sky through a gap in the planking and stars twinkling high up in the heavens. There was anger in his soul now, for if there was a God up there, how proud He must be of His creation. What a disappointment mankind must be to the Maker! If indeed there was a Heaven, then it did not seem to be for the likes of himself or the poor of this world. Only an occasional groan from the wounded man disturbed the quiet now, no-one moved in the stillness until daylight, when the hatches were again lifted off.

'Up on top, every man jack of you! At the double!' The harsh voice penetrated John's sleep, as a ladder rattled down from the hatchway, and the men were compelled to climb out one by one, into the fresh, warm morning air. All were apprehensive of their fate, but John remained with the injured man, reluctant to leave him alone.

'You go up, I can't manage it,' the wounded man muttered through his clenched teeth, 'tell them I need help, and tell them I wasn't doing no wrong.'

The shuffling on deck soon ceased as the men were lined up before the Officer of the Watch, Lieutenant Lowther. 'Count the villains. Make sure you've got them all and let me have the trouble makers.' His temper was short as his sleep had been interrupted and he was annoyed with the guards for their hasty action which would require a written report.

'Two missing, Sir!' the young guard saluted, after counting the men. 'Shall we flush them out?'

'Three of you go below—and watch yourselves, they're bound to be up to no good.' He paused, eyeing the mustered convicts with contempt. 'I want the men who caused all this and I'll not give up until I get them. If I don't, you'll be shut down there for a week—do you hear? In double irons, day and night!' No one stirred, their sullen faces defying the Officer's challenge. 'By God, you'll pay dearly for this insolence! Who was it?' They stood stubbornly refusing to speak. 'Don't worry!' he smiled menacingly. 'We've got weeks ahead of us yet and I'll not be beaten by you filthy scum!'

Having heard the threats, John was already half way up the ladder when a pair of black boots and white buckskin breeches descended towards him, blocking out most of the light. He half expected to have his fingers crushed beneath the weight of the boots, so before the man could descend any further, John yelled out, frantically. 'I'm coming up! 'I've no weapons!'

The guard hesitated, then climbed back up the ladder. John followed the man back up onto the deck, there to be seized immediately and dragged before the Officer.

'You! What have you to say for yourself—skulking like a coward down there against my orders! Are you the villain who caused all this rumpus?' He didn't wait for a reply. 'A dose of the lash will soon alter that! Take him to the mast!'

John lifted his head defensively, 'I did nothing! There's a wounded man down there, injured, by one of your guards. This man did no more than get in the way of your man's shot, and I've been trying to help him'

A guard broke in, 'That's not the same voice, Sir! It was the voice of a foul-mouthed ruffian, last night.'

From below a voice rang out, 'He's over here, the other man! He's been shot in the leg, and a door's been ripped off between decks, it's got blood on it where the devil who did it cut himself.'

'Right, get the surgeon down there! I'll have the man who tore that door off, by God I will!' he growled, turning to stare at the unwashed, unkempt assortment of prisoners. He looked keenly then at John, 'You seem a bright fellow—who started all this?'

Thinking quickly and realising that he was in a tricky situation between two very different camps, John replied truthfully, 'I couldn't see Sir—it was too dark.'

'I suppose it was too dark for any of you to see!' His voice rang with sarcasm and he was shrewd enough to know that the men would stick together.

'Aye, Sir!' mumbled most of the men.

There was a long sea voyage still ahead and the officer was not one to give in easily, he knew from past experience that their rebellious spirits must be conquered soon or there would be no peace or security on the ship for the rest of the journey. 'A likely story! Make no mistake, I'll not tolerate disobedience or trouble aboard this ship and I WILL find the culprit.' He paced the floor whilst awaiting the surgeon's report and kept them all at attention.

A head appeared at the hatchway, 'It's a bad gunshot wound you've got down here Mr Lowther, and I think you'll have another patient up there. Whoever tore the door off its hinges must have cut himself quite badly, there's blood all over.'

A grin spread widely over the officer's face, 'Right you are Mr Oldroyd, I get the message'. Eyeing each man as he walked calmly down the lines, almost relishing his task, he challenged them all as he passed along. 'Right—both hands out in front,' he ordered menacingly, 'Lieutenant! Examine these men. Carefully now, I want to see any fresh wounds immediately.

The men stood with their hands outstretched, awaiting inspection with trepidation, for many had hands which were scarred and calloused, or cracked open with the weather. Separating out those with likely-looking wounds didn't take long; as each suspect was pulled roughly from the line, a look of fear appeared on his face and he glanced around nervously. No-one escaped scrutiny and a sigh of relief could be heard from those who were passed by, but it wasn't long before there was a scuffle, and the guards dragged from the lines one protesting convict with dried blood on his hands. Unable to wash before being mustered he had been unable to rid himself of the evidence.

Once hauled before the officer the man struggled no longer; he was in no position to escape and brazenly accepted the fate which awaited him. One thing he was not willing to do was disgrace himself in front of the other prisoners, especially as he had to go back amongst them afterwards.

'Make an ass of me and my men, would you? We'll see about that!' roared Mr Lowther, before turning to the boatswain. 'Tie him up, Armstrong, and flog him—sixty lashes if you please. And let this be a lesson to all trouble-makers!'

John breathed a sigh of relief. With his faith in justice being so completely destroyed he had felt very vulnerable as he stood in the line for inspection.

The prisoner braced himself for the impact of the lash. Not a word was spoken amongst his fellows; they were just grateful not to be the recipients of such punishment. The flailing cat bit deep into the man's back, opening up the skin to expose a mass of raw bloody flesh below. He jerked, but to John's astonishment and admiration the man did not cry out as the sickening blows gradually turned his back into a bloody mangle of flesh.

His respect for the man deepened as the punishment continued, and John wondered just how he himself would have withstood such pain under the same circumstances. After the first half dozen lashings he was unable to watch any longer, and he let his eyes wander cautiously over the assembly on deck, noting as he did so, that for the first time the entire ship's passengers were also there. This was to let them see the punishment that would be meted out to all offenders and rioters. Each officer at his station was armed with a brace of pistols and a cutlass, ready for action, whilst the two guns on the quarter deck were charged with a round of grape shot and turned inwards on the convicts. Rioting was, however, far from the minds of the convicts who were engrossed in their own misery and saw no reason to further incur the wrath of the soldiers.

Wills had been trying for some time to catch John's eye, and when eventually he did so the surge of emotion caused John's eyes to water. He nodded gently, sharing a moment of real rapport with his friend. Wills looked as pale and drawn as John had expected, and he knew that conditions on the lower deck must be far worse than they were on his own deck. If only it was possible to get Wills transferred on medical grounds! There had to be some way of by-passing the guards without arousing their suspicions, or that of the men around him, in order to see the ships surgeon. But how? Many had been to the sick bay already with headaches, constipation and even boils, but he had none of these. The welfare of Wills was, however, of great concern to him and he had to invent a plausible excuse that would allow him to pass the guards.

As it happened there was little need to invent an excuse. All drinking water was stale and blood-warm in the increasing heat, more and more men were developing diarrhoea and John was no exception. By mid-morning the following day, the pains in his belly were excruciating and his bowels were opening so frequently that he imagined he would never sit comfortably again. He cursed his discomfort, vowing to boil every drop of water he drank for twice the required time, but it was too late, the damage was already done. He soon found himself heading through the bulkheads towards the hospital area.

His prime concern now was for relief of his present condition and, sadly, he realised he would have to postpone his search for Wills, hoping in the mean-time that he would not succumb to the sickness sweeping through the ship.

'Can you give me something to dry up the diarrhoea, Doctor?' he begged, 'I'm hardly able to control myself!'

'It's always the same, as soon as we get near the equator it happens. Your body needs liquid but the water is full of germs and most of you are too lazy to boil your drinking water. Here, try some of this!' The ship's Surgeon handed over a dose of calamine and rhubarb, which John swallowed. 'And don't eat for a day or so, but drink as much as you can or you will dehydrate in this heat.'

The cabin which acted as a sick bay was large and although sparsely furnished was clean and tidy. The natural light which flooded in through the port windows enabled John to see the surgeon clearly. He was not the robust man one would have expected of a medical man, indeed John thought him almost puny, with tired eyes and greying hair, in spite of his obvious lack of years.

'You!' a voice called from within the shadows of the cabin, 'Come here, will you?' The voice was weak and John strained to see beyond the surgeons desk to where it had come from. There appeared to be five or six bunks, but only one held a patient. 'You! Over here!' repeated the anxious voice.

'Can I go to him?' John asked of the surgeon.

'Can't see it doing any harm, he can't move far anyway. He's in no condition to do anything much.'

As John approached the man, he recognised him as the one who had been shot in the leg in the incident two nights previously. 'Oh, it's you!' he exclaimed warmly. 'How's the leg?' In spite of his own discomfort he registered the look of pain which crossed the man's face.

'It aches badly—but I want to thank you for staying with me back there.' The voice was weak and John felt a considerable amount of sympathy for the poor fellow.

'I would not have wanted to have been left injured and alone in that lousy hole myself', John replied kindly, looking keenly again at the man. He looked gravely ill, far worse than he had done at the time of the incident, and John wondered just how bad he really was.

Suddenly, with a stronger voice the man called out to the surgeon, 'Sir—can he play me a tune?'

'Ah!' Recognition dawned on the surgeon's face, 'So, you're the fellow who keeps the guards awake, are you? I think they too welcome the diversion. Quite frankly there's not much to do in an evening except drinking with the Captain, or reading.'

'A book makes a good companion,' John commented wistfully, before being seized once more with pain.

'Take that stuff, it'll dry you up before you get too weak. You're the fifth I've had in here today!' He didn't dismiss John immediately but allowed him to talk to the wounded man until there was little left to say, and John turned to take his leave. 'You like books then?' he enquired studying John cautiously.

'I'm a printer by trade. I love them for their lay-out and style as much as for the words in them!'

'You read a lot then?' The surgeon asked, continuing meanwhile with his notes.

'I did, but I'd be grateful for anything I can get now. I'm not one for philosophy or romance, but if I'm bored, I'll read anything.' There seemed nothing strange in discussing his likes and dislikes with the Doctor who was evidently more than willing to chat. This was the first really stimulating conversation he had enjoyed with anyone since parting from Gervase, and he was reluctant to return to the boring confines of his bunk.

The Doctor raised his eyebrows, 'Can you read this?' His finger indicated the paper in his hand. It held a simple message, 'The patient has gangrene in his leg'.

John raised his eyebrows and his eyes filled with sympathy. 'Can I do anything?' he asked with deliberate lightness, so as not to let the man know that anything was amiss.

Nodding, the Doctor said with a knowing look, 'Perhaps you could help some of the men by writing to their families for them? Few of them can read, let alone write, and my job would be easier if their minds were occupied. Yours too I would imagine? Perhaps you could read to Henry there!'

There was a look of compassion on the Doctor's face which was not lost on John who replied, 'I would indeed be very grateful. Thank you, Sir. May I come back and read or play for him?'

'I'll organise it. I'll have you brought here this afternoon, so bring your flute too.'

Suddenly the pains in John's stomach caused him to double over, 'I can't stay, it's here again—I'll have to go!' He rushed from the cabin, almost colliding with the guard outside the door, and again sought the midden.

By mid afternoon, feeling weak, John lay back on his bed bored by inactivity, and uncomfortable in the heat. His parched throat cried out for cold, clean, water, whilst his eyes watched the blobs of hot pitch poised to drop from the cracks in the beams above. Sometimes the droplets landed on the floor creating a hot sticky mess, and at others on the flesh or clothing of an unwary victim. Tying his spare shirt across the beams above his head to ensure that the hot pitch did not land on his face or in his eyes, he tried to sleep. Nothing moved within the ship, and it was very hot as the vessel lay becalmed. In spite of the open side-scuttles there was no breeze to pass through the crowded quarters and stir the fetid air, unlike in the hulks where the draughts of the damp night air had almost frozen him to death.

'Andrews! Report to the ship's hospital, immediately!' The order rang out through the stillness and reluctantly he rose to obey it.

Why did it have to be now of all times, when he was tired and listless? He had neither the desire to read out loud or to play the flute, and he could have done without the intrusion into his private thoughts. Nevertheless he was well aware of the privilege of the call and slowly moved towards the hatch.

'At the double there! Don't take all day!' The guard was out of humour too.

'I'm coming as fast as I can!' John grumbled to himself as he made his way to where the impatient guard stood.

It was little wonder that the man was irritable, his face was almost as red as his uniform in the sweltering heat. 'Come on, man!' he snapped 'I've not got all day.'

The sick bay into which John entered for the second time that day was cooler than the rest of the deck and the fresh smell of medication was pleasant beyond belief. 'Come in, feeling any better now?' the cheery voice of the Doctor enquired.

'I've nothing left inside me to lose. I just feel so lifeless and fed up, and this heat makes me think of nothing but cold water. I don't know how you can choose to work on a ship like this. I certainly wouldn't.'

'Circumstances, my dear fellow, circumstances!' The Doctor seemed resigned to his fate. 'Now, will you play to your friend? He needs comforting as he's in considerable pain, but I'm not able to give him any more morphine.' He passed another note to John which read, 'I'm going to have to take off his leg!'

A look of shocked disbelief crossed John's face, but he nodded, accepting the inevitable. He was saddened at the thought and was not sure that he could entertain the man whilst concealing such terrible news from him. However, he commenced playing his flute and this helped to ease his worries, but he was relieved when the man finally fell asleep. 'He's gone to sleep—shall I wait a while or go back to my bunk?'

'I'm glad he's dropped off, the pain has previously prevented him from sleeping.' The Doctor spoke quietly, then added, 'I've had a word with the Captain and he's willing to let you write letters for the men—if you wish to of course, but you could make yourself very useful on this ship. It would make the voyage more pleasant for you as well!'

'That is very kind of you Sir, and I'm grateful, but it would be difficult to write in my quarters,' John said, 'and I have no materials or pens! Do you think the men will resent my interference?'

The Doctor shook his head, 'Many men will appreciate the opportunity to send a letter home as most of them cannot read, let alone write. Each man could come to you in turn, but perhaps not every man will feel that he can trust his personal thoughts to someone else. We have supplies on route to the Colony which we can let you have, and we can give you a lantern to work by. Most convicts feel homesick and lost at this stage of the journey, but there are some who have nobody to write to anyway.'

'Thank you again for this opportunity,' John offered, seizing on an idea which was forming in his mind. 'I'm bored out of my mind with inactivity, so the work will do me good. There is, however, one favour I would ask!'

The Doctor eyed him with caution, 'I'm not sure if I can help—what is it?'

'There is a chap,' John said hesitantly, 'a good, simple man, on the lower deck who befriended me in the hulks. I know that the heat and damp are destroying his health. May I write for him, soon, and...' he lowered his voice and gestured in the direction of the sleeping patient, 'if his leg does come off, could my friend take his place on my deck?'

After a few moments of reflection the Doctor replied, 'Well, I do have the power to move men if I feel it is necessary to do so, but I must be satisfied that what I am doing is right! Who is he?'

John hesitated, 'Oh dear! I only know him as Wills—could I point him out to you perhaps?'

'Leave it with me!' A movement from the patient drew the Doctor's attention. 'I must examine this friend of yours first though. I won't promise anything but I'll see what I can do.'

Returning from the hospital John lay on his bunk pleased with his achievement. A sense of contentment overtook him and the usual creaking of rigging and flapping of canvas no longer irritated him, for he felt that it wouldn't be long before he was re-united with Wills. His elation was short lived when he remembered that it would be made possible only if the other man lost his leg. Guilt and remorse brought him down to earth, for he could not in all conscience hope for his own happiness at the expense of another. His reverie was finally brought to an end when he was summoned again to go to the hospital quarter and there told by the Doctor to help in a search for Wills.

The inadequate ventilation and lack of natural light made the lower deck far worse than John had expected it to be. It was impossible to escape the acrid smell of sweat and urine as the Doctor led the way from one compartment to another in their search. During this he informed the men that John could write letters home for those who could not write. Dr Rogerson had little to fear from the prisoners who saw him as their only friend amongst the crew, but the two guards remained at the foot of the ladder, alert and ready in case of trouble.

'I don't want to make it too obvious that we are seeking your friend,' he warned John quietly, 'the men don't like favourites, as well you know by now, and I must satisfy myself also that your friend warrants special attention before I move him!'

John nodded, 'I appreciate your position, Sir, and I'm grateful for your efforts on my friend's behalf'.

'It's my duty to deal with you all in the same light, and try to better your conditions but some make it difficult for themselves, and there are a few who don't deserve much help.' They were half-way along the deck now and Wills was still nowhere to be seen.

'Is there no way to provide more ventilation down here?' John asked. 'The stench is so foul that this must cause the men to feel sick.'

'Ah!' replied Dr Rogerson. 'Before my colleague Dr Redfern in Sydney convinced the Government of the benefit of fresh air and better ventilation, the ships were like cess pits. He still works in Sydney to improve conditions there, but you are right, though unfortunately my powers are limited. The newer vessels are being improved, but I do all I can, that is why I leave the side scuttles open day and night to allow free passage of air.' Together they moved further along the gangway, and the doctor announced for the sixth time, 'Men, I have a man here who can write letters home to your families for you. He will only be able to do a few each day, but with luck, they should be finished by the time we reach Sydney, where they can be despatched on the first ship sailing back to England. It is also important for you all to remember to be as clean as possible in your habits to prevent further sickness.' He looked keenly from one to the other before asking, 'Are there any of you in need of treatment at all?'

Each time they had paused for the doctor to speak, John had looked cautiously into each cell as the men surged forward to listen. They were all eager for any diversion from the endless boredom, but some were too listless to move from their bunks. At first, John did not see the solitary figure lying back in a corner, until he saw the man's feet move at the end of his bunk. The Doctor saw the direction of John's gaze, and they both moved towards the man, who lifted his head weakly at their approach. After a brief examination, Dr Rogerson told John the man would have to be moved to the sick bay immediately.

'Is he in a bad way?' John asked quietly, so that the gathering men should not be alarmed.

'No, but it's fortunate that I've seen him now, before he gets worse.' Turning to the two men nearest him, he said, 'You two—fetch a hammock from the guard immediately.' He then brought his face closer to John's and whispered, 'Is this your friend?' John shook his head.

The figure groaned as it was lifted and bound into the hammock. 'Careful there!' the doctor called angrily at their carelessness, 'And for pity's sake don't drop him when you climb the ladder.' He led the men towards the hatchway and helped him lift his patient up onto the deck above.

Seizing this opportunity of comparative freedom, John walked slowly and quietly past the remaining compartments until, finally, he saw Wills huddled on the side of a bunk.

'Hey, you!' a man challenged roughly, 'We don't want snoopers down here, get back where you came from!'

'The doctor says he can write letters home for us,' another butted in, 'so shut your mouth!'

John raised his hands reassuringly. 'Calm down! I'm not here to cause trouble, I'm a prisoner like you. If there is any disturbance I won't be allowed to help you.' As he spoke he watched Wills, hoping he would recognise his voice without being called.

'My old lady's better off forgetting all about me,' a disgruntled voice called out.

'Well, I'll write to your mistress then!' John called back good-humouredly, and there was a roar of laughter. Wills lifted his head and smiled. John chattered first with one man, and then another before thinking it was safe enough to approach Wills. 'Cheer up, my friend,' he said softly, 'I'm trying to get you out of here but don't let on to the others. At least if I fail I'll be allowed to come and see you occasionally.' He touched Wills lightly on the shoulder, noticing as he did so how thin and pale he was. 'You must tell Dr Rogerson straight away that you are sick.' He made to leave, but the look of regret on Will's face held him back. 'Don't worry, I'll soon be back', he said quietly.

Wills held out his hand. 'I've missed your company. Thanks for trying to help me.'

John quickly released Wills hand. 'Don't tell anyone else about this,' he urged, leaving Wills then to resume his thoughts once more.

Later, on returning to the lower deck they found Wills flushed from a bout of coughing. The damp atmosphere of the lower deck was undermining his health and eating into his lungs. Dr Rogerson immediately realised that Wills was in need of medical attention and transferred him to the hospital, leaving John below to write letters. These were sad and sometimes angry letters, but he kept his thoughts to himself and endeavoured to be of service to the often bitter, unhappy men. After a while the unaccustomed exercise made the joints of his fingers ache, but he was now at least occupied and this made him feel brighter in spirit. It was almost eight months since his capture but it felt like a lifetime. He well knew just how difficult it was to maintain any links with the past.

'Fresh air is really the best thing for your friend', Dr Rogerson advised John next morning. 'He must be moved out of the lower deck permanently or he will not reach Sydney. I'll get him transferred within a day or two onto your deck, but you must encourage him to spend all his time in the open instead of sitting on his bunk. I'll get his spell on deck increased to help build him up a little.' He shook his head, 'I'll keep him here until tomorrow but he needs sunshine more than anything. Come to my quarters later and you can talk to both men for a while!'

'I'm most grateful,' John's voice was filled with emotion, 'I've not met much kindness this past eight months. Thank you!'

Dr Rogerson raised his hand, 'Just make sure I don't regret it that's all. I, too, deplore much of what goes on in the penal system, but if it wasn't me here it could possibly be someone much worse.'

Once free of the verminous and claustrophobic lower hold and with the improved food in the hospital, Wills perked up. He was finally lodged only four compartments away from John's own and even their turns up on deck now coincided, restoring them to their former companionship.

Although Wills had improved John was under no illusion, for he knew deep down, that his friend was ill, but he tried to cast these thoughts to the back of his mind. Together they fashioned fish hooks from old bones and dangled them from twine over the ship's side for hours on end whilst they talked. Occasionally they spotted sea birds, whales, even flying fish in the endless blue waters. There were moments, when the winds were light and the swell gentle, that John forgot his predicament. At this time he felt at one with the elements, but when the squalls came they were ferocious and ugly, reminding him of his own insignificance and helplessness. His mouth was sore from the lack of fresh fruit and vegetables, and in spite of the allowed dosage of lemon juice he was troubled by his teeth, poor Wills had already lost some of his.

On September 30th, 1818, when the ship crossed the Equator, John and Wills watched with interest as the seamen performed, as tradition demanded, the ceremony involving Neptune and his wife for the passengers who had not previously crossed the Equator. To John this amusing charade in the baking heat symbolised the mysteries of human nature. Here for the first time he observed the wives and children of the military men on board and wondered what on earth possessed their men folk to bring them on such harrowing journeys. Some of the youngsters were pale and drawn, it was little wonder that they cried in their sleep; yet it had been the screams of a woman which had disturbed the whole ship last night with her childbed wailing. John had covered his ears to block out the sounds of her pain but it had been sunrise before the woman was finally released from her torment. As a result, the ship's passengers were almost as exhausted as she was herself.

Looking out across the water, he pondered on the future and wondered if ever he would be the cause of such agony in a woman. Was Botany Bay to be as lonely as he had heard tell?

As they drew nearer to Botany Bay Wills appeared to be getting weaker, 'Will you not let me write to your family, too?' John offered, trying not to show his anxiety. 'I've done it for most of the others and I'm sure your family would appreciate a word from you!'

Wills' face became drawn with pain. 'What is there to write about? I have nothing to offer, no hope to bring. I have let them down.'

John shook his head sadly, 'No, you haven't! These are savage times and men are tried beyond their strength. Life for the poor is terribly hard and unjust, if you haven't any money then you are tempted to do things which you wouldn't normally do—brighten up your family's life a little, if only to show that you haven't forgotten them.'

'My wife, she can't read,' Wills' voice held a sob, 'they are alone, left to fend for themselves and I will never see them again.'

'Shush! Don't say that! Time will pass, then perhaps you could send for them.' John noted again the despair in his friend's eyes.

'And commit them to this journey?—I think not—I am dead to them.' His face was lined with concern and John feared that perhaps his friend was right, much could happen in seven years.

'I was a fool,' Wills blurted out suddenly, 'such a fool! I've never been dishonest in my life but when things were bad after the war and flour was too dear, we couldn't manage. My wife was with child again and the children were sick. I was desperate. The estate had so many crops and vegetables that I didn't think they'd miss a few, but I'd reckoned without the sharp-eyed overseer. Each night I took some home until it became a habit. They near hanged me—it's a pity they didn't, it would have been better than this.'

'Nonsense—to your family you are still alive and that alone offers them a kind of hope.' Yet John knew that the future was bleak. At least he had no ties, unlike his friend. Of course there was Fanny, but he was having difficulty now picturing her in his mind, her face, surrounded by a halo of golden hair, was becoming indistinct. 'We must not separate, you and I!' he said to Wills encouragingly. 'We have to meet up again wherever we are sent. Perhaps I could see you from time to time?'

Wills sighed, 'I am merely a shepherd and you are an educated man. I would only drag you down'.

John shook his head. 'It makes no difference if we all end up in the quarries! I can't think of any man on this ship with whom I'd rather spend my time, other than you. Friendship cannot be separated by background— we need each other! I hear that they need shepherds out there, perhaps if you tell me a little about the ways of a shepherd and his flock I could, perhaps, join you on a farm.' He had no intentions of losing Wills again and was willing to go to any lengths to stay by his friend's side.

A wry smile flickered across Wills' tired countenance at the simple faith of his friend. 'They can be stupid creatures, can sheep, and try the patience of Job. I suppose anything is worth a try, to keep us together that is! You can only learn about sheep by handling them but there is no harm in my trying to teach you what I can. But what will you do if we are separated and go to different farms? Another shepherd would soon realise that you're inexperienced.'

With a reassuring grin John quickly replied, 'I'm a good learner, and will face that problem when it comes, if it does. At least it gives us something to hope for—a future.'

The Cape of Good Hope was behind them and the last leg of the journey was becoming more miserable with each passing day. Frequent squalls tossed the vessel violently, whilst rain lashed her decks. In these wearying conditions it was impossible to keep warm, and men who had stupidly disposed of their clothing earlier in the journey now rued the day, for they were left without protection against the weather, and no man's clothing was safe from marauding thieves. Thick fog clung to the ship as she rolled in the waves one day and John found himself preferring to remain in the hold rather than be surrounded by the ghostly wet blanket up on deck.

He watched Wills with concern, for he appeared to be getting weaker than ever, complaining of feverishness. His face was alternatively flushed, then pale, and the arrowroot gruel supplied by Dr Rogerson offered no solution to his general condition. He coughed incessantly, irritating all within earshot and when it was obvious that something was seriously wrong he was transferred to the hospital.

Captain MacDonald was exceedingly pleased with himself as he stood surveying his ship. With 108 days sailing behind him and only five or so more to go they had made good progress. It had been a relatively trouble-free voyage, as voyages went, and they had not entered port once, enabling him to cut almost ten days from his previous record. Few fierce storms had hindered the vessel, and the winds had been mostly fair, but he was no fool and knew that until he was safe in Sydney Cove anything could happen. To him the sea lived, like some powerful mistress, toying with him, challenging him to a duel. He felt that one day she would tire of him and sweep him to her bosom but until that day came he would continue to fight her and give her good sport. He had no desire to end his days in an armchair by some fireside, he would much prefer to die at sea than become old on land.

He stood on the bridge proudly, allowing the breeze to tug at his clothes. A soldier approached and halted, saluting the Captain. 'Sir!' he said.

Reluctant to break off his communication with the sea, Captain MacDonald turned, 'What is it then?' he barked.

'Dr Rogerson's compliments, Sir, and could he see you in your cabin as soon as possible, please?'

'In my cabin you say? Very well, you may return my compliments, and say I will be down directly.'

'Aye, Sir!'

Leaving the bridge with some regret, he followed the soldier and headed below to his cabin. He had a good surgeon in Rogerson and could be sure the fellow was not about to waste his time. However, a sense of foreboding darkened the Captain's thoughts, for the good doctor would not have sent for him without good reason.

'Morning, James!' he said, entering the cabin apprehensively. 'Got a problem have you? I hope it's not too serious, we've had a good trip so far—don't spoil it for me now!'

James Rogerson came straight to the point. 'I'll not beat about the bush—we've a bad outbreak of dysentery on board. I'm endeavouring to contain it, but will you warn the crew to be careful what they eat, and to wash their hands in vinegar before handling food, AND after relieving themselves—every time!'

'We haven't lost a man so far this trip but we're not there yet James, so do what you can—do your best, man!' He reached out and opened a nearby cupboard. 'Will you take a brandy with me, James? It may ward off the devil. I was just congratulating myself on the speed and efficiency of this journey, and now this happens!' He was lucky. Dr Rogerson supervised the *Speedwell* excellently, endeavouring to instil good hygiene in the convicts but there was always an element of the unexpected on any voyage.

'Flies don't need much encouragement in these conditions' James replied. 'As you know, we always sprinkle chloride of lime around the water closets to minimise risks, but to be fair it is not easy for the men in those conditions.'

There was little point in debating the matter further, Captain MacDonald concluded. He just prayed that they would be able to contain the out-break, and he knew that if any man could do it, it would be James Rogerson. 'Do your best, man, that's all I ask' he repeated gravely.

James thought for a moment, then remarked, 'I think it would be a good idea to stop them fishing, as the sick men were doing a few days ago. They may not have gutted the fish thoroughly, or cleaned up properly afterwards.' Sipping his brandy, the Doctor continued, 'Fish stinks enough without being careless about it, and their quarters are foul-smelling as it is. The flies will have had a field day!'

The Captain readily agreed to James' suggestion, adding with a sigh, 'What I wouldn't give right now to eat a freshly-caught trout!' He could almost taste the flaky texture of the fish which he used to catch as a youth in the river Tay. 'We're in the Bass Straights now, and must be no more than five days away from Sydney, less perhaps if the weather is kind. Keep your fingers crossed that we don't have trouble at the last minute, then we shall be able to dine in style when we disembark.'

In his weakness it had been Wills who had gone down with dysentery first, and as John held the horn tumbler of barley water to his friend's lips he had prayed that the sickness was merely due to his having malnutrition. However, next day, two more men from their compartment developed similar symptoms, all three were taken to the sick bay, leaving John alone and in a despondent mood. Before long, he too was removed to the now cramped hospital. He was becoming as sick in mind as in body in his delirium, and in moments of clarity he began to want nothing more than to die.

It wasn't long before the Doctor had ten sick men on his hands and the Captain approved the plunder of the *Speedwell's* private medical chest in an effort to check the out-break. He breathed deeply with relief when, as the strong westerly winds drove his vessel along the familiar coast of New South Wales, he finally saw one morning, the entrance to Sydney Cove.

By eight a.m. he had every fit man mustered on deck as his ship dropped anchor between the heads of Port Jackson and, within the hour, a pilot arrived on board to guide the *Speedwell* into Sydney Cove. However, it was after noon when she finally came to anchor in the shelter of the cove and Captain MacDonald's job was nearly done.

Chapter 4

*O*n *the deck* of another anchored and battered transport ship, the *Lord Eldon*, stood one more weary exile. This was a man banished from Sydney for the past eight lonely years and separated from his wife and daughters, who now returned to a land whose inhabitants had turned their backs on him, hoping never to set eyes on him again.

The gout-ridden figure of John Macarthur observed with apprehension the dramatic changes which the intervening years had wrought upon the face of Sydney Cove. Gone were the decrepit and ramshackle houses which had in the past greeted many a reluctant and often near-dead voyager. In their stead were imposing new edifices raised as though in defiance of the 'Old Rebel' of Botany Bay, who now leaned against the side of the ship for support.

The tall white lighthouse silhouetted against the clear sky on the South Head of Port Jackson seemed to offer a warning, rather than a welcome. It was not that the Colony's progress in his absence irritated him, but rather the fact that he was aware from letters and reports that even now the old strife was still there, gnawing and festering away amongst the inhabitants. Internal politics were no longer his affairs, and his long battle for permission to return from exile had been granted on the promise that he would not meddle in the running of the Colony. He had every intention of keeping his word in this matter.

Macarthur was no longer the young energetic subaltern who had come of his own free-will, accompanied by his wife and baby son, with the Second Fleet to Botany Bay in 1790. His joining of the New South Wales Corps had rewarded him well, for the opportunity of promotion and welcome increase in pay had come quickly to this man of humble origins, a man with ideals and determination. Now, twenty-seven years later, at the age of fifty, with hopefully the last wearisome voyage between the Colony and England behind him, his body seldom free from pain, and his mind often beset with melancholia, he was left irritable and irascible. He had seen in this harsh and forbidding land possibilities for prosperity, but Governor after Governor had chosen to ignore his suggestions, or had only half-heartedly accepted his ideas. Ideas which he believed would have brought wealth and security to all.

Always in the background there had been envy and greed, and policies which left the Colony vulnerable in times of drought or flood. He had eventually quarrelled with successive Governors, those weak-minded men with their simpering wives, and the ill-trained and unqualified Judge Advocates. The last clash, with Governor Bligh, yes, the very same who had been unable to govern his own ship, had brought about his downfall. None of them had recognised that Macarthur's dedication to the rearing of pure thoroughbred sheep with fleeces of finest wool was not just for his benefit alone but for that of the whole Antipodes, to provide them with a much needed exportable commodity. The Mother Country needed good wool, and Sydney needed mutton. But no, he was seen instead by most as a power-greedy and quarrelsome landowner.

The loud-mouthed, vicious and vulgar Governor William Bligh became his arch enemy, seeking every opportunity to thwart and hinder the sound proposals he put forward. The jealous and spiteful gossips of Sydney had fed Bligh well with their tittle-tattle and lies, until too late they realised that he was strangling them all with his crafty and mean ways. Towards the end of his ineffectual and tyrannical rule he had tried to seize their property and then illegally arrested Macarthur on a trumped-up charge of importing two liquor stills, before jailing him for alleged treason. The people had finally seen the light on that hot evening in January 1808. Enraged citizens and military alike had rebelled over the shambles of Macarthur's trial, and set out to seize Bligh. As they ransacked his house, the stout, broad little man had been found beside the bed, under which he had most probably been hiding, with dust and feathers stuck to his coat and 'bed fluff' on his rear end.

John Macarthur could well understand why the mutineers on the *Bounty* had risen all those years before against the self-opinionated and arrogant Captain, but what he could not understand was why, knowing the man's history, His Majesty's Government had been foolish enough to send out Bligh in the first place as Governor of New South Wales. The insurrection caused by Bligh's illegal act ended his career as Govenor in the Colony.

After two and a half years Macarthur took a trip to England where he was finally charged as an instigator in that riot and was prohibited from returning to New South Wales and his family. Exile in England, however, had not left this sheep-rearer entirely without ambition nor had he wasted his time whilst there. Not only had he battled constantly against ill-health, but he had persistently pestered the Government to accept his ideas about the sheep industry, until after eight and a half years they had agreed to his repatriation on condition that he kept out of politics. During those years he had prepared carefully, following the market trends, and judging the quality of product and consignment methods of foreign importers. As a result, through letters sent home to his wife in Sydney he had been able to improve the methods on his own farm.

There had been no threat to his liberty whilst living in England, but if at any time he had returned to Sydney Cove he would have immediately been arrested for his part in instigating the uprising against Bligh.

Armed now with a promise that his liberty was assured he was returning, but there was no triumph in this return, only relief and an eagerness to put more of his ideas into practice. The return of this forceful, quarrelsome owner of Elizabeth Farm would not be welcome news to many people in New South Wales, he knew that, but in the past they had been given several chances to rid themselves of him. They had not stirred themselves sufficiently when he had offered to sell them his land and live-stock, at low prices, and now he was coming back with Government promises of yet more land and additional convicts, increasing the resentment they felt for him.

The English Government had generously constructed a greenhouse on board the *Lord Eldon* to enable him to transport his precious cuttings of vines, fruits and flowers which he hoped would benefit the Colony. There was much to do in the months ahead, but the prodigal would need to keep his part of the bargain, lie low and act with caution.

It was seven o'clock in the morning on the *Lord Eldon* and the pain from his gout was excruciating as John Macarthur attempted to scrawl a brief note to his beloved Elizabeth. Poor Elizabeth, for nine long years she had run his estates and done a magnificent job by all accounts. How he missed her! He had written frequently, but in his heart he knew that he would be facing a stranger. Had he managed to sell his New South Wales properties and stock he would not have returned to this God-forsaken land, but would have bought a gentleman's farm amidst the lush green vales of England and brought his wife and the girls home. Perhaps the miserable English winters would have finished him off and then they would have buried him in England's soft, gentle soil. Instead he had to live with a painful and tortured body and prove to the world that he had been right to devote his energies to sheep.

James Macarthur took his father's letter and added a postscript, for he and William, his brother, were to proceed to the farm in the first available carriage, leaving their father to follow when the heat of the day had past. Their youthful impatience had already been stretched to the limit as the adverse winds had slowed the final part of the voyage. They were eager to return to their childhood haunts but children they no longer were, for they were now strong, tall young men of sixteen and eighteen years, well educated, but with no desire to remain at a distance from Elizabeth Farm any longer. What had started out merely as a visit to England had in the end sadly separated them from Elizabeth Farm. The big cities of Europe had provided adventure for the boys but proved no match to the call which the wilderness of home offered to these sons of an empire builder. Home, that place where they had roamed freely amidst the harsh challenging landscape. The bush held no fear for them, they loved its wild woods and ungiving land with its strange creatures and exotically plumed birds. Their freedom had been that which most men would only have dreamed of and they had missed it dreadfully.

All morning the two Elizabeth's, mother and daughter, watched the road from Sydney until eventually in the distance they saw the dust rise and billow as the carriage came nearer. Finally, when the rumbling wheels entered the farmyard, Elizabeth Macarthur trembled with emotion to see that the shapes in the carriage were indeed those of her sons. For nine long years she had been parted from them and now they were returning home. Time had wrought its changes, turning them from children into men, but she too had changed with the responsibilities of the farm resting firmly on her shoulders for so long. Yet, she was nervous also, not over the boys home-coming but of meeting the stranger who was her husband. It was therefore, with mixed emotions that she waited impatiently for the carriage to stop before the door, and then, in a flurry of excitement, two splendid young men climbed down and seized her.

'Mother!' was the only discernible word in the babble of excited voices. Then, nine year old Emmeline threw herself with childish glee upon the brothers she had only heard about. They towered above Elizabeth, strong and powerful, dwarfing her as they clasped her again in their arms. 'It's so good to be back home,' they chorused, and she wasn't sure which voice belonged to which son as the tears welled up in her eyes.

When finally they released her from their embrace she drew back. 'Come. Let me look at you both!' she cried, unable to keep the ring of pride from her voice. Whatever the future held in store for the farm and family, Elizabeth knew now that she would no longer work alone. She clasped the hands that were young, eager and capable and led them towards the house.

'Please, Mother!' James begged, holding her back. 'Let's walk in the garden amongst the smells that we've missed all these years. You've no idea how different they are from anywhere else!'

She smiled indulgently, listening to James talk as though she had never even seen England, although it was true she had given up hope of ever seeing her native county again. 'I have never forgotten the smells of Cornwall,' she replied, turning towards the precious garden.

'We've had enough of being cooped up,' sighed William. 'After the stifling heat of the tropics and the foul air on board ship still in our nostrils, the sweet smell of grass and eucalyptus is like Heaven.'

They strolled contentedly through the fruit trees and vines of the well-stocked garden, and Elizabeth remembered her hateful journey years ago, when she had been virtually a prisoner in the stinking, filthy cabin, with a tiny sickly babe pressed to her breast. This whilst trying to hide from the crude and vile antics of the convicts in the holds. 'Surely times have changed since my voyage here? Nothing could still be that bad or inhumane?' she asked hopefully yet she knew from tales which circulated in Sydney that ill-treatment still persisted on the transport ships. She didn't go to Sydney as often these days, preferring the tranquillity of the farm to the pathetic and often degrading sights which met even the least delicate of eyes there.

'We were lucky, we travelled as free men and with some respect on a good vessel, but I understand that on some ships many evils still persist. It seems that on some convict ships, men are treated more like animals than the impoverished beggars which some of them are.' James paused, old for his years, then continued with more youthful eagerness. 'The gardens are delightful! If the farm is as well taken care of as this, then I think father will be well pleased!'

'How is he?' she asked tenderly, 'Is the gout as bad as he says it is?' She could still hardly believe that her husband was at last returning.

'His health is gone, and you are bound to find him changed. We are hoping that the warmth of this place will help him, but he is often sorely depressed and racked with pain. Even his letters to you have often drained him of strength and we have been obliged to finish them off for him.' James spoke cautiously, wondering if his mother was aware of the real extent of the melancholia which disturbed their father. 'He will come as soon as it is cool enough for him to travel. He didn't mind us coming on ahead in the heat of the day.'

'Will Papa really be here soon?' begged Emmeline, pulling at William's coat.

William playfully caught his sister in his arms and lifted her high into the air. 'Yes, he'll be here by tonight. My, you're not at all as I imagined you to be. Can you ride a horse?'

'Of course I can,' she replied indignantly, 'better than you can!' Her mind raced on excitedly, 'Tell me about England!'

'I'll tell you all about it soon, and tomorrow you shall ride with me far out into the bush and down along the river to show me the farm and pastures.' He was impatient to ride again into the wild countryside, but he knew he ought not to absent himself from his family so soon after his return. 'Come, little sister, I'm thirsty. Let's see if I can remember where the kitchen is!'

Watching her fledglings as they hurried away, Elizabeth smiled and turned back to James. 'Your father has fought long and hard for the farm and this Colony. It will be almost impossible for him to forego his battles with the community here, but he must remain quiet. I am older now, and tired.' She sighed, bending to remove a wilted head from a rose before she spoke again, almost to herself. 'The years, whilst he was away, were peaceful for me, and I have no desire for conflict or political connivances. I am now socially accepted in Sydney, with kindness, and on my own merit.'

They wandered slowly, alone now, enjoying the silence. Elizabeth wondered about her husband; he had always been full of kindness to her and the children but he could be stubborn and troublesome when people crossed him. She knew too how this harsh climate and life was gradually affecting the minds of those earlier settlers, who had sailed in cruel conditions, fighting for survival against many odds. Would he too become irrational in his pain and suffering, just as so many others had done, and be tormented in his mind?

Later, as they stood watching the sun sink behind the eastern range of the Blue mountains awaiting the 'Old Rebel's' return, she considered her own fortunate life. The good Lord had given her four admirable sons, all intelligent and of good countenance. John, who was at this moment studying law in London was of excellent character and a vigorous supporter of all that his father stood for. It was years since he had been home, and in spite of his regular correspondence Elizabeth pined to see him again, but she had to be content with the friendly features which she could see on the portrait he had sent with one of his informative letters.

'Is John well, does he take care of himself? Will he never marry?' she asked wistfully. Questions poured out in quick succession, as she sought to satisfy her curiosity about the family which seemed fated to be forever in a state of separation.

He smiled readily. 'Many a fond parent would like to snare him for their daughter and the ladies contrive to effect a marriage, but he is single-minded and works hard, and seems to have no preferences. No, he is quite content, and Elizabeth Farm is never very far from his mind. He is very respected in London, and has been a pillar of strength to father, striving constantly to clear his name and hasten his return home. He fought hard to make the Government see the sense in father's ideas, and although it took a long time he was determined never to falter in the struggle until he succeeded!'

'And Edward? His visits are so infrequent, between campaigns. Is he happy?' his mother enquired.

James nodded. 'He joined us in Europe, but then we wrote of it. He's the adventurous one, and enjoys life to the full on his travels with the Military, but I think he will come home to stay eventually. However, I fear that John will always remain in London.'

How like her he was, she noted, with his dark wavy hair and serious eyes. A warm pleasant smile played on his lips and his mother liked what she saw. Edward, the soldier, was the fair, gallant one, whereas William seemed to have more than his share of good humour. She loved them all.

Suddenly, James lifted his head, looked out into the distance and exclaimed, 'I believe father is coming now!' He raised himself from the rail upon which he was leaning and Elizabeth touched his arm as if for reassurance, as she too peered out along the road.

The single-storey dwelling that was Elizabeth Farm overlooked the gentle, peaceful Parramatta River. Its elevated position protected it from the occasional flooding which destroyed crops growing along and near the river. John Macarthur watched as the carriage drew him nearer to his homestead and family and vowed to himself that never again would he cross another ocean as long as he lived.

Every bone in his body ached from the jolting of the carriage and he longed for the peace and tranquillity that only Elizabeth and the farm could offer. There was no sign of disorder or neglect anywhere. Fences were well maintained and everywhere there was evidence of good management. He had Elizabeth to thank for this.

The man, old before his time and worn out, still found himself anxious to begin the final stage of his great plan to build a giant corporation, which would supply the English market with the finest wool. In order to do this he needed the land promised him, and also the extra convicts to work it. He could not rest until all was done. He was home!

It took John Macarthur two weeks before he could bring himself to make the customary call upon the Governor of the Colony. To Governor Macquarie, who was still pestered by the troublesome colonists, the thought of meeting yet another, possibly the most troublesome of all, gave him little pleasure. Yet he wasted no time in granting the 'Old Rebel' his grazing land and the convict labour he desired, which had been promised in London.

With these acquisitions safely in his grasp, and having quickly discovered that political life in New South Wales had changed little in his absence, John Macarthur retired to his farm at Parramatta, and for two years endeavoured to live in peaceful seclusion from the outside world. He rarely visited the capital and left his family to socialise with his old enemies.

Chapter 5

John Andrews was oblivious to the sight of the white light-house on his arrival at Sydney Cove. He could see nothing for the glare of the hot sun which hurt his eyes as they carried him from the *Speedwell*, with little or no care for his comfort, to the long-boat which lay alongside the transport ship. Nor had he been aware during the last stage of the journey of the storms which had constantly washed the decks as they sailed the half-charted coast of New South Wales. Land-breezes had caused the ship to be tossed and battered by tempestuous waves, but he had been beyond caring, praying only for the angel of death to release him from his miserable state.

He was just as unaware of the other prisoners who were lined up on deck for inspection by the Colonial Secretary and the Principal Superintendent of Convicts. They were all, to a man, scrubbed clean, hair newly cut and faces shaved as they stood in the heat of the day dressed now in coarse, arrowed trousers and jackets, unsure of their fate and resentful of their predicament. Each man was wretched from the shortage of good fresh food and clean water, and although they were relieved to have ended the harrowing journey and to quit the filthy holds, the uncertainty of their future loomed before them. Some stared sullenly round whilst others gazed blankly out across the shimmering water towards the town.

Minor officials followed obediently in the wake of the Superintendent with their large assignment books, endeavouring to discover what talents if any the prisoners might have. Through mismanagement on leaving England no paperwork had been despatched with the *Speedwell's* cargo other than a list of names, and it would be the prisoners' own statements which determined their lot. The men, however, were unaware of the missing documents and had no reason to lie, for it would achieve nothing. Only a few had a trade to follow, and some of those were useless to a Colony which needed brawn rather than brain from the convicts. It was only the literate who stood any chance of avoiding the digging and rock-breaking of the construction gangs.

Having delivered his human cargo James MacDonald sat below deck once more, writing with satisfaction in his journal. With great pride he wrote; 'Total days at sea 113 (10 days off my record). Prisoners behaved very quietly and readily obeyed orders, and are delivered safely, at little expense to the Government, (I flatter myself)'.

There had been no sign of mutiny, he had made sure of that by quickly imprisoning possible offenders. One prisoner had run amok but that was only to be expected in such confined conditions. Two deaths had unfortunately occurred during the voyage, of dysentery, one only last night, and the lives of two more hung in the balance. Both were in the Colonial hospital with Dr Redfern.

He closed the journal, rose and left the stifling cabin, his duty almost complete. Once on deck he surveyed his vessel. She looked more like her old self again, with decks freshly holystoned and her holds swilled out thoroughly.

His Excellency Governor Lacklan Macquarie climbed aboard. He was, at times, in spite of his hard eyes and determined jaw, a likeable old soul, though sometimes a little too self-righteous. He was perhaps over-dressed for the heat, his gaudy tunic trimmed with gold, and his collar so high and stiff that it seemed to support his ears. After exchanging salutes, Captain MacDonald greeted Governor Macquarie heartily. He was eager to get the formalities over and done with, in anticipation of what Sydney could offer in the way of good food and female company.

John could not have cared less had they dropped him into the sea, for he considered that drowning must be preferable to the ghastly state in which he found himself. He was acutely aware of the stench from his body, and had no strength even to shield his eyes from the blazing sun. The jolting and swaying of the boat seemed never ending, and finally out of weakness, he fainted.

How long he had lain in the cot he did not know, but the bustle of activity and voices gradually woke him. At the same time, he was aware that the foul smell of the holds which had surrounded him for so long, had finally gone. He turned his head and in focusing his gaze saw Wills in the cot alongside his own. The face of his friend was white and emaciated, his body almost skeletal, and he lay still, staring at nothing but the white ceiling of the Colonial Hospital.

When his strength finally allowed, John whispered, 'Wills—can you hear me?' He was sure his voice was loud enough but there was no reply from the frail human by his side.

'Now laddie, take it easy,' came a voice, firm but kindly.

John looked about him and encountered a tired, careworn face. 'Oh, God! I wish I were dead,' he cried out piteously, reaching out to touch the man's arm.

'The worst is over, my friend, get some sleep,' Dr Redfern urged, looking down at the pathetic wretch in the cot before him. He knew his patient was weak, but not beyond recovery. He found little satisfaction in his ability to revive men, only to see them brutalised later by the penal system. He had done his best to improve things but when Captains deprived men of decent provisions on board ship in order to sell what was left at a fat profit, he was left to repair the damage. Yet these men had travelled on the *Speedwell*, and his good friend James Rogerson was noted for the excellent care he took of prisoners, while MacDonald was known for his humane captaincy.

Dr Redfern knew the real score more than most, having been a convict himself! Only his skill as a surgeon had saved him from the dreadful humiliations and degradation which existence in this Colony subjected transportees to. What was he saving the lives of these men for? What good did it do if they were then worked to death or abused like animals? He looked intently at the man lying before him, whose eyes beseeched help. The gaze was so frank and honest that he turned away, lest he read too much in it or gave hope, where there was none to give.

The hand weakly plucked at his sleeve, 'Please, is he going to get well again?' John begged hopefully, indicating the other bed, 'he's a good friend of mine!'

The older man shook his head sadly. 'He's very weak. You're younger and stronger than he is, but you both need plenty of rest!' The lilting highland voice softened its usual brusqueness. he was not a hard man but circumstances compelled him to avoid becoming too interested or involved with his patients, for his own sanity's sake. Yet he did much more for them than he needed, he had organised, and was running, an out-patients surgery in his spare time. He wondered, again, why he bothered, when, at every opportunity some drowned their miseries by consuming endless gallons of grog. He had learned to steal himself against their guile, but in the really sick there was in truth, only a pathetic cry for help. He turned and left, disturbed by the feeling of futility which had come over him and by the state of the young man who had impressed James Rogerson so much. When would this evil system end? When would the mother country cease to spew out her dross and, instead, cure the evils on its home ground? Moving swiftly, he left John and proceeded to give his attention to other patients.

John realised that his only friend in the world was dying. Without him there was nothing, no comfort, no hope, and no one whom he could trust amongst the thieving scoundrels with whom he had voyaged. His disenchantment and disillusionment with human nature had long since convinced him of his isolation in the world. Turning slowly, he looked at Wills again but sadly realised it was too late. Wills was dead. He tried to call Dr Redfern back, but he was nowhere to be seen. There was no one now! He was truly alone in a strange and forbidding land, without friends, and he grieved over the sad loss of this unassuming man who had defended and encouraged him so much. John lay back and closed his eyes, hoping and praying that he too would not see the light of day again.

His sleep was fitful and disturbed. He was walking once again, in his dreams, amongst the precious hills with Fanny by his side. He could even smell the bracken and the perfume of her hair as they moved towards each other, but as she smiled and he reached out to touch her, she faded into a mist which descended suddenly and she was gone!

He woke with a start. Fanny had been almost there and he had nearly touched her. Closing his eyes he tried to recapture the dream but the harsh reality of his situation drove it rapidly from his mind. Tears came to his eyes. There would be no Fanny, no hills or mist for him ever again. What right had she to invade his dreams, bringing back the image of her youthfulness and spirit, when he was doomed to live without her forever? Now Wills had gone too, leaving him in a well of misery from which it was impossible to escape. He stared around at the white walls, his mind in turmoil, and with the will to survive slowly ebbing away.

In the days that followed, John was too weak to leave his bed but when he finally did so, his legs were barely strong enough to support him. Those men who had left the Speedwell on their feet had been similarly affected as, accustomed as they were to the pitching decks, the solidity of the wharf side upset their balance, and their legs buckled beneath them.

Each time Dr Redfern passed his patient's bed he noted with concern the lack of response in the young man's eyes. Then, as time went on and John's dreadful pallor began to disappear, he was equally disturbed by the fact that the young man was so listless. William Redfern had no favourites amongst his patients, indeed he dare not favour one man above another amongst the unlovable scallywags, and in most cases he was powerless to do anything other than return them to their miserable lifestyle. However, he was reluctant to move John back amongst the others, even though his infectious period was over, fearing for his mental state.

Slowly, with great patience he drew out answers to his questions, questions about the old country, for he was eager for news from the old world that was not distorted by the bigotry which the isolation of the Colony bred. He liked the fresh-faced young man, recognising in him something which he too had once been. He phrased his questions simply at first, taking care not to drive John back into melancholy. Then, when he thought he saw an interest in life returning, he took pleasure in seeking his company.

In a moment of quiet confidentiality he said, whilst buttoning his coat, 'I too, was a convict once. It seems a lifetime away now! John stared at the old doctor in disbelief.

Doctor Redfern ignored the surprised look on his patient's face, saying deliberately, 'It isn't easy, the life of a convict, or Government men as we are called over here, but you would survive best if you could steel yourself against the demon grog!'

John watched the old man as he went quickly about his business. What had brought the good doctor to this sorry existence?

'I see I shock you,' Dr Redfern said, 'but life has its strange twists. I remained here after my time was up because I had no ties in the old country and I felt I was needed here.'

Recovering from this surprising disclosure by the doctor, John declared bluntly, 'It's difficult to believe you were capable of any crime!'

'I don't consider I committed any crime, young man, but it is sometimes easy for one's acts to be misunderstood.' His answer was suddenly brusque as if he had said too much, yet he noticed the interest brought about by his words. He was not in the habit of telling his story, though many knew of it. 'We'll soon have you out of here, now,' he said, changing the subject. 'I'm afraid you will have to join the others soon, I can't keep you in isolation any longer.'

Sensing the doctor's reluctance to say more about himself, John said with deep conviction, 'I was framed'. William Redfern looked sternly into the young man's eyes, he had studied many men in his time and considered himself to be a reasonable judge of character. Perhaps he was getting soft in his old age yet he found himself believing the young man's statement.

He uttered a word of warning, 'So many men say that, but no one believes them. The old lags will resent you and make your life a misery if you persist with your story. You will just have to accept life as it is.'

'I know that already, but I thought you of all people might understand?'

The doctor shook his head sadly, 'After a while in this Colony one doesn't know what to believe, and if you are innocent you'll never prove it here—just try not to let it make you bitter'. It was a hollow statement. In the long years ahead how could a young man in his prime of life be expected to accept its cruelties without becoming bitter and twisted?

'They accused me of stealing a silver watch, but I had one of my own, a finer one than the one they say I stole! You know, I always believed in justice and that the poor should stand firmly together so as to get a fair deal for a hard day's work. I see nothing admirable in a system which prospers while its poor starve, or sends innocent people to the other side of the world on the word of a ruffian.' John's eyes flashed with indignation. It had been many months since he had spoken out with such feeling and this left him drained.

The fire had not been missed by Dr Redfern. Oh, to have such feelings of youth again! He reflected on his own adolescence and it seemed a hundred years or more since those exciting days. He then said, not unkindly, 'Rest now, perhaps we will get another chance to talk alone before you leave.'

'I do hope so,' John replied, gratefully.

Turning away, Redfern sighed deeply. It was a sad fact that only a short time in this country would be needed to extinguish any fire or passion brought about by his patient's return to good health. He had seen it happen all too often, signs of rebellion were immediately crushed. He must guard himself against involvement with this young man as friendship with a prisoner was impossible.

Throughout the night William Redfern tossed in his bed disturbed constantly by his thoughts over the fate of the young man in his dispensary. Try as he might he could not forget, and by daybreak he felt that he had gained little benefit from his slumbers; he resolved to remove John Andrews into the company of his future companions that very day.

John waited impatiently for the doctor's return, longing to talk again with a man of such compassion. He was tired, not from lack of sleep as was the doctor but from inactivity and boredom. He was, however, disappointed for when Dr Redfern re-appeared he was reluctant to talk, although eventually he spoke kindly enough.

'I'm afraid I will have to move you now after all!' he said apologetically. The crestfallen look on John's face spoke volumes, so he added, 'Unfortunately it had to happen sometime. They're a rough lot in the main ward but if you don't alienate them you'll be alright. However, it's not just the lads you'll need to guard against you know'. Lowering his voice he advised, 'You're an educated man and sound as though you have radical leanings, my friend. Take heed, interference is not appreciated here. Some of us have spent years battling for convict emancipation for those who have served out their time, but it is a hard battle. There are those who fear that they will become outnumbered by industrious ex-Government men. Take care not to make enemies of them, for they don't suffer trouble-makers, free or otherwise, for very long.'

'Surely there is hope if men like you take up our cause?' John replied.

'It has taken me years to bring about reform of medical conditions here in Botany Bay and on the transport ships, yet even these results fall far short of what is needed and I still tread warily.'

'I think,' John said passionately, 'that there is far too much corruption and self-interest in the world. It suited some men very well when I was got rid of!'

The doctor sighed. 'I was sentenced to hang, but they thought me young and rash, and gave me a reprieve.'

John shook his head in disbelief, 'What did you do, a man in your position?'

'I was a Naval Surgeon in '97' and there was a mutiny. All I did was try to get the men to be more united amongst themselves, but they said I was their leader. I was not.'

'So we are both guilty of trying to get men to fight for their rights! Things have not changed very much in all these years, have they?'

Someone was approaching and William Redfern drew himself upright as if his examination was complete, and brusquely informed John that he would have to remove him from isolation into the main body of the hospital.

'Thank you Sir, thank you for listening to me.' John murmured, and watched him go with a pang of regret, for he was going to miss the old man's company. It was obvious that the doctor had not had an easy time of it but he had managed to survive his ordeals, and he had to do the same. The thought of joining the other convicts did nothing to raise his spirits, the noise and general disruption from their ward serving only to remind him of the coarseness he had endured since leaving Sheffield.

After tidying his bed, he walked to the window opposite and looked out over the infamous Botany Bay. It was not at all as he had anticipated whilst on board ship, and the calming beauty of the splendid scene, with the ships lying peacefully in the shimmering water was one that gladdened his heart. Paling fences surrounded the houses, enclosing colourful gardens, and grand buildings could be seen standing proudly in the distance.

John then saw that a veranda ran the length of the hospital below his window, but there was no door opening onto it. How he longed to stand out there and breathe deeply of the clear air, that same air which had been so healing each morning as he climbed out of the ship's hold.

Only then did he fully appreciate that he was not in chains, and that he could walk comfortably without restraint. The floor did not heave beneath his feet anymore but the unaccustomed exercise made him weak and he sought the support of his bed once more. His rest was cut short, however, when an orderly instructed him to gather his things and go immediately to the other ward.

A row of unfriendly faces greeted him; most were resentful and careworn, others apathetic or as blank as the hospital walls. He had hardly been there more than a few minutes, when a voice called out from the adjacent bed, 'New here are you?' John turned to find a gnarled face watching him with the wary stare of a cat. The old lag then winked and grinned, revealing gaps where his teeth should have been. 'You'll not be here long, they'll have you in a gang as quick as lightning.' A ring of glee was in his voice and John recognised that there was no real friendship offered by the man.

'What's it like out there in the gangs, is it as hard as they say?' John felt obliged to enquire.

'Not arf! Day in day out, sweating amongst the perishin' flies, or drenched by the soddin' rain.' Sitting up, the old lag lifted his shirt, gingerly at first, then with a flourish as he turned his back on John. 'See these!' he boasted and, hearing John gasp said with pride, '150 lashes and not a squawk! And it's got me a few days rest in here!'

John stared, appalled by the angry red weal's which criss-crossed the man's back, the repulsive patches of dark, congealed blood patterning his skin, and he sat down weakly upon his own bed.

Quite suddenly the man lay back and cried, 'I can't move, me back's broken!'

An Orderly who had just entered the room eyed him contemptuously and growled 'You'll be back in the gang tomorrow you old fraud, and well deserved too.'

Doctor Redfern shook his head as he followed the Orderly in, quietly observing all that went on. In spite of the painful lashings meted out to him the old lag persisted in getting into trouble. That any man would willingly suffer so much for a few days rest amazed him, yet he had to admire the man's courage and determination.

When both the Doctor and the Orderly had passed through the ward, the old lag addressed John once more. 'They might well jeer, they think we're soddin' horses, pullin' and heavin' from dawn till dusk. If we're not breakin' up rocks then we're shiftin' the bloody things about.' There was no response to his tirade which only made him more irate. 'Not been out there yet, have you? I saw you come in, you'll wish you'd died along with that other fella!'

John sensed that he was being goaded into an argument but saw no point in retaliating; he had no facts upon which to speak yet he knew that he was expected to answer. 'Will we be chained all the time?' he asked lamely.

'Not everybody, not all the time. There's no place to run to. There's nothin' out there except bleedin' natives and starvation, just outback for hundreds of miles. Some think they can get to China if they walk far enough—silly buggers!'

'Do we get any spare time?' queried John.

'For grog and women, you mean?' he chuckled wickedly, 'There's nowt else!'

'Are there no other jobs but quarrying?' John asked hopefully.

'Sheep! Sheep watching, but who wants to be stuck out in the bush for hours on end, away from the women? Not that you've got any choice as to where they stick you!' He fell silent, having exhausted his repertoire and litany of complaints. The sound of heavy boots on the wooden floor roused him again. 'They're comin' for yer lad!' he crowed.

The Superintendent of Convicts entered, accompanied by two soldiers. 'Name?' he asked, opening the large assignment book which he had placed on the table in the centre of the room before looking across at John.

'Andrews Sir, John Andrews!'

'Guilty?' came the sharp question in reply.

What was the use in arguing? 'Yes!' he answered meekly.

'How many years?'

'Seven.'

'Trade?' The questions came thick and fast without compassion. John was merely another convict. 'Trade, man, trade?' The Superintendent repeated impatiently.

John thought quickly. If only he could get out of town into the hills he could think more clearly, get himself sorted out. He'd had enough of the heavy work in the dockyards at Portsmouth.

'Are you alright?' the voice asked again. A soldier made towards him.

'Shepherd!' he lied. Why not? He could learn, and Wills had explained quite a lot about the creatures as they had chatted together on the voyage. 'I'm a shepherd!' he repeated, with added conviction. It sounded good and he had no desire to work for another six and a half years in quarries which would damage his health, and maybe his hands. Hands which were capable of delicate art and printing skills.

The Superintendent raised his head questioningly, half in disbelief, 'Not another shepherd,' he sneered, 'England must have more shepherds than it has sheep. Come on! A likely young lad like you must have done more than mind sheep.' Then he fired a final question, 'What estate were you on?'

There was no going back, so John thought quickly. It was obvious from the questions that they had little or no documentation on him and his mind raced on in an effort to recall where Wills had worked. He couldn't remember, so in desperation gave the name of the nearest large estate he could recall in the area when he had lived in Sheffield. 'Wentworth—in Yorkshire.' He had remembered that the Magistrate, the Earl Fitzwilliam of Wentworth who had been the man to commit him, had a large estate somewhere north of the town.

'Hmm! Interesting!' muttered the Superintendent, 'D'Arcy Wentworth is connected with that family.' He shut the ledger quickly and led the soldiers away.

'What happens now?' John asked, turning to the old lag.

The toothless grin appeared once more. 'They'll assign you to a farm in the bush. They don't waste much time.' He winked evilly, but without malice, 'Shepherd be damned—we've all tried that one.'

Perhaps it had been foolish to lie, especially as he wasn't a good liar and now there was someone here who could possibly expose him for the fraud he was. 'Who is D'Arcy Wentworth?' he asked cautiously.

'I think he's a landowner or something hereabouts. It'll be a laugh if you get sent to work for him.' His words were accompanied by a low chuckle which made John even more apprehensive.

'What do they do with craftsmen and educated people, or those too weak to work in the quarries and unsuited for the bush?'

'Some go as servants,' the man shrugged, 'some work in the Military stores, others as clerks—that's if they can read and write! But you're only a simple shepherd.' he said sarcastically.

A shepherd indeed! thought Dr Redfern who had been working nearby during the interview. James Rogerson had told him that the young man had been writing letters home for the transportees until his sickness. He was pleased he had not been involved in the discussion as from his observations the fellow was well-educated. The young man was foolish, for his talents could probably have been put to good use in the Colony. However, it was too late now—being branded criminal was one thing, to be found to be a liar as well would only add to his disgrace. The fellow had sealed his own fate.

The road to Parramatta was out of the doctor's way but he felt a strange compulsion to visit his old friends the Macarthur's at Elizabeth Farm. Nearly a month had passed since he had seen old man Macarthur who was certainly keeping his word by remaining secluded on his farm. All through the 'Old Rebels' exile, William Redfern had kept an eye on the health of the Macarthur family, and at one point practically saving the life of the sickly daughter Elizabeth. They had in return always welcomed him as a friend, and in a letter from England John Macarthur expressed his heartfelt gratitude for the care he had taken of his family during his absence.

Hoping to reach Elizabeth Farm before nightfall, Dr Redfern spurred his horse on and was relieved when the low building finally came into view. Dismounting near the river below the farm he allowed his horse to drink before slowly leading it up to the house. It was indeed a remarkable place, it was not with idle hands that the Macarthurs had achieved so much, but with years of sheer determination. He secretly admired Mrs Macarthur, and respected her devoted loyalty to that stubborn husband of hers throughout the long lonely years of separation. She was as handsome a woman as she was shrewd in business, and had things been different he would not have been averse to wooing her himself.

Life in the Colony suited him well enough and in spite of his convict background, his skills as a surgeon had earned him a great deal of respect. He had devoted his life here to improving the lot of his fellow man but still managed to maintain his privacy and not become personally involved with any of the transportees, at least until now. He was strangely moved by the plight and waste of this fervent young man who reminded him so much of his own past self. This land was a cruel and crushing one, but he had seen it change, and watched its people take on a mantle of respectability, but it was still a brave man who could rise up from his lowly state and make something of himself. Life was not easy for ex-Government men, even those whose spirit had not been crushed by oppression.

Tying his horse to the fence he marched resolutely up to Elizabeth Farm, knocked on the door and waited patiently, no longer unsure of the wisdom of his decision, and determined to achieve his aim. Macarthur was in need of good reliable men, well, William Redfern would see that he got one.

There was no escape from the burning sun and parching dust as the five sweating Government men marched cheerlessly, in single file, along that same road to Parramatta. Flies buzzed irritatingly and persistently around their faces, sucking greedily at the beads of perspiration which ran down from under the straw 'issue' hats which the men wore. Sydney was long since behind them now and the picturesque harbour town through which they had passed had faded into the distance. During their march to the barracks that morning it seemed as though in every direction men toiled, gaunt and miserable, sweating and dirty. Their issue garments, marked with the telltale arrows of smudged paint, identified them to all, as they struggled, yoked like oxen to wagons filled with gravel and sandstone rocks. These rocks were to be hewn and dressed to build the new barracks which were rising slowly behind its perimeter wall on a hill above the town. Every building which rose in architectural splendour owed its existence to forced human toil.

John hated flies. They seemed to offer him greater attention than anyone else, and the more he tried to whisk them away the more they seemed determined to attack him. His fair complexion was not suited to this type of climate, and he longed for water, clear, pure, refreshing water. Heat had always sapped him of his energy but today, added to the weakness of sickness, it caused rivulets of perspiration to seep from every pore of his body.

Mounted guards rode front and rear of the column, missing nothing and knowing full well that any attempt to escape would be immediately foiled. No human being could outrun a horse, and any man not recaptured before reaching the bush could soon become lost and die in agony through lack of water. In the end most dragged themselves back to civilisation, their desire for freedom tempered by the futility of it all. Those who did not return were either butchered by the natives or died from starvation or other causes.

Slowly the richly pastured flats of Parramatta came into view, the lush grass appearing as manna from heaven to the foot-weary men now nearing the journey's end. The gentle slope, leading up to Elizabeth Farm, with its neat fences and well-stocked gardens, reminded John of his native Nottingham, and he envied the ducks as they floated contentedly on the man-made ponds.

Chapter 6

*L**ittle stirred across the vast landscape* except the grey woolly sheep that slowly foraged through the sparse grass of the bush for food. This monotonous scene only changed when birds of prey soared on outstretched wings over the flock or hovered in the hope of stealing a lamb.

John watched constantly, his eyes glazed with the tedium until each long day finally drew to a close. Shepherding had not come easy to him but he strove to remember all that Wills had taught him. It was his sixth day at Camden, a property some distance from the main farm, and already he was afraid for his sanity. He had seen shepherds who were nearly deranged after years of loneliness out in the bush and he could quite understand their strangeness. He had seen the signs in the man who had shown him his duties on the first day. Now there was no one to talk to, no escape from the heat and flies, and he must never doze off. Only once in those first days had he allowed himself to fall asleep, then was suddenly jolted awake by the frantic bleating of his flock. In that moment between sleep and awareness he had seen the eagle hanging there, its giant wings gracefully spanning the sky against the sun, casting a huge shadow over him, the wing tips looking like black evil fingers ready to swoop. Too late had he recovered his senses, for the bird swooped on a lamb and lifted it bodily into the air, ignoring the threshing legs, before flying off with it into the distance. Had it not been for the plight of the lamb and the fact that he was supposed to be guarding the sheep he would have marvelled at such an act of nature. Instead, he waved his crook angrily at the eagle and shouted, 'You thieving swine!' so angrily that he disturbed again the already frightened sheep.

It had been with some trepidation that he returned the flock to the farm that night, knowing full well that if he did not report the loss, the shortage was bound to be discovered and he'd be punished in some way.

He fastened the gate of the enormous pen and headed for the manager's cottage. Even before he reached the building he heard angry voices from within, and he hesitated whether the time was right to admit his error.

'There is too much carelessness and laziness about this farm, and it has to stop here and now, do you hear?' the well-spoken voice thundered. 'I'll not have any more of it. Get the men together before sunrise and leave them in no doubt about the consequences. We treat men well here and this is the result!'

The voice was obviously that of an enraged young man and John hastily pulled back, hoping to slip away unnoticed and to postpone his errand, when the door swung open. It was too late, the keen-eyed youth caught sight of him and hailed, 'You there! What do you want?'

John hesitated, unsure of himself. 'I'm one of the new shepherds, Sir!' he called back respectfully, without the usual convict insolence.

In the weeks since his return from England young James Macarthur had confined himself mostly to the farm. He took few trips to Sydney and mixed little socially. He intended to learn as much as possible about the farm and its management without delay, but this left him little time for diversion or contact with other young men of his calibre. The respectful bearing and apparent sincerity of the young man before him calmed his anger somewhat, and in a quieter voice he asked, 'Right then, what's your problem?' He saw John hesitate. 'What do you want?' he repeated, the anger having gone from his voice.

John answered honestly, 'I'm sorry, Sir. I made the mistake of dozing off in the heat and an eagle took one of the lambs. I know that there is no excuse for this but I promise it won't happen again'.

'It had better not! Those lambs are of best Merino stock and their fleeces will be worth a good deal of money in a couple of years.' He was well aware of the hazards of shepherding and found it very difficult to be angry at the man's admission, as here in New South Wales deceit and concealment were second nature to most of the population. 'What's your name?' he asked.

'Andrews, Sir. John Andrews.'

'Ah, Redfern's prodigy.' James muttered beneath his breath. 'Alright, but you must pay for the lamb out of your earnings. We can't have rules for one and not for another. Report to the manager in the morning.' His voice was stern but not unsympathetic.

'Thank you, Sir.' Relief flooded over John for he had heard many tales of ill-treatment by masters here in the Colony and although it was a bitter blow to lose a good deal of money he accepted that it was just. Half turning to go, he paused as James Macarthur spoke again.

'Life in this part of the world is hard, and shepherding here has special but quite natural problems, but I know my mother has prided herself on treating men fairly if they are loyal to her. Keep your honesty, Andrews, and it will do you nothing but good in the long run.' James nodded his dismissal and strode off towards the house.

How long would it take him to pay off the lamb? John wondered, as he returned to his sleeping quarters. He tossed and turned during a restless night, considering his future. His dream of America was the only thing which would keep him sane in his loneliest hours, and he was determined to buy a passage out of the Colony when his sentence was over. He would need capital, far more than he could possibly earn, so had taken Doctor Redfern's advice and sworn off liquor. His regular bonus of wine was sold to less prudent men in order to save all he could for the day when once again he would be free. However, these efforts alone would not be sufficient and his stay in New South Wales could be prolonged indefinitely.

After many hours of careful deliberation, he resolved the problem by deciding to sell his skills in writing letters, as he had done on board ship. This occupation would surely keep his mind alert and perhaps save his sanity, but dare he risk using what small sum of money he had to buy the necessary writing materials? He instinctively fingered the little bag which hung round his neck to reassure himself that it was still there. The silver flute was there too, hidden and unplayed since his illness and the despondency which had afflicted him on his arrival. At one point he had feared the worst when waking in hospital and finding it gone, but James Rogerson had kept it safe and handed it to Dr Redfern for safekeeping until John was capable of taking care of it again.

Once out on the ranges, he tried to retain his enthusiasm but nothing shortened the long, lonely hours. He tried to while away the time by fashioning a whistle from a piece of wood, but to no avail. He played the flute, frightening the flock at first until eventually they accepted it and thereafter ignored it. At first the animals had fled his clumsy attempts to round them up, but as the sun began to go down they seemed instinctively to head for the safety of the farm, encouraged by the eerie sounds of the wild dogs. Even he was disturbed by their noise and was relieved when the sheep were finally secured in their pens.

By day came also the added threat, not just from the animals and birds of prey, but from Irish bush rangers greedy for mutton. John was at risk from these men as they were not averse to violence to get what they wanted. He knew he must be vigilant at all times.

As he played the flute to himself he mused on his plans, but the sharp memories of the past kept flooding back, memories which pained him. When he had pen and paper he would write to Fanny and tell her of his long solitary days, but what was the point? He did not doubt that she would remain loyal to him at the cost perhaps of ruining her own life, and that he would not allow her to do. She must be released from such a burden, especially as he now had no plans to return to England ever again.

The idea of writing to express his thoughts began to obsess him, and that evening, immediately he had returned the sheep to their pens, he approached the stock shed. The heavily-built store keeper was still at his work, despite the lateness of the hour, and although he was noted for his quick temper when provoked, his keen sense of humour came easily to the fore.

Patrick Kelly was as Irish as his name, good at his job, and was not easily fooled even by the most cunning of the convicts. His red hair blazed in the light of the lamp and his blue eyes twinkled merrily as he raised his bushy eyebrows to see who had entered the store. 'What can I do you for, young fella—not lost another sheep I'm thinking?' he asked in his thick Irish brogue.

John looked round hopefully, 'Is it possible to buy pens, ink and paper, d' you think?' The room was well stocked with farm implements and kept in a most orderly manner, as was the open ledger on the table which showed evidence of a neat hand.

'And what may I ask would a simple shepherd be wanting with writing materials?' came the reply. 'Is it the sheep you'll be writing to, or a fancy line to a filly?' There was a chuckle as his lilting Irish voice filled the shed.

John shook his head, and replied with a smile, 'I haven't written to England, apart from letters for other men, since I left York Castle. I had thought to earn a little by writing letters for men who couldn't write!'

'I can get supplies—but it'll cost you, mind,' offered Patrick, ever the business man.

'Can you get me something to read too? I live in fear of going mad out there with just the sheep and the heat. Anything will do, old newspapers, a bible, anything to pass the hours,' John begged.

'And just what will the sheep be doing while you're occupied with the reading? You're here to work, not to amuse yourself. You've only been here a short time and already you've lost a lamb'. Patrick Kelly's patience was fast disappearing.

'I would be less inclined to fall asleep if my mind was sufficiently occupied. I've tried whittling wood but I'm not much good at it.'

'Well it's harder you'll have to try then, my man.'

John tried another ploy, 'I have money to pay for the goods,' he pointed out.

The Irishman's eyes twinkled a little brighter at the mention of money and the chuckle came back into his voice. 'Will you be wanting a desk too? And someone to carry it?'

'No thank you. The pen and paper will do just fine,' John bantered in reply.

'I'll have no sauce young man, Patrick Kelly does no favours for the English for nothing.' He fell silent for a few seconds before adding seriously. 'If you have the cash, now that would be different. I can get what you want from Sydney within a few days. It'll cost you, and a little bit extra, if you know what I mean?'

'About how much extra?' John asked suspiciously, knowing full well that he would have to pay above the odds, but he was desperate, and these supplies were beginning to symbolise peace of mind to him.

Patrick Kelly had been quickly calculating just how much he dare ask for his profit margin, and took a chance. 'Say two shillings extra—eight altogether?'

Dismay showed on John's face as he realised that there would be very little of his treasure left after the transaction but he knew there was no other way to obtain what he wanted. 'Very well then, you get the things and I'll see you alright.'

'Ah, no! No y'don't—it's cash it is, or nothing doing.' The hand of providence stretched out across the counter, leaving John with no alternative.

In spite of the fact that the money hung around his neck, John replied cautiously, 'I'll bring it in ten minutes.' Then he left the store to wander where he thought no one would observe him before removing the cash from the purse. He shook the coins free, glad that he had the presence of mind not to reveal too much to the canny storekeeper. He slipped out of the shadows, returned to the Irishman and handed over his precious eight shillings.

'Would you be wanting a wife too?' Patrick Kelly mocked, pleased with the evening's business, 'I have two daughters who'll be eligible soon.' His eyes were dancing now, reminding John of the little people the Irish were so fond of talking about. Then suddenly the man's eyes became serious, and he bent closer to whisper. 'If it's a woman you'll be needing to warm your bed just ask Patrick now.'

'I might want a wife one day—but I'll not be paying for one', John said, imitating the man's brogue. Then, out of curiosity he asked. 'Do they allow us to marry out here?'

The Irishman shook his head in amusement, 'You've a lot to learn, me lad. There's nothin' for a man to do round here at night and you'd be lucky to find a spare female this side of Sydney. If you find one, grab her quick, and providing the Master gives his consent, you can wed. They like to think a woman anchors a man down, and makes him more dependent and reliable. It works too—if you can manage to find a woman that is!' He rubbed his fingers through his beard, and scratched at his chin before adding, 'You'd be better off concentrating on your sheep, my boy.'

Leaving the shed for the second time that evening John wandered slowly back to his quarters, content with his achievements.

Patrick Kelly kept his word. Within the week he obtained the precious commodities for which he had been paid, and about which John had enquired anxiously after work each evening when he returned to the farm. In the meantime in preparation, John knocked together a small wooden box in which to keep the pens, ink and paper, and utilised scraps of rough hessian which he begged from the shearing shed to make a bag in which to carry it.

However, the weather was changing, leaving him little opportunity to do more than his job. Quite suddenly it became stormy and unpredictable and it was as much as he could do to keep warm and dry. He would return each evening too exhausted to write, and fall asleep instead.

Without warning one particular afternoon the sky darkened, and gloomy storm clouds gathered with increasing speed as he watched, bringing with them heavy rain. Not the light, fine English showers which he was used to, but heavy torrential rain with drops so forceful that he was almost flattened to the ground by them. The air darkened rapidly as if it were night-time and it was only when huge flashes of yellow lightning lit the sky that he could see. The crackling and rumble of thunder scattered the frightened sheep, and he was drenched before he could seek the shelter of the hut which he had located a few days before. Now he could not even see where it was, for a sheet of falling water obscured his view.

Ploughing through a sea of mud he found himself stumbling over roots and stones as he sought the hut, but it was not to be found. He was completely engulfed by rain and his wet clothing clung heavily to his cold, soaked body, hampering his every movement, so that he felt he might have been better off naked against these elements. Nevertheless he plodded on rather than stay immobile and vulnerable, he found the ground becoming increasingly muddy and treacherous until he realised he could not stop his downward slide into the creek. He snatched frantically at anything within reach but could not halt his descent into what was now a fast-running stream.

Above the noise of the rain he could hear an unfamiliar roaring which frightened him, then the stream began to flood! As water swirled around his ankles, pulling at his trousers, he froze. The stream was becoming a torrent, or had he wandered towards the river which itself was becoming swollen by the storm? He was stuck at the bottom of a muddy bank being engulfed by the fast-rising water and was in danger of being dragged along by the debris which came sweeping by with increasing power. Something crashed against his leg, knocking him off balance, and he frantically tried to climb back the way he had come. There was no time to spare and unless he moved quickly he knew that it would be too late and he might end up in a watery grave.

For one brief moment only, did he consider the relief that drowning would bring, but his instinct for survival proved greater than his desire to end it all. He clawed desperately, seeking to seize roots or branches on the banks above before it was too late and he was swept away. The deafening roar was increasing, coming closer now, its awesome power numbing his mind, but, reaching out one last frantic time, his fingers caught the stump of an old tree. He hung there a moment, gasping for breath, and then strove to lift himself out of the current.

Slowly and painfully he inched upwards, his cold hands tearing on stones and roots, his feet scrabbling in the mud and debris. His water-filled boots hampered his progress but eventually he found himself above the raging torrent. Continuing upwards he had only seconds to spare before a wall of water swept the bank below him with terrifying force, taking with it anything and everything which was not anchored down by deep-seated roots.

Taking no chances, John climbed even higher, allowing himself no rest until he was satisfied that there was no danger even if the river did continue to rise. Every muscle and sinew was taut, strained and aching as he moved cautiously to the safety of the bank top where he lay panting, listening and afraid. Afraid that the water would rise over and beyond the top of the bank; he had cheated death, and for what? He quivered as much from shock as from the coldness of the wet clothes which clung to him.

Through the thinning rain, flashes of lightning illuminated the bush, revealing dead and twisted eucalyptus trees, their trunks gaunt and ghostly in the brilliant light. The shock of the flash flood had left him exhausted and weak, yet he knew that he had to find his flock and see how they had fared. Here and there scattered through this desolate scene stood a pathetic and bedraggled animal or two, but where were the rest of them? He had no horse or dog with which to round them up; if he didn't find them all it could prove financially disastrous.

He pushed on, allowing the rain to wash away the thick mud from his clinging clothes as he sought the sheep, and to his joy found that they had, after all, survived remarkably well. Having nowhere else to go after bolting a short distance in panic, most had simply huddled together instead of wandering blindly as their master had done. He found one carcass but was too exhausted to count the rest so, taking his flute he played softly as he went, and the simple creatures merely followed.

The bedraggled group reached familiar territory and eventually John located the hut, lifted the flap-door and sought refuge within its four bare walls. Removing the tallow candle from the bag which still hung round his neck, he found to his relief that the tinder-box had not let in water, so it wasn't long before the candle was alight, allowing him to locate the wood which he had previously stored in the hut. After several minutes he had kindled a fire on the earth floor, and was standing up removing his sodden clothes, which he then hung up over the fire to dry. He was shivering now, both from the cold and nervous reaction but the fire's growing heat slowly seeped into his body, bringing with it the need for a meal. Eating greedily from the ration of food which he had been given at the farm, he marvelled that his small wooden box of writing materials had come to no harm in the storm, in spite of everything that had happened.

It was obvious that the hut had not been disturbed since his last visit, and for once he hoped that for a while at least he would be left in peace. He sat on an old tree stump which someone else had previously left in the hut, and gazed comfortably at the flames of the fire. Drowsiness crept upon him but he dared not sleep for he had to return the flock to the farm, count them, and then if necessary go back to find any that were still missing.

A feeling of hopelessness soon replaced that of drowsiness, leaving him empty and forlorn. He wondered how long he could stand the loneliness before losing his reason, and how much longer he could endure this terrible isolation. For fourteen hours each day he followed the mindless sheep, in the hot sun, or rain, without sight or sound of another human being. His heart was heavy as he leaned forward to lift the hessian flap, but nothing stirred in the dark blanket of drizzle. In utter desperation, he took the flute from the bag hanging around his neck, knocked the water from the reed, and played softly to himself.

So haunting was the sound that it reminded him of Fanny. He sighed, resting the flute on his knee, trying to make her image go away but she was all around him now, the memories painful, and he could find no peace. He had almost drowned in the swollen, muddy river but he had fought hard and survived. There was no going back and it would be unfair to expect her to wait for him. He decided that the kindest thing would be to release her, for this was no place to bring her and he intended eventually to go to America anyway. Tomorrow he would write to Fanny telling her that it was over, then perhaps she would haunt him no more. Thus determined, he rose and resumed his duties.

At the first opportunity he rested some paper on the lid of the writing box he had made and balanced this on his knee as he sat on a mound of earth. It was not as easy to write to Fanny as he had imagined the day before, and the more he wrote the sadder and more bitter he became. 'Oh, my darling Fanny,' he murmured, 'you will never know how much I need you at this moment, yet I have to let you go out of my life forever!' He stared out across the plain, watching the sheep as they meandered about, cropping the meagre grass. What worries had they save the immediate need to feed, and be on the alert for danger? If only he could emulate their placid nature, but he was not old or infirm, only deprived of all his natural physical and emotional outlets. Oh, that he could be allowed to satisfy those desires! What torment he suffered now in his need of Fanny. He was near desperate in his desire for her, and tears of frustration misted his eyes. He forbade himself ever to think of her again, and increased his determination to be resolute in the personal disciplines which so many others in the Colony chose to ignore.

He had squirmed with disgust at the obvious sounds of depravity taking place at night on the hulks. It had not been any better on board the *Speedwell* either, when desperate men had sunk to disgusting levels, willingly or unwillingly, as they sought satisfaction. He, personally, had rejected such acts but youths such as Joe had not. He managed to maintain his self-respect but the scars on his mind would remain forever to haunt him. Where, here, could he find a woman as innocent as Fanny? Perhaps one day in America he would find someone, if death or dishonour did not claim him first.

His handwriting was not what it had been; the rolling seas had not helped before, and now the cramped sitting position did nothing to make it more legible. It mattered not under the circumstances whether it was scholarly or plain and unpretentious, the message it contained would be painful enough. With great deliberation he wrote:

Camden
15th February 1819

My dear Fanny,
I would have written sooner but I could not find a person suitable to trust with the delivery of this letter. I am now sending this care of the Reverend Fox who will ensure that it falls into your hands only. He visited me in prison and permitted me to write to you through him. You will scarcely believe this to be my own handwriting, my knees being my desk and the grass my seat having written it in the bush. My Master's estate is about fifty English miles from the capital (Sydney) where I am tending a flock of sheep, which are very little trouble but very confining as every day is the same thing, both Sunday and Holy Day with the exception of Christmas Day when our Master allows us to put the sheep in the fold a little earlier. This is his own goodness as other Masters do not allow such indulgences.
I am starved of news and reading matter, and despair for the next few years as we follow the sheep from sunrise to sunset often over fourteen hours.
I beg you Fanny to forget me. I feel very much injured at being here in this state that I am in, and the Mayor of Nottingham has forgotten his promise to me. I have been unjustly treated as you know, and was sent with such haste from the Old Country. The journey on board ship defies description and I will not trouble you or bore you with details, except to say that it was a most cruel and miserable time and before I landed I was sick almost unto death. If I had been in the hulks for any length of time before

sailing I fear the worst would have befallen me. Instead
I was well before starting out. I could never return to a land
which treats its people so unfairly and at the first opportunity
I shall catch a whaler to America and stay there.

I shall not say any more on the subject, but thank you for
your friendship. I beseech you to think no further of me for
I am consumed with loneliness, my flute being my only
comfort, and if my Master gives consent I may be forced to
take a companion to wife.

There are many birds of beautiful plumage here which
you would enjoy, and reptiles. I have seen a bird of prey
called an Eagle Hawk, which took a young lamb. I feel
myself like that lamb. I cannot write again for the past is too
painful and I admonish you to marry another who can care
for you.

My sincere wishes to Gervase and your mother and all
enquiring friends.

> *Yours in despair,*
> *John Andrews.*

He did not address the letter directly to Fanny but sent it via the Reverend Fox. The cost of sending the letter reduced his capital even further and once despatched to Sydney was irretrievable. In moments of reflection he began to hope that it would never reach its destination but at other times he knew that he had done the honourable thing. Now Fanny could start a new life.

Time dragged slowly by and after fifteen months in the Colony loneliness was still his worst enemy. He owed his sanity to his reading habit and devoured anything in print, from newspapers to pamphlets, even the Bible which had been given to him by a passing Minister of the Church. Whenever he could he wrote letters for other men at a fee which was increasing his 'escape' fund very nicely, although the further he was sent out with the sheep the less opportunity he had to write.

He had rescued his sheep from marauding natives and been beaten almost senseless by thieving bandits, but the flock was no longer a burden to him; indeed his work had been made easier by his use of the flute, for the simple creatures seemed mesmerised by its gentle sound which could be heard from a distance. However, the days were eternally long and monotonous causing him to worry and examine himself for signs of eccentricity.

In spite of his mental state he was lean and bronzed, and together with hair that was bleached blonde by the sun he was almost handsome.

However, this availed him naught for he rarely saw a woman who was free or even pleased him.

The Macarthur farm was prosperous and well-organised, a fact which he appreciated, and he had to admit that in comparison with many other employers the Macarthurs were fair-minded. They were at least mindful of their workers living and working conditions and few, except the dishonest and defiant, were punished. Yet it was important to keep on the right side of old man Macarthur for he was extreme in his views. John suspected that he was becoming ever more cantankerous and strange in his ways as the months went by, but as he was away from the farm so much these days he was affected little by the old man's oddities.

James Macarthur, however, was entirely different from his father and when out riding in the bush would often pass the time of day with John. Their first encounter had been as a direct result of the flute, he had been drawn towards its unfamiliar sound as he explored the property, checking the stock as he did so. He found John sitting on a mound of earth overseeing his flock, the flute pressed to his lips. Over the months a mutual respect had developed between the men, who discovered that they were both lovers of music and verse.

In spite of John's constant writing on behalf of the other men, he himself had received only one letter in the two long years since leaving Sheffield. It had been a feeble apology from his uncle explaining why he had been unable to see his nephew before the ship had sailed. He had been too busy!

It was therefore something of a surprise when a second letter arrived, written by the Reverend Fox. John had not expected a letter from Fanny, let alone one from Fox, so he was rather puzzled as to why one should arrive at this time. His hand shook as he opened it and eagerly unfolded the page.

Mr John Andrews   *Sheffield*
August 12th, 1820

Dear Sir,

    I received the letter from you which I forwarded to Miss Garnett as requested. I am obliged to inform you, however, that the young lady in question has since married and I was compelled to leave the letter with her brother until such time as he could let her have it. It saddens me to have to be the bearer of such tidings, knowing as I do your feelings for the lady, but I think the matter must now be dropped.

    I ask God's blessings on you in your difficult circumstances and exhort you to keep to the Lord's ways, as a result of which you find Him a comfort to you. Nothing in this life is ever easy and we are sent tribulations to test our faith. Do not lose heart, time will pass and very soon you will find yourself a free man again. Look forwards not backwards and prepare yourself for the future.

I trust this letter finds you well. Under the circumstances I cannot allow myself to pass on further letters to the lady concerned.

Remember to pray to God for strength and deliverance.

Your humble servant in God,
Richard Fox.

The words glared back at him from the paper. He could not believe his Fanny had married! Even though in his letter he had told her to forget him, and had stated that he might indeed need to take a wife, it was a blow to realise that Fanny had already married before she had received his letter. He could not suppress the sense of disappoint nor the bitterness he felt, for in his heart of hearts he had dreamed that Fanny would always remain loyal to him. It mattered not now whether he returned to England or stayed in the Colony; he had no ties, no responsibilities, and no one who cared about him.

He kicked the earth viciously with his foot, causing a cloud of fine dust to rise and renewed his vow to reach America before he died.

'Bad news?' The voice of a horseman cut into his black thoughts as he stood in the stockyard.

'No more than one can expect, I suppose, but it is of no consequence now,' he replied. Nor was it of course, and he opened the gate of the pen to release the sheep. Wool, that was all he could see as the endless stream of animals stretched out before him heading for the plains. Turning to the horseman once more, he said, 'I wonder what the poor blighters think about all day long? There are times when I wonder if we wouldn't have been better without brains. Thinking only causes trouble.'

The horseman laughed. 'If they had brains they'd sell us the wool off their backs instead of letting us take it.' He turned the horse and rode off, leaving John to follow the flock.

For almost four hours he walked in the heat and dust, as each day or week he went further in search of fresh grass, sometimes staying in the bush all night. The greedy 'box' eucalyptus dried out the soil, restricting the growth of fresh grass so that the sheep were ever forced to graze over larger distances in search of food. He was compelled to travel as far as ten miles sometimes in search of better grazing and this in itself brought fresh problems. The mongrel-like dingo's stalked the unsuspecting flock, waiting cunningly for any opportunity to seize not one but numerous sheep. To the roaming aborigines the temptation of a bellyful of mutton would also be too much and one would stalk, spear the animal, and disappear as quickly as he had arrived. Night-time, however, brought some relief for the sheep were rounded up and surrounded by hurdles. With the flock thus protected he could leave them in the hands of the watchman who had prepared a meal ready for him.

However, it was now mid-morning and the letter about Fanny was still uppermost in his mind. Had he not been so preoccupied he would have been aware of another sound beyond that of the squawking parakeets. It was several minutes before he realised that the bleating was growing more irate and the flock was becoming more restless. Moving swiftly but carefully, trying not to stampede the sheep, he could see that it was neither rustler nor aborigine for the latter would have speared and felled a sheep with great accuracy before disappearing quickly into the bush. It had to be a pack of cunning dingos. He could not hear the animals but he knew that they were there, stalking the sheep. It was not the loss of a sheep or two which was so worrying but the fact that the wild dogs carried an incurable disease which ruined the wool and checked breeding. The Macarthur Merinos were a pure breed which had to be guarded from straying or neglected flocks, and particularly against the risk of this dreaded infection which the dingo could spread so rapidly. Not that he could afford the loss of a single sheep anyway, as Elizabeth Macarthur was meticulous in her book keeping; she knew exactly how many sheep were in each flock, how many were killed or sold, and once every two weeks she insisted that the stock levels and condition were thoroughly checked.

The sheep were scattering now in blind panic and there was little time left if he was to do anything to prevent disaster, in addition the location of the attack was difficult to determine because the animals had been grazing amongst the eucalyptus trees. He was always nervous when the sheep moved into this area of scrub beyond the Nepean river, as it was so easy for trouble to develop in that vast territory.

Any sudden action or noise he made now could only make matters worse for the sheep, as the terrain itself was dangerously fissured by the river, so his normal technique in dealing with the dogs with well-aimed stones would be to no avail.

Walking as quickly as he dared in the direction of the snarling and bleating, and with his crook held firmly, he was fully alert. Parrots and other birds added their cries to the increasing turmoil, so he reached into his shirt for the flute which he hoped might calm and reassure his flock.

It was not easy to walk and play at the same time, especially with the crook tucked under his arm at the ready, then suddenly, he tripped on a protruding root which caused him to expel air sharply through the mouthpiece, so piercing the air with a shrill note. There was a momentary silence as the shocked creatures of the bush ceased their raucous cries, but within seconds the noise began again. However, the note had the same effect as a gun, but the sheep were used to the flute and the dingos weren't. Taking a chance he deliberately blew three more piercing blasts on the pipe and the sky became alive with the flapping of wings as with a loud screeching the parakeets and clouds of green budgerigars flew in panic from the trees.

Quickening his pace he moved on in time to see the dogs slinking back into the shelter of the scrub, leaving the bloodied carcass of a sheep on the ground. Picking up first one stone then another he hurled them wildly into the bush in the direction of the retreating dogs. Then, raising the crook menacingly he followed, driving them even deeper into the trees, where he found a second dead animal. Rounding up the flock he judged that while ever the dogs had the two carcasses to devour they would be content, but it had been a costly blunder on his part and one that he would have to account for to Elizabeth Macarthur.

As he calmed and regrouped the sheep, he cursed his negligence and the effect this would have on his hard-earned savings, with the consequent risk to his future plans.

During the next few months he pushed further south, ever seeking fresh pastures in the new territories of Mossvale and Goulburn, but never could he accept that any of these areas might one day become his home. His mind dwelt on his eventual release and the American whaling ships which docked regularly in Sydney harbour. One day, one precious day, he would board such a vessel, a free man, travelling to a free country.

Chapter 7

It was a sombre, thoughtful man who walked the road to Collingwood farm. During the three years in which John could have obtained his Ticket of Leave for good behaviour, allowing him to move employment, he had chosen to remain on the Macarthur Estate. He could not leave the Colony until his seven year sentence was up, and so, instead of risking his chances elsewhere, he had decided to stay where he was well-fed, clothed, and free from the temptations of the convict system, particularly by keeping away from Sydney. Whilst serving his time in the bush he was at least out of harm's way, safe from the temptations of the flesh and the evil rum. Only once in seven years had he been back to Sydney, and that had been with shipment of fleeces. From that visit, and rumours which occasionally reached him about the behaviour of other 'Government men' there, he decided that it would be healthier to keep away from the drunkenness and debauchery altogether. The sight of the work gangs had convinced him, for in the bush he could at least maintain his dignity and save his money, without the opportunity to fritter it away.

His only indulgence in all those years on the farm had been to buy an occasional book when it had been impossible to beg or borrow one. That one journey to Sydney had been useful, as he had carefully noted the homestead belonging to an American whaling Captain, which lay halfway between Camden and Sydney. He intended returning there on his release to ask for advice on how to get to America.

Now, free at last from the confines of his sentence and the security of the Macarthur farm, he was walking briskly along the road back to Sydney. He was heading for the American's dwelling place.

Eber Bunker, the whaling Captain, had been settled in the Colony for many years, and although he had built a fine farmhouse, John could not understand the man's reason for choosing to settle permanently here. However, over the years John had learned all he could about the man, his likes and dislikes, for in him he saw salvation.

He had known that the path back to normality would not be an easy one. He knew too that many pitfalls awaited him, but the jubilation which he had expected to feel was not there. For seven years he had dreamed of this day, had been told what to do, had been forced to relinquish all responsibilities for his own life, and now he was free and heading into uncertainty. He was close to panic! Were his plans merely dreams? Was he capable of dealing with the aggressive and greedy world into which he was walking? At this moment he felt as vulnerable as the animals which he had protected for so long. He left the road and headed for the friendly cover of trees, taking comfort in the bush which he had come to know as well as hate.

Night was falling fast and dark, leaving him prey to any marauding native or bush ranger who might take advantage of him, and strip him clean of everything he owned. Tiredness was making him fearful, and he glanced round nervously. Was he as soft in the head as many other shepherds were, had he not tried to maintain his sanity against all odds? Perhaps he had waited too long before making the change? He was lonelier now than he had ever been as he huddled beneath a gum tree, clutching the canvas bag close to his knees. He should locate a creek and wash the dust from his face, but it was already too late to wander further in the darkness and he decided not to move. The eerie stillness of the night was broken by the occasional screech of a bird or the snap of a twig and he drew the coarse woollen blanket tighter around his body, as if for protection.

He was no longer the brash, energetic youth of yesteryear. The lonely experiences of the past seven years had robbed him of some of his confidence, leaving him defenceless in an unknown, cruel world. What comforts had he without a wife or loved ones? 'Oh, Fanny!' he cried out, 'I am lost.' The hard ground offered little comfort as he lay watching the stars in the sky above, fighting to hold down the sobs which he considered to be unmanly, before he finally drifted into a troubled sleep.

He woke stiff and cold after the long night and moved from the shelter of the tree into the warmth of the morning sun. His clothes felt damp from the night air but as he stretched out his limbs towards the sun his spirits rose. He would go on, he must! Gathering up sufficient wood to make a fire he boiled the remaining water from his leather canteen and made a brew of tea. The bitter liquid and the dried-up remainder of his bread and cheese did not dampen his renewed enthusiasm and he wondered why he had been so afraid the night before.

On the road once more, he lengthened his stride, intending to reach Collingwood farm before nightfall; however it was further than he had realised and he found the afternoon drawing to a close with still some distance to go. He had fresh provisions now, purchased from a wagon heading for Camden, and when the road crossed a lively creek he decided to camp whilst there was still sufficient light. Following the water-course he found a sheltered spot which completely concealed him from the dusty road, and he lowered his few belongings to the ground.

With water close at hand and sufficient food to see him through the night, John relaxed, stripped off his clothes and sat naked as a babe in the shallows of the creek. The water ran between and over his hot sticky feet as he lay back, allowing the flow to soothe his body. He was better prepared tonight to meet the oncoming darkness, and he was glad that he had stopped before he was too tired to relax. That had been his trouble the previous night and one which he must not repeat, for it lowered his morale and sapped his confidence. Tonight he would build a fire for company, extinguishing it just before he went to sleep, but for the moment he was content, his body clean and his belly full. It was the thought of mingling with the crowds in Sydney which overshadowed the night now, there was more treachery there between his fellowmen than amongst the creatures of the bush!

He had one secret fear. He had heard that sedition was rife once more in the town, and young master Wentworth was stirring up feelings for radical reform amongst the convicts. John wanted nothing more to do with reform, and hadn't he told the receiving officer that he had worked on the Wentworth Estate in England? Young Wentworth's pen flourished too in the form of 'pipes' and publications. No, Sydney was no place for him, the dangers of re-conviction there were too great and he had had enough of sheep! If his plans went well then he would merely sail from Sydney Harbour on his way to Hobart, in Tasmania, and beyond with whaling ships. Tonight, however, he was happy enough to be alone under the vast canopy of stars, and watch the reflection of the rising moon dance on the waters of the creek, driving away all fears. Collingwood could not be too far distant from his camp and he was determined to reach his destination in good spirits. He slept without nightmare or disturbance and awoke fresh, full of hope, and began re-tracing his steps along the creek back to the road.

The final leg of the journey was very pleasant. At one stage, climbing a high vantage point, he looked down its verdant slopes and saw the George's River flowing freely. The small town of Liverpool lay to the north and although it would lengthen the journey there he preferred to follow the river to the town rather than walk the dusty road. There was a luxury and freedom in his walk now and he watched the fish dart to and fro in the strong current. The waters teamed with grayling and bass but try as he might his attempts to catch one failed. His heart was full and he would have remained there longer, enjoying his new-found freedom but Collingwood lay within his grasp, enticing him on.

There at last, before him, lay the Bunker farmstead, beckoning in the bright sunlight, yet he hesitated, afraid to take that final step. Years of isolation in the bush had left him reluctant to approach strangers and he stood immobile, torn between his desire to achieve his goal and bewilderment. In the end his courage failed him and he retreated the way he had come. Before long, however, his senses returned, along with the knowledge that he was without supplies, so he gathered himself together and headed for the farm. He was a free man yet he walked hesitatingly, as if fearing the challenge or command of a superior. But he was free, free to put his life in order once again!

With letters of credit sufficient to buy himself a passage on a whaler, and references from the Macarthurs, his hopes were high. Rather than work aboard ship he preferred the security of buying a passage from a respectable owner, as too many men had been caught by the duplicity of shady captains, and had ended up being shanghaied. Eber Bunker was a respectable man and there was no reason why he should turn down good money when it was offered.

Sydney was a place of contrasts, a labyrinth of jumbled stone terraces dissected by tiny winding streets and alleyways running down towards the harbour. Above the Cove, in contrast, stood fine dwellings which reminded him of England, yet he knew that they were the breeding ground of petty quarrels and intrigue.

The steep dirty streets which led down to the water's edge were lined with grog shops, spilling and spewing from their doors the dregs of humanity. Tipsy, disorderly women accosted him laughingly, tempting him in lewd ways to join them. The stench of stale rum and tobacco offended his nostrils, and he hurried away towards the quay where he found a chandlery and a canny owner eager to take his money.

Browsing warily amongst the crammed shelves he selected a beaver cap to replace the battered straw hat which had shielded him for so long from the blazing sun in the bush. His woollen frock and fustian jacket he exchanged for a box jacket, similar to the ones worn by the seamen on the quayside, but he refrained from purchasing any item not essential for the voyage. Finally he bought a useful warm woollen overcoat which would double as a blanket in cooler climates.

Once equipped for the journey he stood on the quayside breathing deeply of the fresh, salty sea-air. It was winter time and the onshore winds were damp and cutting but it did not matter, he was as free as the wind and no man could take that away from him.

A fleet of whaling brigs lay moored out in the bay ready to sail, first to Hobart and then with their cargo of whale oil in an easterly direction towards Nantucket Sound, on the East American coast. The sheltered bays and estuaries of New South Wales teemed with fur seals, black and sperm whales all of which mated and calved in the same waters, so providing rich pickings for the whalers. John gazed out at the brigs, wondering which one would serve his purpose and return him to sanity. His very soul quivered with excitement and hope. It had not been difficult to persuade Eber Bunker to find space for him on one of his ships, as a good fare added to the profit of the voyage. The fare had not been cheap but he had refrained from haggling with the good Captain for fear of crossing him.

Everywhere it seemed, was clatter, bustle and speed. The closeness of passing carriages unnerved him, and his head swam with the unaccustomed noise and clamour. Loud voices seemed to come at him from every direction, and he found himself half longing for the peace and quiet of the bush. He did not relish the long gruelling voyage ahead, although he looked forward to the solitude which the vast oceans offered.

As the sheer, black walls of the tall ships loomed over him he shuddered, remembering the times when he had been forced to climb the sides of the filthy hulks. Today, however, he clambered out of the long-boat willingly and with hope in his heart, ready to face the challenges ahead. Was he really on his way at last? It was as though this was all a dream, from which he would wake soon and find his hopes dashed.

He turned his head away as the whaler left Sydney Cove, away from the life and land that he could never forget, but his heart was heavy too, as he was not without feelings for the miserable wretches who must remain behind in the Antipodes forever.

'God, help them!' he whispered, with a depth of emotion that shook him. 'God, help them all!'

He closed his mind to the past and John Andrews was no more.

Chapter 8

1844

Adam freed the linen sheet which had ensnared his neck as he had tossed and turned in the night. In doing so he was released from his nightmare, but his body was bathed in sweat and his mind still reeled from the shock of the clarity of his memories. For some time he lay trembling in the strange room, fighting to control his emotions. It had been some years since he had been confronted so vividly with the past but time had not lessened the impact, nor taken away the pain. He could not sleep for the turmoil which had woken him; all he could do was to take comfort from the soft feather pillow and the fragrance of the clean sheets, simple things which he had missed so much all those years ago.

It was not the morning sun which heralded the dawn of a new day, for the house lay in shadow, but the trotting of horses and the rumbling of carriage wheels which woke him finally from the shallow sleep into which he had fitfully drifted. He left the bed and went to the window, half afraid to face the once-familiar scene. Parting the heavy curtains he compelled himself to look out into the street below, then beyond towards the Church and graveyard. In spite of the passage of time he could see that little had changed but he knew that if he were to remain in the town he could not hide away from things which reminded him of the past. There was no escape and for his own peace of mind he would have to find Gervase and Fanny in order to reassure himself that they were fit and well. That done he could get about his business and let the past be buried forever.

After dressing, he left the room and knocked on Luke's bedroom door. Receiving no answer he entered, only to find it empty and the bed made. He closed the door and made his way down the stairs where he found Luke already devouring his breakfast.

'Good morning, my dear,' Mrs Fisher said, welcoming her guest with a cheerful smile. 'Did you sleep well?' she asked, bidding him to sit to the table.

'Yes, thank you Ma'am,' Adam said politely. It had not been Mrs Fisher's fault that he had suffered the nightmare. 'I was a little too travel-weary to relax properly, but the bed is most comfortable,' he attempted to reassure her.

'I have a good reputation in the town, especially for my cooking,' she said proudly. 'I have ham and eggs cooking already, as you no doubt can smell. I trust they will be to your liking?'

'They are to mine,' Luke chimed in, appreciatively. 'My mother is an excellent cook too but the food on the journey was far from good.' His youthful gratitude was not lost on Mrs Fisher and she smiled as she disappeared from the room.

On her return with Adam's plate she commented, 'I don't fancy all that travelling myself. All that water does not appeal to me, but you are young enough to put up with the inconveniences, I'm too old to be gadding about the world'. She paused for a moment, 'Tuck into that,' she said proudly, 'good food makes a world of difference to your day'.

'Thank you, Ma'am. Most welcome I assure you!' Adam was hungrier than he had realised and immediately started to do justice to the lady's cooking.

Luke finished first and sat back contentedly, 'What are we going to do first, Father?' he asked eagerly.

'Well, first I finish my meal, that's what,' Adam smiled, happy to see Luke so full of life. 'Then I wish to satisfy myself that two of my old friends are safe and well before going out to meet our members. You take a look around the town, but watch you don't stray too far. Keep to the main streets, d'y'hear? No adventures mind, and be back here at one o'clock!'

'Yes, sir!' Luke replied and left the room to return to his own, leaving Adam to continue his meal in peace.

Mrs Fisher returned. 'The young man had enough, has he?' she enquired on finding Luke's chair empty.

'Young people can't be still for very long, Mrs Fisher, but I gathered that he enjoyed an excellent meal. I thank you too, Ma'am.' Mrs Fisher never failed to respond to compliments and she smiled with delight. 'May we leave our belongings here until after lunch?' he asked, 'I have a little business to see to in the town before proceeding.' He ought really to tell her of his Mission but first he needed to find Gervase and Fanny, and to save himself a lot of hard work he required her help. 'Do you have a gazetteer or Trade Directory of the town, Mrs Fisher? That I could consult?'

'I do indeed. One moment!' Opening a cupboard in the chiffonier Mrs Fisher withdrew a book which Adam instantly recognised. Gervase had sold the very same in his shop. 'I'm in it, of course,' she stated proudly. 'Leave it on the table before you go out. I take it that you will require lunch before leaving, Mr Johnson?'

'Why, I'd be most grateful to you. Will one o'clock be in order, I should be back before then?'

The long-case clock in the hall struck nine, and Mrs Fisher turned to leave. 'One moment, if you please, Mrs Fisher! There was a printers and stationers in the High Street many years ago, called Webster's, it appears to be in different hands now.'

Mrs Fisher thought for a moment before replying. 'Oh, dear, you are going back many years. I remember it because the shop burned down a long time ago. There are other stationers in the High Street but perhaps I can provide you with writing materials?'

'You are most kind, but it is not that which I require. I wish to contact Mr Webster. That is why I need the gazetteer as he may not be in business any more. He must be sixty now!'

'Oh! They are still in business, indeed they have a rather prosperous concern in Rockingham Street and are quite respected in the town. Mr Webster has been dead for many years but the family live in a rather grand house up on East Bank, across the River Sheaf, not too far from the old deer park. I don't know much about the family but as it is a pleasant day why not take a walk up there? The fresh air will do you good and it is a most pleasant part of town.' She turned to leave once more.

'My grateful thanks, Mrs Fisher. I shall indeed take your advice, the day is bright and a stroll is just what I need.' Adam was delighted at his good fortune to have located Gervase so soon although he wasn't sure if it were Gervase who was dead or his father. The more he thought about it the more he remembered. It had to be Gervase, the father had been dead some years. There was a sadness at the realisation but he still needed to find Fanny and he did not know her married name. He took his leave of Luke, after admonishing him once more to be aware of danger, then set out to cross the town towards the river.

He had walked this same direction many times with Gervase but now the town had sprawled out much further and the rows of terraced houses almost flanked the river. For all that, the walk was still pleasant though he was disappointed to see man's intrusion into the outlying pastures. From the river he could see several large houses on the far hillside but in his excitement he had not asked Mrs Fisher the exact location of the Webster's house. He was left with no option but to enquire at the nearest house in the hope that someone would be able to point him in the right direction. He need not have worried for the Webster's were well-known and as his eyes followed the man's pointing finger he could not mistake the large, fine house, standing on the slope beyond the river.

Following the gravel pathway Adam climbed the gentle slope until he reached a boundary hedge. He peered over out of curiosity, realising that this was where Gervase had ended his days and acknowledging that business must have been good to provide such a sturdy mansion overlooking the town. Turning round he looked back towards the town and was amazed at the growth which had taken place over the years. The valley was being filled with tiny houses and smoking factory chimneys and yet from the distance it was not entirely without charm. He had forgotten the dirty haze which hung over the town like a mantle. Forgotten too the many small rivers which cut and separated the valleys of the area. To his left, luxurious meadows still stretched out towards the wild hills and he savoured the rich smell of clover that wafted over him.

He would have liked to have ridden up the winding drive in style, but he was in possession of no worldly goods on this Mission, and had merely sufficient clothing to sustain his needs and a little money to keep him out of trouble. The members of the Church would provide his living or, if not, hopefully friends made on his travels would offer him accommodation. Here, however, with Gervase dead he would merely be a passing stranger calling to pay his respects.

On reaching the porticoed entrance he stood hesitatingly before the heavy oak door, afraid to lift the knocker. Finally, summoning his courage and chiding himself for his fears, he knocked and waited until the sound of heavy footsteps rang within the confines of the house. The door swung open to reveal a man-servant in his mid-forties.

Running his eyes over the strangely attired visitor the man enquired politely, 'Can I help you, Sir?'

'It's a little difficult for me to explain' began Adam, 'but I will try.' He was aware of the strangeness of his own voice. 'Many years ago I was a friend of Mr Gervase Webster and as I was in the area I thought I would call and renew his acquaintance.'

'Mr Webster's dead, Sir,' interrupted the man. 'He's been dead some time now.'

'Yes, I understand so, and I am very, very saddened to hear it, but I understand that he has a family to whom I would pay my respects and enquire also of the whereabouts of other friends with whom I have lost contact!' Would they even know of Fanny, he wondered?

The man hesitated, intrigued by the strangers peculiar accent. 'Won't you step inside, Sir, whilst I tell young Mr Webster of your request. Who shall I say is calling?'

Adam was suddenly unsure of himself. What did it matter what he called himself to these strangers? 'Adam Johnson!' he replied.

'Wait here a moment, Sir.' The man briskly crossed the hall and entered a room, closed the door and left Adam to wait, deep in thought.

The hall was not as luxurious as one would have expected but was highly polished and simply furnished. A portrait caught his eye. A woman of classic beauty stared hauntingly down at him, her features almost romantic and Adam guessed her to be a relative of Gervase, so alike were they. A rustling sound caught his ear and, looking up, he saw to his surprise that he was being observed from the upper landing by the haughtiest pair of eyes he had ever seen. The youngish woman nodded politely before turning away and disappeared into one of the upstairs rooms. The incident disturbed him. The woman's obvious aloofness reminded him that he was a stranger, perhaps unwelcome at the house.

The servant returned, and, asking Adam to follow, led him towards a large study full of commodious furniture whose walls were lined from top to bottom with an impressive array of books—something Adam expected in a house which Gervase had owned.

Standing by the window which overlooked the scene so admired by Adam on his climb out of the valley, was the figure of a tall, confident, even proud young man. He was not handsome, nor was he unfriendly, which pleased Adam, but he was certainly Gervase's son. A lump rose in Adam's throat. So many years had passed but the resemblance was strong enough to bring back fond memories, although the young man was not dark like his father had been, his hair was auburn yet the strong features and firm jaw were familiar, and resembled also those of the woman in the portrait.

'It is kind of you to see me,' Adam offered, shaken by the meeting. 'I am from America but I was a friend and employee of your father, Gervase Webster. It seemed a pity not to seek him out during my stay here.' Adam held his hand out to meet the strong handshake offered to him.

'My father is dead,' the youth replied, 'but I am pleased to receive you.'

In spite of the ready smile there was a graveness about the eyes which reminded Adam of something, something which baffled him. 'I am terribly sorry but I have only just learned of your father's demise. He was a good friend to me and I am sad not to be able to renew his acquaintance. Perhaps your mother may have heard him speak of me?'

'My mother is dead too—perhaps you have not noticed the emblems of mourning about the house, she died only a month ago.' The youth's eyes became sad, making him look older then he perhaps was. Suddenly he apologised, 'Do forgive me, I did not introduce myself. I am George Webster. Please sit down, perhaps you will take a glass of wine with me?'

Shaking his head Adam declined, 'Thank you, but I do not take alcohol'.

'Then shall I have the servant bring you some tea?' His host offered, a little surprised by his guest's reply.

'Thank you, but I don't take tea or coffee either, just a glass of milk or water would do nicely.' The young man looked most bewildered. 'It is a habit I acquired in America. I am sorry to be such a nuisance', Adam explained.

Concealing his inquisitiveness, George nodded. He'd never met anyone from America before, nor had his father ever spoken of having friends there. He turned and walked across the room and took hold of the velvet bell-pull which hung on the wall by the fireplace. 'Father never mentioned a friend in America' he said, returning to the window as the door opened and the man-servant entered. 'Would you get Mary to bring our guest a glass of milk, please, Henry?' he asked.

Before Henry had a chance to close the door it was thrust open wider, revealing the figure of a smiling young woman. Adam drew a deep breath, for the girl was beautiful, her hair a rich auburn colour rather like Fanny's had been, yet deeper. He rose and stared in fascination as the laughing eyes met his.

'Mr Johnson—this is my sister, Sarah', George Webster explained. 'Sarah, Mr Johnson is from America—he did not know of father's death and came here to see him.'

Slowly she came towards Adam, hand outstretched and smiling warmly. Once again he sensed something familiar about the features which he could not explain. 'I saw you coming up the drive and stop to admire the view. It is beautiful isn't it, Mr Johnson?' she stated proudly. 'I love to look out over the moors!' She was almost before him now, 'I am very pleased to meet you!' Her young face was alive with enthusiasm and she asked, 'Do you like our country, Mr Johnson?'

He bowed slightly and took her hand. 'I am English, and lived in the town in my youth, working for your father. But yes, I too am fond of the countryside hereabouts.' Then he added more soberly, 'I'm very saddened by the news about your father and mother'.

The two young people fell silent, suddenly at a loss for words. Adam felt uncomfortable, as if intruding on their grief and broke the silence by asking, 'I wonder if you could help me find someone else?'

Relief flooded over the youth's face. 'If we can, we will! Who is he?'

'It's not a man—but a woman! I don't know her married name but your father was friendly with her family, the Garnetts. Her name was Fanny!' A strange look appeared on the girl's face, one of both shock and sadness. 'You know of her?' Adam questioned.

'But Mr Johnson, she was our mother!' Sarah cried out. 'Didn't you know?'

Adam reeled at the news, his face blanched white with shock. Fanny, his beloved Fanny! He couldn't take it in. He looked first at the man and then at the girl, no wonder the eyes had fascinated him so much—they were Fanny's eyes! She had married Gervase—all this time they had been together, his best friend and his beautiful Fanny. He was stunned.

They stared back at him, this foreigner who stood so shocked before then and were unsure what to do. 'Please do sit down again—are you unwell?' the youth enquired as Adam lowered himself in the chair.

Suddenly Adam felt very old, very foolish; something inside him had snapped leaving him empty and vulnerable. He placed his elbow on the chair arm and put his head on his propped hand. All these years he had known that Fanny was married, probably the mother of children too, but never in his wildest moments had he imagine her married to Gervase. He had loved them both in different ways, thinking of them now and then when times were bad. Now they were both gone. Fanny—his Fanny—was dead, he could not believe that she no longer existed.

Concerned at his guest's strange behaviour, George Webster came across to him, embarrassed by his own youthful inability to cope with the strange visitor. 'Please, you seem so distressed, can I help in some way? Perhaps a tot of brandy would help?'

Shaking his head weakly, Adam refused. 'No, thank you. I am sorry to have been such a bother, I think it is the shock of finding out that both my friends are dead. I had better return to my lodgings–my son will be worrying about me!'

'You must let us send for the carriage—it is too far for you to walk in your state. It is the least that we can do for you!' Without waiting for Adam's reply, George rang the bell again and Adam attempted to rise. 'Please, Mr Johnson, it really is no trouble and we would feel happier knowing that you were safe.' Adam wanted desparately to be alone to think, but he was grateful not to have to walk at this moment. Henry re-appeared before any more could be said. 'Henry! Tell William to prepare the carriage for town. I want him to take Mr Johnson home, he is unwell.'

Adam could not explain why the blow had been so shattering, for to do so would only upset these kind young people. It would be a relief to leave as soon as the carriage was ready. Feigning illness now, thus preventing the necessity of answering awkward questions, he nodded acceptance and lapsed back into silence leaving his host to stare out of the window.

'Ah! The carriage is out in front!' George exclaimed suddenly.

Adam rose slowly. 'I thank you most kindly for your hospitality—I shall not bother you again. May the good Lord go with you!' he muttered, his head held down to avoid those searching grey eyes which seemed to reach into his very soul.

'You will be alright, won't you?' Miss Webster asked, her voice full of concern.

'I will, my dear—it is perhaps the travelling that has caused it. Good-bye and thank you' he murmured softly.

George Webster handed Adam into the carriage and bade him good-bye. As the vehicle rolled away along the drive he commented, 'What a strange affair, Sis. He hardly seems to be father's type at all, and what an unusual character, did you see his odd clothes? I bet he has a tale or two to tell!'

Sarah laughed, 'It's quite exciting, but sad, too, I suppose'. Then in a more serious tone she added, 'I do hope that he will be alright'.

'William will see to it, I don't doubt.' He entered the house and spoke to Henry, 'I think I will take some tea after all this disturbance. It has broken my routine'.

'If you'll pardon me, Sir' Henry spoke out, 'I'd be wary if I were you.'

'Whatever do you mean, Henry? It's not like you to be so outspoken' George remonstrated, not unkindly.

Henry reddened, 'I should not have spoken out, Sir!'

'Well now that you have you'd better continue—what mystery are you concealing, Henry?' George persisted.

'He looks like a Mormon to me. Best keep away from his kind and their queer ways. I've seen them in the town preaching, a brazen lot, as though we don't know who God is over here!'

'Oh, Henry, you gossip too much' Sarah chided. 'He seems harmless enough. I feel sorry for him, and you shouldn't believe everything you hear in the alehouse.'

'It's nothing to do with me Miss, but I heard as how they drag people off to America, particularly young woman' he said pointedly.

'What rubbish' she laughed. 'How can they drag people off if they don't want to go?'

By now Henry was quite adamant, 'It's a spell they say that's cast over them!'

'Well,' George broke in, 'charms didn't do much for him here, did they? Fetch that tea into the study as soon as you can, the whole episode has left me with a thirst.'

'I'll take some too,' his sister added, 'so much excitement has left me quite distracted.'

'Where to, Sir?' The driver of the carriage asked, without taking his eyes from the road ahead. He too was fascinated by this unusual visitor to the house.

'Church Street, please.' Adam's head was throbbing and the meadows which had held such charm earlier in the morning seemed to lack lustre now.

Slowly they approached the town until the carriage was engulfed by red brick and gritstone buildings, and the bustle of town life.

'Here! Drop me here, please. My lodgings are just across the road there!' Adam pointed to Mrs Fisher's door. 'I'm most grateful for your assistance.'

'That's alright, Sir. Given me a chance to come to town it has!' the driver replied, leaping down from his seat to pull out the steps for Adam to climb down. He glanced at his passenger, but on seeing the foreigner half-concealed beneath his turned-up coat collar, and not wanting to leave the horse unattended, decided Adam was capable of handling himself and left him to cross the road alone.

Adam mumbled his gratitude again and fled to the shelter of his lodging house. Mrs Fisher answered his knock, and seeing that he was unwell suggested delaying dinner for an hour to give him a chance to rest.

Once within his own room he leaned wearily against the closed door. Now he was alone and there was no longer any need to control his bewildered emotions his face became twisted with sadness and reflection. What he found hard to accept was the fact that Fanny had been dead only a month! The earth over her was barely settled, he had arrived too late. It was almost as though fate had deliberately taken her away from him again. Yet he had not wanted to cause trouble but had merely needed to make sure she was being taken care of. Well, she was safe enough now in God's hands, safe from the perils of this harsh world and all its ills. Gervase would have taken care of her, he knew that, but he couldn't help wondering what kind of relationship theirs had been. His two best friends had taken care of each other, their lives had been fruitful and comfortable, what more could he have wished for?

In spite of his bewilderment there was no trace of jealousy in his heart; instead there was a kind of peace. There had always been, within himself, a feeling of guilt at having left her alone to face the future but if he had known the truth earlier he could have accepted it and been a better man for it. Instead he had used Fanny as a prop in difficult times. Now he felt more guilt from the fact that he had always kept a part of himself for Fanny at the expense of his own wife and family.

Suddenly he felt drained and tired and longed to feel the comforting arms of his wife around him. Was he always to be a dreamer? All his life he had chased the impossible, always living for tomorrow. At least now he was free from temptation—he was also free to concentrate on his work here, then to return home to his family. He stretched out on the bed, grateful for its softness and was soon overcome by a deep slumber, undisturbed by dreams for the first time in years.

There was a tap at the door which woke Adam from his sleep. He climbed from the bed, straightened his shirt and necktie and called out, 'It's not locked! Come in.'

Luke's flushed face peered into the room. 'Ah, you are back! I thought I heard someone earlier but as you didn't come to my room I presumed it was someone else. Did you find your old acquaintances, Sir?' he asked politely. Then, noting the strained look on Adam's face, he asked, 'You're not ill, are you?'

'Just overcome, my boy—but I'm feeling better already. I had some bad news that's all, but there is nothing to be done about it, I'm sorry to say my friends are both dead. I have decided to ask Mrs Fisher if she can put us up for a further night as I can't face the crowds today. Meanwhile we should do some preparation for tomorrow.'

Luke nodded and replied, 'I have spent a pleasant time amongst the shops and streets, and have seen some magnificent hunting knives which are made in the town. I also found the people quite friendly, not at all as I expected, I almost believed that they would have two heads after all the tales you told of them!'

Adam shook his head. 'Perhaps I was young and foolish in those days. The people were hungry and fighting for reforms after the French Wars and I thought I could help solve their problems by encouraging them to defend themselves.' He felt calmer now, 'It doesn't always do to involve oneself too deeply in matters which don't concern you—it didn't do me much good in the end!'

Luke smiled, 'I think you'll find, Sir, that they are not at all as you fear. I'm quite looking forward to preaching to them tomorrow'.

'It may not be that easy, Luke.' He looked at the fine son whom he adored; his face was fresh and clean cut. He was as honest as the day was long and Adam recognised in him much of the young 'John Andrews' he had been. He could not recall ever telling the boy of his affection for him, such an effect his lonely years in the bush had wrought on him. He must try to let the boy know how he felt. 'You're too old to call me Sir, Luke. In the streets call me Elder but when we're alone call me Pa! I'd like that, son.'

There was something strange about Adam that Luke couldn't fathom but a loud tone rang out from the gong below. 'Not before time! We'd better make our way below before Mrs Fisher comes looking for us', he said, still puzzled. Adam brushed back his hair and checked his appearance before following Luke who had already gone ahead.

Together they entered the cosy room where Mrs Fisher waited expectantly. 'Why, Mr Johnson' she exclaimed, 'you look much better now, the rest has done you good.'

'Yes, Mrs Fisher, I have just woken from a very refreshing sleep and feel relaxed. I heard some sad news this morning about my friends but their family were kind enough to send me home in a carriage. I think exhaustion and sadness took its toll of me. However, life goes on and I would ask a small favour of you?'

'If I can help, I will', she replied with concern.

'Are our rooms vacant for one more night? I really think the rest would do me good. Then we will depart in the late morning, if that is convenient?'

Never one to miss an opportunity of adding to her income, Mrs Fisher was delighted. 'The rooms are all yours, Mr Johnson, the pleasure is all mine. Will you take high tea tonight?'

Adam's response delighted Luke, who was very much enjoying the comforts of Mrs Fisher's lodging house, particularly the food. 'You have a very hilly town here, Mrs Fisher' he piped up, 'it is extremely flat where we live. I have quite worn myself out, and have a huge appetite.'

Laughing, she shook her head, 'A young man like you, worn out? Why, a long walk on the moors would do you good. Why not take him, Mr Johnson? Hackney carriages run from outside to Endcliffe Woods and you could walk through the valley on such a beautiful afternoon'.

'Mrs Fisher is right, Luke. Come! Eat up and we'll go. I know the way from when I lived here.' He had no desire to work today, and rather fancied taking the opportunity of improving his relationship with Luke.

For the cost of two shillings Adam and Luke were carried by the hackney cab from the heat of the town up the long road to the old toll bar. On reaching the gate Adam refused to pay the outrageous toll to go through, paid off the cab and led Luke along the twisting Porter Brook. They walked for some time enjoying the peace and solitude, until they reached the old forge where the hammering and grinding within disturbed the silence. 'I walked these valleys and hills many times in my short year in Sheffield and one never forgets their beauty or smells. Around every corner there is a surprise known only to those who venture out to find it.' Adam spoke softly as though afraid to disturb the peace. 'Even in summer the lush green does not disappear and countless small flowers grow in abundance everywhere.'

'It isn't difficult to see why you loved it, nor why you were bitter at the injustice done to you' Luke replied. 'To be wrenched from all this and taken to the wilderness of the bush must have been terrible.'

'Yes.' Adam agreed, 'It made me very angry and bewildered, but that was a long time ago. Enjoy it now while you can for there are other people who can no longer enjoy it, some who have loved it better even than I.' He thought of Fanny and Gervase, almost imagining he could hear their voices in the rustling of the trees. Suddenly he was enjoying the company of his son. Since Luke's birth he had been busy, too busy, building his business to give the family security, and to some extent burying the past.

They had reached the pastures at Fulwood Head with its scattered farms and grazing animals. 'Come!' Adam announced. 'We must start back, for there may not be a carriage available at the Bar and we could be forced to walk back to town.' These were precious moments; his face glowed with the freshness of the air, and all around the ghosts of his friends seemed to walk with him in silent companionship.

Luke did not break the silence, for he knew that Adam was enjoying the peace; instead he occupied himself in his own dreams as well as admiring the beauty around him.

Adam had been right, there was no carriage and so they walked slowly back, noticing as he did the changes, good and bad, that had occurred during his twenty-six years absence. Sturdy, stone houses were beginning to fill what had once been fields and orchards, as people sought to escape the squalor of spreading industry.

On returning to Mrs Fisher's, Adam sighed with contentment. 'I shall retire early tonight, Luke. I suspect that sleep won't be long in coming,' he said.

Luke smiled. 'I'm quite looking forward to Mrs Fisher's cooking first, then I shall enjoy a good read.'

There were no bird songs to awaken Adam next morning as a misty drizzle hung in the air. Shortly after ten, when he had decided that all languishing and pleasurable pastimes should be put to one side, Mrs Fisher knocked on his door. 'Is there something amiss?' he asked, observing the slight frown on her brow.

'I'm not sure' she replied, 'but there are two ladies below asking after your welfare.'

A furrow creased Adam's brow too, 'But I don't know two ladies in the whole of the town. I think perhaps you are mistaken.'

'It was certainly Mr Johnson they asked for,' she said, moving aside to allow Luke to enter the room. 'Your father has visitors.' she told him, passing a card to Adam, 'You were asking after the Websters, it would seem that they have come to you! You may use the parlour if you wish as I do not allow ladies in my guest's rooms. I will put the ladies in there until you come down.'

Adam shook his head, 'I didn't know there were two Miss Websters, I met only one yesterday at the house but I guess there could be more. We'd better go below and solve the mystery, although I don't see what they would want with me'.

Entering the room he saw immediately that it was indeed Sarah sitting on the sofa, and with her was the older woman who had looked down on him with such disdain the previous day. She rose as he entered and came forward to greet him with hand outstretched. 'Mr Johnson, I am Becky Webster. We were not introduced yesterday but I understand from my sister that you were taken ill in our home and she wished to be reassured of your recovery.' She was not as tall as her younger sister, nor as beautiful, but her hair was fiery red like Fanny's had been and there was the same look of proud defiance in her eyes. The sisters were very different from each other yet there was no mistaking the eyes or colouring of skin and hair.

Adam bowed. 'It is indeed kind of you to take such trouble on my behalf, the mere stranger that I am in your midst.' He turned then to Sarah with a smile, 'Good morning, Miss Webster, your concern is most heart-warming'. Sensing the presence of Luke behind him he drew him forward. 'Let me introduce you both to my son, Luke!'

Sarah beamed warmly, her eyes alight with girlish charm as she acknowledged his greeting. Luke strove to conceal his confusion at her open friendliness, and bowed shyly hoping that no one would notice the deepening colour in his face. When he did raise his eyes from the floor he was aware only of Sarah, of her abundant curls and her radiant face, the prettiest thing he had ever seen. The admiration on his face did not, however, escape the elder Miss Webster's keen eyes nor did the response in the eyes of her sister and she resolved to make the visit as short as possible. There was a restraint in her voice when she spoke to Adam. 'Are you moving on from Sheffield soon?'

Sensing some hostility in her voice, Adam was at a loss to understand what on earth he could have said or done to cause such a reaction in this stranger. Her manner was in sharp contrast to the open warmth of her sister. He observed her closely as he answered, 'As far as I know we shall stay and work here for several months, teaching the people about our religion'. He thought he saw her stiffen at his reply and saw that she made no effort to resume her seat. Realising that she had no wish to prolong the visit, Adam spoke again. 'I would like you to thank your brother for his kindness to me yesterday—I fear I would not have reached here without the carriage.'

She nodded in acknowledgement and indicated to Sarah that their meeting was at an end, 'Come, Sarah, Mr Johnson has much work to do and we had better leave him to get on with it'. Shaking hands with both men she led Sarah into the hall. 'I wish you luck in your work,' she stated coldly, 'but we are not heathens here, Mr Johnson, and there are enough religions in this town already, squabbling and fighting to keep the Lord busy for years to come.'

So, Adam thought angrily, the old narrow-minded bias against change still lingered in the town, yet he had not expected to face it so soon or from such a quarter as this. Holding back his feelings he replied politely, 'There is only one God, and it seems such a pity that men assault each other on the path to meet him!'

'With that I am entirely in agreement!' Having said that, Miss Webster drew herself up proudly, 'Come, Sarah, the carriage is waiting'.

To Adam, such pride in a woman verged on rudeness, something Fanny had never been guilty of, he reflected, as with some relief, he handed her up into the carriage. She was as formidable as Sarah was charming, a state of affairs which disturbed him greatly and he was not sorry to see the pair of them leaving.

With a smile that sent Luke's heart fluttering, Sarah allowed him to hand her up into the seat next to her sister. 'Thank you,' she said pleasantly before turning to Adam. 'I am so pleased that you are well, Mr Johnson. You must come and visit us sometime and tell us about Mama and Papa when they were young.'

He caught a glimmer of irritation in the older woman's eyes at the offer but not wanting to offend the younger he replied, 'If we get an opportunity I assure you that we will.'

'It will be nice to have foreigners in the house.' Immediately she had spoken, Sarah realised the impropriety of her remark and glanced down at her hands which were folded in her lap, blushing furiously.

Adam smiled. She was so like Fanny, impetuous and outspoken. 'You are most kind, and so like your mother' he said, covering her embarrassment. 'Yes, I believe I shall look forward to the visit.'

The carriage rolled away and Sarah waved impetuously to the two men who watched them go.

Luke was first to speak. 'Phew! what a contrast they make! I'm not very enamoured with the elder Miss Webster.'

Adam chuckled, 'But the other is not too bad, eh?' He saw the colour rise in Luke's face and promptly let the matter drop. They were here to work and he did not want Luke distracted by any pretty woman, no matter who she was.

As the carriage turned the corner, leaving Church Street behind, Becky cautioned her sister. 'Sarah, you are too generous and familiar with strangers, and your rudeness in showing open curiosity about foreigners does nothing to applaud your upbringing.'

'Oh, Becky, you are stuffy' Sarah retorted, 'Why, he's a most friendly man and if he looked like his son when he was younger I shouldn't wonder if mother didn't take a fancy to him either.'

A look of shocked disapproval appeared on Becky's face. 'Really Sarah, this is too much. Your outspokenness is outrageous and will surely land you in trouble one day. I insist that you let the matter drop and do not make the mistake of inviting them again. If the man has any sense at all he will heed my coldness and stay away. I have no time for religion or fanatics. Why, even his dress marks him out as a crank.'

'That's not fair, Becky, they *are* foreigners' Sarah defended passionately.

'Enough, Sarah! I do not wish to meet them again or discuss it further.'

Sarah obeyed but beneath her dutiful submission lay an irrepressible delight at the prospect of seeing Luke again. She caught hold of Becky's hand and squeezed it in a sisterly fashion. 'I'll try and be better behaved' she promised. However, Becky was not deceived by her sister's sudden submission and vowed she would keep a watchful eye on the lively minx.

With the need to economise on their expenses, Adam and Luke settled on a cheaper lodging house in a back street which lay to the north of the town, and, free of his past, Adam set about converting the citizens of Sheffield to his way of thinking. He knew there would be problems, and that as a Mormon missionary he would not be welcomed by the town's intolerant Ministers or their flocks who were resentful at the success of previous missionaries. He had also been warned that open-air meetings were getting livelier and rougher. However, it was not for himself that he worried, he had stood before boisterous crowds in the past, it was Luke over whom he had fears.

Almost before their first meeting began, he sensed trouble in the air. The gathering crowd was sullen and quiet, he stood outwardly calm before them whilst inwardly he was filled with apprehension. He began his opening remarks in expectation of the usual mocking response, but there were none. Pressing on with his oration he was not aware, unlike Luke who watched the crowd carefully, that several rough looking youths were ringing the crowd and edging closer. Without heckling they slowly pushed forward, jostling the more sober citizens, until Adam and Luke were surrounded by an inner ring of unsavoury characters.

'Brethren!' Adam continued, concealing his fears. 'God has shown himself through his son Jesus Christ, to his followers in America.'

'Oh, yea!' A coarse voice rose from the crowd. 'Why didn't he come here then instead of sending you!'

Adam was momentarily caught off guard. 'Would he have been welcome, my friend? That is the question!'

'Not bloody likely—where's religion got us anyway?' A burly man called out. The crowd roared with delight. 'Tell him to bring his loaves and fishes here—it's food what we want, not words!'

There had been times in Adam's radical days when he had been in such a crowd as this, even stood before them here on the same spot, and he was not unsympathetic to genuine grievances. However, he was not a Government representative nor was he in a position to make economic or political points. He was here to offer hope and comfort in another way, to give them what he felt other religions failed to provide. 'That quarrel is between you and your Government representatives,' he continued, 'God wishes to feed your souls with hope. He wants to lighten your burdens.' Something whizzed past his ear, landing with a splat against the water pump behind him.

'Go back where you come from, we're not here to listen to rubbish', a woman yelled gleefully.

'Yes,' agreed another, 'I've got kids to feed, you can't eat words!'

He sensed the growing resentment within the crowd but made one final effort to get his point across. 'I offer you a better future, through God.' His voice was firm but lost in the cat-calling of the crowd, and he knew he was vulnerable as he stood on the raised steps before them.

'Get down and shut yer mouth, or we'll pull you down!' someone challenged.

'No! I think not, my friend. I've as much right as you to be here today' he shouted back, deploring his own inability to control them and realising that the youths were advancing on him.

Luke looked on helplessly as two men seized Adam. Two more then pinned Luke's arms behind his back and, struggle as he might, there was nothing he could do to help his father.

'Let's baptise him!' one ruffian jeered jubilantly as they thrust Adam's head under the spout of the pump. There was no escape as the creaking of the pump handle violently heralded the outpouring of icy cold water. The crowd roared with laughter but Adam could not hear it through the noise of the water. He was bereft of his tall black hat and his head and shoulders were drenched, when suddenly he was released without further violence and allowed to go free. Seizing his hat and making sure Luke was by his side, he beat a hasty retreat, to the jeering of the crowd, down Coalpit Lane and to safety.

No one followed. Finally they stopped to regain their breath and Adam saw Luke's ghastly white face. He realised what a pair they made and knew that they had merely been the butt of a bored crowd. He had run away once before, at the time of his arrest, but then he had been alone and frightened, now he was a middle-aged man tormented by a gang of hooligans seeking excitement. He would return, they could bank on that! He looked at Luke and shook his head, 'Oh, lad! What a pair we make.' He chuckled. 'This will be a tale to tell your grandchildren.' Luke grimaced. He wasn't so sure.

They hurried home, taking the quickest and quietest route, grateful that the incident had not been more serious than it had. Adam considered that the towns people hadn't changed much over the years and were still easy to arouse, but for the most part were merely simple hardworking folk out looking for distraction. The grubby, ragged youths were the victims of a system which had hardly changed in decades. His quarrel was not with the people at all but with that system.

Two days later he read with some amusement a small report in the local newspaper entitled 'Scene at the Pump in Barker's Pool'. Tearing it out he placed the scrap of paper between the leaves of his bible, as a reminder should he ever forget his humble station in life. The incident, however, left Luke quite shaken and at a loss to understand the way Adam had accepted the situation. Such mobs back home in Illinois frequently attacked members with vicious thuggery and he had quite feared the outcome at the pump.

'You forget that I understand these people, Luke. Tomorrow they will probably listen quietly, although I am not so foolish as to ignore all that has happened. We'll let things cool down awhile and try again tomorrow.'

However, when Sarah Webster read of the affair in the *Independent* later in the week she was most distressed at the possibility that the two men might have been Mr Johnson and Luke. Such aggression, she lamented to George, was unforgivable humiliation of two harmless strangers.

'But, Sarah,' he remonstrated, 'that's the risk they run if they will stick their necks out like that.'

Sarah was indignant. 'That's not funny, about sticking their necks out, under the circumstances. How would you like to be so treated in public. What ever must they think of us? I do hope that they have come to no harm.'

'Really, Sarah. They weren't hurt by all accounts. Besides it may not have been Mr Johnson and his son at all.'

'Oh, I know it is' she protested. 'I just know it to be so. Won't you find out if they are alright? I did say that they would be welcome to call on us. Could we invite them to dine with us?'

'Alright, alright,' he laughed, trying to calm her. 'I'll invite them if only to convince you that it will make amends for the incident. You know, I've seen these people perform before—it's something they have to put up with, and there are people who resent them taking away their congregation as well as others who don't appreciate them using our town squares for their own propaganda. I suppose it does no harm and if people are foolish enough to follow them they deserve all they get.' He looked at her keenly and added sternly, 'I do hope, Sarah, that you don't intend getting mixed up with this strange religion of theirs—it can only bring trouble'.

She shook her head, 'No, of course not. I just feel sorry for Mr Johnson. He seems so nice, and I would not like to be humiliated like that myself'.

'But you wouldn't put yourself in such a position, although I must say that it takes some courage to stand before a mocking crowd and to speak out like that. How can we invite them? Do you know where they live?'

Sarah's eyes lit up. 'Why couldn't we leave a message at their Meeting House? Surely someone will pass the letter on and it is only just down the road from the Works.'

True to his word George sent a message round to the Meeting House, with instructions to the boy to push the letter under the door if there was no-one there. It was therefore several days before Adam actually received the note requesting the company of Luke and himself at Bank House. It was a formal note to which he replied in similar fashion, accepting the invitation.

He was somewhat apprehensive about the visit, fearing to recall old memories and he was not enthused by the thought of meeting the cold forbidding eyes of the elder Miss Webster. Yet he felt drawn to these young people who were offering him their friendship.

Sunday dawned damp and dull and was brightened only by the service at the Meeting House and the invitation to Bank House. They were not expected until six thirty in the evening but by this time the mist had cleared and he was able to show Luke the fine views as they climbed the hill to the house. As the warm inviting lights from windows beckoned, Adam could not help but wonder how he would stand up to the evening. He would be expected to discuss Fanny and Gervase at some point and this could be very awkward; it was almost as though he was about to deceive them. Perhaps he had been unwise to accept the invitation?

There was no mistaking the warmth in George Webster's welcome, nor that of his sister Sarah and, on the face of it, the older Miss Webster was certainly polite. To his relief, George took to Luke immediately and it wasn't long before the two young men were deeply engrossed in conversation, leaving Adam with the sisters.

It was not difficult for him to relax in Sarah's presence but he was convinced that had she not been there it would have been a trial to communicate with her sister. Sarah's lively spirit left him with no time to dwell on the past as she switched from one topic to another like a charming butterfly.

'Mr Johnson,' she exclaimed, 'before the light goes I must show you the garden. If the weather had been better we could have sat out. We have a small pond with all sorts of creatures in it, frogs, fish, even newts. It lies beyond the formal lawn that mother laid out there. Do let us walk there and look at it.' It was almost as though it were Fanny standing there, her enthusiasm and precocious charm reminded him so much of her mother.

'But, Sarah, it is too damp outside,' interrupted her sister, 'and dinner is almost ready to be served.'

Although deep in conversation, George raised his head, and remarked, 'There's time, and it wouldn't take long but we must keep to the path or we shall all end up covered in mud'.

In spite of the conditions, Sarah's enthusiasm for detail captivated Adam and he knew that if he closed his eyes, it would be as if Fanny was there. So Fanny had planned this garden, with the same loving care that she had organised his room above the shop in the old days. Across the lawn, beyond the well-stocked pond was an orchard of various apple and pear trees, and where the drive rounded the house there stood an impressive array of stables and out-houses. He was sure that if they had not all been neatly attired, Sarah would have had them exploring the hay lofts as well.

Captivated as he was with her, he was completely unaware of Luke's obvious admiration too, until suddenly he turned and caught an unguarded glance. It was a sobering moment for he did not wish to have the worry which an affair would bring. Luke was here to serve the Lord and should not be distracted. Watching Sarah he took heart in knowing that she was unaware of the spell which she was casting over Luke's affections.

For almost twenty minutes they wandered pleasantly, chatting freely in the musky evening air before George offered to show Adam and Luke round the interior of the house. 'We had better scrape the mud from our feet before we go in,' George pointed out, 'or there will be the devil to pay from Mary if we don't.' Leading the way, he took them first up the wide, polished oak staircase to the landing on which the elder sister had stood observing Adam on his first visit.

Adam was surprised at the loftiness of the upstairs rooms, for the house from the outside had given him the impression of being much more compact. The overall neatness of the house impressed him but, on realising that he was about to be shown into Fanny's room, was greatly relieved, when from below stairs, a dinner gong rang out, calling them to dine. As they reached the foot of the stairs and crossed the hall, once again Adam caught sight of the portrait which had intrigued him so much. 'What an elegant woman,' he remarked, 'who is she?'

'One of father's forebears, can't you see the family likeness in father?' George bent a little closer and whispered, 'I'm afraid she was quite a character, wild in fact—but my sister won't hear a word against her'.

Joining his sisters in the dining room, George Webster seated himself at the head of the table and placed Adam and Luke on either side of himself. 'Welcome again to our house, Mr Johnson, and Luke,' he said, 'I must admit that when you called the other day I was surprised and confused, but the more I thought about it and with Sarah's badgering, I felt that it would be pleasant to get to know you better. We would love to hear about mother and father when they were young.' He waited until the servant had finished serving him. 'How well did you know our parents?' he asked.

'Well, I worked for your father in the early days when he was starting out with the business. He had premises in the High Street then. We got on very well and spent many hours out walking together. I had a great deal of respect for him. Your mother would often accompany us on our jaunts and I must say that Sarah remind me very much of her. Then I left the country.'

He glanced fleetingly at Luke, warning him not to enlighten them further. 'And that was twenty-six years ago.'

'Ah!' The elder Miss Webster remarked, 'Perhaps that is why we have not heard of you; it was before we were born and before the new premises in Rockingham Street were taken on.'

Adam continued, 'I hear that there was a fire—what happened? Your father was always particular about fire hazards.'

'I understand that it was possibly a leaking oil lamp in the workshop', George explained. 'Father had been very busy and had intended changing the lamp, but never got round to it. We don't really know for certain and it is such a long time ago. He rented the Rockingham Street premises, before he finally bought them. Since then we have expanded and prospered very well.' There was pride in George's voice but no conceit. 'Wine, Mr Johnson?'

Adam shook his head, 'I thank you, but if you remember I don't take alcohol. I would appreciate water or fruit juice, whichever is more convenient'.

'You intrigue me, Mr Johnson. I know that you are a Mormon and have meeting rooms in Charles Street, but I read in the paper of an incident at the pump—it was you I presume? I'm afraid your kind are not always popular hereabouts.'

'Yes, that was us! We are often misunderstood, but are only here to explain to the people what we believe in. If what we preach causes so much fear and resentment to other religious leaders then perhaps they should look to their own beliefs to see what is lacking there. If they have nothing to fear from our message then why do they throw stones at our meeting house windows and chant loudly while we are holding services inside? I haven't witnessed such actions personally, yet, but I understand some of the sisters are so frightened by it that they dare not leave the premises unaccompanied.'

Luke spoke up, 'I have it from one of the brethren, that it is perhaps the bad weather today which stopped them. They have no liking for their own discomfort'.

'We do not attend chapel regularly ourselves' the elder Miss Webster spoke out. 'Father never forced us to go, although I suppose we are Unitarians if the truth be known. Mother always said that there was too much cruelty and injustice in the world for there to be a God, and that when she met him she would tell him so.'

Fanny! Miss Webster was telling him about Fanny as though she had been a stranger to him. He wanted to cry back at this prim young woman across the table, 'I loved your mother—she had such spirit!' He tried to calm his violent reaction by changing the direction of the conversation. 'I did get the impression the other day, Miss Webster, that you had strong views on religion, not that you were against it.'

'My sister is against anything which is dictatorial or diversive. In this town religious squabbling causes more trouble then enough. But enough of religion. Whereabouts in America do you live?'

'Navoou, Illinois, although at the moment the persecution and intolerance there is far worse than anything you could imagine over here.'

'What line of business are you in?' George asked.

A smile crossed Adam's face, 'Would you believe that I am still a printer? Not it would seem as prosperous as yourself but we get by. If we didn't have to keep moving on because of persecution the business would be bigger'.

'Would you care to visit the Works sometime?' George enquired, 'You might find it quite interesting. I'm there most of the day—call whenever you wish.'

It was only after Adam had agreed to visit Rockingham Street that he wondered if it was such a good idea after all. George's enthusiasm had caught him unawares.

As conversation fell to ordinary topics and fragmented into several different discussions between the four of them, the evening passed pleasantly. It was only when Adam glanced at the chiming clock on the mantelpiece that he realised how late it had become. 'My, we seem to have stayed longer than planned. I hope we haven't outstayed our welcome.' He realised that it was already pitch black outside and he had not brought a lantern with him. He had thought to return home before nightfall. 'May we borrow a lantern? I'm afraid once again I must fall back on your good nature—it was foolish of me not have brought my own with me.'

George waved aside Adam's plea. 'We have taken care of the matter already Mr Johnson and have arranged for the carriage to take you home.'

'Once again I am in your debt—and am most grateful.' Adam said, rising from the table. 'This has been a most enjoyable evening.' He shook hands with Sarah and turned to face the serious grey eyes of her sister who was watching him, there was no real warmth in the eyes. Throughout the entire evening Adam had tried to break through her reserve but she had responded with nothing more than polite smiles. Her fingers, when he took her hand in his, were stiff and formal.

'Good evening Mr Johnson' she said, politely.

Once in the carriage Adam pondered on the strange, almost arrogant Miss Webster. She was so unlike either Fanny or Gervase in her manner that if it were not for her colouring and the familiar defiance in her eyes, he would have thought her to be someone else's child. Fanny had been a rebel but never unkind, and Gervase had been firm but gentle, even with the most exasperating people.

Chapter 9

After that first confrontation with the crowds in Barker's Pool, Adam adopted a different technique—he would match their sport word for word, indulging the people with sparks of humour, beating them at their own game. He welcomed their boisterous challenges and insults, returning them with lively quips which resulted in even larger crowds gathering. Gangs of youths gathered to harangue his preaching yet never again did they touch him. This popularity had its effect and a slow trickle of converts tramped down to the murky river and bravely entered the waters for baptism.

Luke, though in awe of his father's success in these confrontations, had not the stomach for it, yet he knew that it was only a matter of time before he too would have to take the stand. His shy, self-conscious disposition left him quaking with nerves. Adam was aware of this and chose carefully the best opportunities for Luke to speak, ever watchful for signs of trouble when he would intervene with timely eloquence.

Adam had not forgotten George Webster's invitation, and soon found time to call at the Works, realising at the same time that it would be an excellent opportunity to introduce himself to yet another section of the population.

The frontage of the Webster's establishment was quite modest, belying the spacious accommodation existing behind the facade. From the street it appeared to be merely a house with an adjacent archway allowing horse and cart to pass through into the courtyard. However, on entering the courtyard Adam was surprised at the spaciousness of it and to see stabling incorporated within. He gathered from the washing strung up in one corner that several buildings were occupied as dwellings.

Crossing the cobbled yard, Adam and Luke approached a youth carrying a number of parcels, obviously completed orders. 'Is Mr Webster anywhere about?' Adam asked.

The youth indicated a door at the far side of the yard. 'Go through that door at the end Sir. I don't know if Mr Webster's in but the foreman will tell you all you want to know.' He slipped, almost dropping the parcels, Luke steadied him just in time. 'You'd better watch your step too—it's a bit greasy underfoot', the youth warned, before going about his business.

Peering through the half-open door Luke was impressed by the size of the machinery within. 'This really is something' he exclaimed in admiration. 'It makes our workshops look small.'

Adam sighed, 'If we didn't have so many interruptions and have to move so often we would be able to buy more efficient machinery. You know the problems we have'. The sound of their voices brought a figure from behind a machine. Adam was startled.

'Now then gentlemen, can I help you?' the man enquired with suspicion, eyeing Adam and Luke carefully.

A look of amazement crossed Adam's face and he stared in disbelief at the man. 'It's Tom Linley! It is you isn't it?' he gasped, involuntarily, hardly believing what he saw.

'It is! And who might you be?' There was no recognition on the foreman's face. 'Have we met before?'

'Tom, it's me, under all these whiskers, you old devil!' There was suddenly a light of awakening in Tom's eyes and he stared in bewilderment. 'John! John Andrews—you remember?' cried Adam.

Tom scanned Adam's face, not once but several times before it dawned on him that Adam told the truth. 'John?' he gasped. 'How? We thought you were dead! Miss Fanny always said that you would have been back before now if you weren't.' He stared hard at Adam, then, with tears streaming down his face he came forward. 'All these years!' He cried as the two men clasped each other in a warm embrace, 'I have never had a chance to tell you how much I admired you.' There was a mixture of joy and regret in his voice. 'You left a big hole in that old shop when you went.' He clasped Adam again, 'God! It is good to see you!'

Adam was aware that Luke had stiffened and knew he was as shocked as Tom. What could the boy be thinking? Adam had told no-one his real name, not since boarding the whaler off the Coast of New South Wales. He had completely concealed his old identity and apart from his ticket of leave which he kept locked in the safe in his office back home, there was no evidence that John Andrews was still alive, except for the man standing before him. Through the emotion and tears Adam heard himself saying, 'Tom—you old friend, it's good to see you too'.

Luke stood, as if frozen to the ground, no longer sure who his father was. He had never before seen him show signs of deep emotion yet here he was in tears in the arms of a stranger, and calling himself John Andrews! He turned instinctively, needing to get away, away from things which he could not understand. Half walking, half running, he left the yard in a state of embarrassment and shock.

The sound of Luke hurrying across the cobbled yard released Adam from his trance and he let Tom loose. 'Wait, Tom. My lad's upset, he's had a shock. I've got to go after him and when I've sorted things out I'll come back.' He hastened through the archway after Luke, leaving Tom in the doorway of the printing shop, stunned by the suddenness of it all.

'Luke, wait!' Adam called frantically, as Luke hurried blindly down the road. 'Wait son—I'll explain it all if you'll only let me!'

Luke had no idea why he was running, no idea where in fact he was heading. He stopped, waiting for Adam to catch up, unable to speak.

'Listen, Luke!' Adam pleaded. 'It isn't as bad as you think!'

'I don't understand you any more—you're supposed to be my father, yet now you say you are someone else' the boy cried.

The look of bewilderment in Luke's eyes upset Adam and he put his hand gently on his son's arm. Luke shrugged it off, not out of anger but from distress. 'I think,' said Adam, kindly, 'that we had better return to the house where I can tell you all about it.'

It wasn't easy for Adam to even begin to relate to Luke the tangled story of his life, for he'd always felt that no one would understand or believe him. However, he began at the beginning, where his mother had drowned herself, leaving him in the care of a very busy uncle. As a child he had felt himself to be a hindrance to his mother's brother but the man had done his duty and provided all the necessities of life, except the love that a boy needed.

He explained about his exploits as a radical in Nottingham, and his banishment to Sheffield. How, on reaching Sheffield on a cold miserable winter's day, Adam (John) had been met by the resentful Tom Linley, but as time went by a strange kind of friendship had developed. Gervase Webster, their employer had been a mixture of father and brother to John, and together with Fanny, a family friend, they had formed strong bonds. John and Fanny (he spoke of the past as though it were someone else's), saved a boy from death at the hands of a mill overseer. As a result of John's evidence the man had been sent to York Castle but even from that distance he had taken his revenge by having John cruelly beaten one dark night. Not once did Adam tell Luke of his love for Fanny.

John had re-joined the radicals in their plans for reform but the overseer, once released from gaol, struck again, having him framed for stealing a silver watch.

At first Luke felt little sympathy as he listened to Adam's story. He felt that he had been deceived all those years, yet as the story unfolded he became intrigued by its incredibility. For three hours he sat listening as Adam unburdened himself about his trials in the hulks, the voyage and his lonely life as a shepherd.

'But what happened after you left New South Wales?' Luke enquired. 'How did you find the Church, and mother?'

'I remember that at first I was a solitary figure on the decks of the whaler, keeping myself to myself. I watched people, almost stared at them, but could not bring myself to do more than mumble 'good day' to them. I must have appeared very odd, for I know that I had strange little habits through being on my own for so long. Even now I am no great talker, except when forced to it and I wonder if that is the reason why the Elders chose to send me here, to place me where I have no choice but to speak up.

'You do well on the streets' Luke pointed out.

'Ah, but then I feel the spirit!' Adam replied. 'However, on the ship I was a paying passenger and as such they left me alone. There were storms on that voyage too, natural and man-made, and tempers flared in the heat or wet, but this time I was not battened below nor was I humiliated by the filth and squalor of it all. The fleet had already been away at sea for almost three years and I could sense an air of excitement and expectation amongst the whole ship's crew as we neared home port. Life was rugged enough and comforts few, yet I found myself liking those simple but strong-minded seamen. By the time we reached the shores of Nantucket Island I had shed some of my hermit ways and can still recall the jubilation we all felt as we drew alongside the jetty.

The fact that I had finally reached America was in itself an amazement to me. I, John Andrews—now Adam Johnson, for that was the name which I gave myself the minute I left Sydney, had finally reached America! My feet seemed to float on air as I walked down that gangplank and I would have knelt and kissed the ground had I not been afraid of appearing foolish.

My first inclination was to catch a ferry to the mainland but the long sea voyage had eaten a large hole in my savings and I realised I needed to find work as soon as possible. It also occurred to me that many years had passed without my being at liberty to explore, and having left Sydney with all haste I had never observed the workings of a port.

I stayed in Nantucket several weeks, walking miles across the island, savouring the sweet-smelling heather of her moorlands whilst the salty air blew my over-long hair into a constant tumble. In the end I tied it back into a pigtail like the sailors did. My confidence increased as did the money in my coffers, and I became tempted to remain amongst those patient people.

Nantucket, with her weathered grey cottages and wharf side structures jutting out into the magnificent sheltered harbour, entranced me. I even bathed in the warm sea from the soft sandy beaches. I worked hard too, earning my keep by off-loading endless barrels of whale oil from the bowels of the ships which came in a constant stream into port.

On the voyage I had been befriended by a sailor who offered me lodgings with his family. This was my first taste of homelife in nearly nine years and when the time came for me to leave I left a little of my heart with those sturdy, forbearing people. With the women too, who constantly waited for men who had fathered children whom they had never seen. I knew the anguish of their absences but each seemed to accept his lot as a way of life and to put their trust in God. It was perhaps on that Island that I began to feel strangely closer to God, as I shared their Quaker homes and learned that I was not alone in shaping my destiny. I had been allowed to come this far and I was thankful for my preservation.

Soon I had sufficient savings to press on, and because I had been warned that American winters could be harsh and long, I decided that I should move inland and seek permanent employment as soon as possible. This knowledge, combined with my burning desire to discover America for myself, forced me to leave the shelter upon which I knew I was becoming increasingly dependent. I had to move on before it was too late.

I re-lived the joy of arrival again when I landed on the mainland and was surprised to find New Bedford also to be a thriving whaling port. There were barrels everywhere. The whole waterfront seemed to consist of nothing except barrels, full ones and empty ones. Nor could I believe my eyes when I saw the vast quantities of whalebones laid out to dry along the piers. My fancy was tickled when I realised that much of it was destined to end up closer to woman's bodies than I had been for eight years. I could not for the life of me imagine why any woman would want to be so torturously encased in whalebone corsets for vanity's sake. Yet I knew that a slender waist appealed even to me.

At first I wandered the cobbled streets, exploring every alleyway like a child. A most pleasant smell appeared to be constantly in the air and I could not resist asking a weather-beaten old man who was sitting on a barrel on the waterfront, where the odour came from. I had been encouraged by his smile earlier as I had disembarked.

'Melted down blubber, my boy, makes fine-smelling candles,' the old mariner replied. 'Not from this area then?' he went on to ask.

I liked the friendliness of this old man and invited him to share some ale with me. He grinned, a toothless grin, which I imagined he had used many times before to charm a drink from a passing stranger. Not such a bad way to end one's sea-faring life, I thought, to sit watching others taking all the risks.

What tales that old man could tell! I sat spellbound for far too long when I should have been seeking accommodation and work.

Realising that time was passing, I seized my hat and made to rise. 'Much as I am enjoying your company, I must go' I told him, 'but I have left everything rather late already and have nowhere to stay the night. I really must go. Thank you for your time and company.'

The toothless grin appeared afresh. 'Why not share my humble shack?' he proffered. 'I could do with an extra dollar or two. Take me as you find me—that's all I ask.'

There was no reason for me to turn down his offer. He was clean, and too old to be dishonest, so I considered myself, a stranger, more of a risk to him than he to me. 'If you're sure I won't be a trouble to you!' I insisted, grateful not to have to search for lodgings.

We entered his wooden, one-roomed cabin and I stood there in amazement at the orderliness of it all, yet the room was far from empty. I would say rather that it was crammed with possessions without giving the appearance of being cluttered. A bed, pushed into a corner displayed a colourful quilt of the most exquisite patchwork design, whilst on the floor around the pot-bellied stove were animal-skin rugs. 'You can sleep on the rugs piled on top of each other' he indicated, seeing my interest.

Sitting by the warmth of the stove which he had lit immediately we had arrived, for the evenings were chilly now, we talked well into the early hours of the morning. 'My father was Danish', he informed me, as if explaining the reason for the coffee pot which simmered all the while on the stove.

Everywhere I saw evidence of the life of a sea-farer. I could not but admire the many engraved whale bone pieces which were placed here and there about the room, so fine were they in detail. 'Did you do these?' I asked, 'I saw men on the ship working with much dedication on similar pieces!'

He nodded. 'Each one represents a voyage, and when I got bored of scribing then I used to sew' he said proudly.

'Did you make the quilt on the bed?' I asked.

'Every inch of it I did—as good as any woman's work, though I say it myself.' His crinkled face was as interesting as the quilt and I was full of admiration for him.

'Dare I ask how old you are?' I ventured.

He smiled, 'Born in 1734 I was!'

I did a quick calculation and came to the astonishing conclusion that he was even older than he looked. 'But that makes you ninety-two!' I gasped.

He laughed, 'Now don't you go thinking that I'm past it—I cook for myself and clean. When I get short of money I tell a tale or two on the pier, or sell a piece of my scrimshaw'. He picked up a piece of the delicately-carved bone. 'They'll be no good to me when I'm gone.'

I looked round once more at the orderliness of his small home, and marvelled. 'Have you no children?' I dared to ask.

'Never married. Didn't think it fair when I was always away at sea. Had a woman or two in my time, mind you. But they all wanted me to stay on land too long. Now I'm too old to sail or put up with a woman! As for children—who knows?' A wicked glint appeared in his eyes and we laughed in harmony together. We sat, by the light of the stove, well into the early hours, exchanging tales, but I never told him what turned me into a traveller, and he never asked, though I suspect that the wise old man had his ideas. He told me that it was a fair trek to Providence where mother's relatives lived, and that there were many lakes and swamps to cross, yet I could not afford the more direct route by boat into the top reaches of Providence Bay.

I was still young and strong enough to make it on foot. I stayed three nights with him and became quite fond of the old sea-dog but I had stayed longer than I had intended. The mariner and I exchanged a brief embrace as we parted and I knew that I would never see him again.

It took me two weeks to reach Providence, hitching lifts and working my way from farm to farm. I found people of all nationalities who were warm and friendly, confirming my original thoughts that this country was the place for me. Everywhere the land seemed to be ablaze with colour such as I had never seen before, not even in England. Trees with leaves rich in all shades of colour, especially the reds and golds. They stretched on for mile after mile, shimmering against the frosty autumn skies. There were hickory, oak, beech, birch, maple and white pine trees all arrayed in their finery, but as I approached Providence they were beginning to wither and fall, forming a multi-coloured carpet beneath my feet. I knew that I had only just made it before the onset of winter.

On reaching Providence I found that my enquiries as to the whereabouts of my mother's cousin, Samuel Slater, brought a quicker response than I had expected. He had prospered, making the task of tracking him down fairly easy and had I known of his elevation in life before arriving I might have questioned the wisdom of my descending upon him unannounced. In the event I need not have worried about my welcome.

It was no great distance from Providence to Pawtucket where he lived. The town was situated on the banks of the Blackstone River where wooden-planked houses and two mills clung to the water's edge. Although I had seen enough water to last me a lifetime, I stood on the long wooden bridge spanning the Pawtucket Falls, fascinated by the thundering, foaming water which drowned out all other sound, and marvelled at its awesome power. There were giant boulders being pounded by the incessant flow and I could see that the owners of the mills either side of the river had chosen their sites well. Nowhere else, apart from the sea, had I seen such natural forces at work, and harnessed so well. There would be no seasonal fluctuations in flow here to disrupt work, and I could almost feel the power transferring itself to me, driving me on.

As I approached Samuel Slater's impressive house I took a deep breath, knocked on the door, removed my beaver cap, and awaited a response. It was, of course, a servant who opened the door, and I found myself facing a young woman with a most charming smile. Although she was of ample proportions, the girl was not unattractive and I suddenly found myself tongue-tied. Such a reaction shocked me. Here was I, a man who had not given much thought to women for years, floored by the simple smile of a young girl. Over the years, in my loneliness, I had nursed my ideal of womanhood, one which was warm and comforting, and did not remind me of my beautiful...' He stopped suddenly—he had almost admitted to Luke his love for Fanny! With care he continued, 'The young woman epitomised all my dreams.'

Concealing my thoughts and discomfort, I proceeded to state my business. 'I am from England and am seeking a kinsman, a Mr Samuel Slater. Would you be good enough to inform him that the son of Elizabeth Stone, his cousin, of Belper, begs to see him.' The words were hesitant and stumbling and the girl, sensing my shyness, smilingly replied.

'He doesn't like to be disturbed at this hour normally but I'll see what the Mistress says. Please wait here', she said.

I waited patiently for some minutes until I began to believe myself forgotten entirely. Eventually the young woman returned, her features pleasant and welcoming. 'You are to come with me, Sir, if you please.' She led me to a very comfortable parlour where a small man in his late fifties, who bore no resemblance at all to my mother, came towards me and shook my hand. 'Good morning pleased to meet you!' he said, searching my face, perhaps looking for a family likeness. After all I was a stranger.

He was not unfriendly but I felt myself under scrutiny and knew that I should quickly explain my unexpected appearance at his door. 'I apologise for arriving at an inconvenient time, but I have journeyed many miles to meet you Sir. My mother, Elizabeth Stone from Blackbrook, Belper, was your cousin, and although it is many years since you last met, the family often spoke of you and your achievements with pride. It was through their tales of you that I got my childish dream of coming to America—a dream which never left me.' He had not as yet invited me to sit down and I began to wonder if I should be obliged to leave.

He rubbed his balding head. 'Yes, I remember Elizabeth as a child but I don't know what became of her. My mother did write once saying Elizabeth had married.'

'She married a Nottingham man and moved there, but I was only nine when she drowned!' I stated simply.

'Oh! That is a shame,' he sighed, 'she was a quiet girl as I remember.' Then, as if recalling his position as host said, 'Do take a seat! I'm afraid I didn't catch your name?'

So far I had avoided giving him my name, but now that I knew the extent of his knowledge about my mother's life I felt safe to use my new name. I had no desire to lie but I did not want to risk ruining my chances of starting a new life. 'Adam Johnson!' I was used to the name now and no longer stuttered it hesitatingly. 'I did not give it to the girl earlier as I knew it would have meant nothing to you. I came to America because I saw a chance to better myself and besides I have no ties in England anymore.' I sat down as I spoke.

'There is great scope here for a person who is willing to work—I presume you have a trade?'

'I am a printer, but I am willing to do almost anything to get established. What I want more than anything in the world is to move westwards for a while, exploring this vast land. I do have a small amount of money but really I need to find work before winter sets in—so that I can acquire more capital. I'm not looking for charity,' I assured him, 'but if you could recommend something hereabouts I would be most grateful!'

'Do you know anything about cotton at all?' he asked. I shook my head. 'Do you know anything about iron works or carpentry? There are many forges around here which may take you on', he offered.

Once more I admitted my lack of experience. 'No, but I am willing to work hard and learn—given the chance' I added quickly.

'I don't know of anything else around here but if you are willing to stay in Providence I might be able to put you onto something, perhaps labouring in the boatyards there. Mind you winter here is not the best time in which to seek employment, so many others are doing the same thing.'

'I would be grateful for anything that you can arrange', I assured him, for I had the feeling that he was doing this for my mother's sake rather than mine.

He relaxed, and smiled. 'We have eaten already but if you are hungry I'm sure Henrietta will find you something in the kitchen,' he offered kindly, 'we also have a small room which you are welcome to use whilst you are here. Have something to eat and we will talk about it later.' He rang the bell and waited a few minutes for the girl to appear. 'You must tell me of England, and how she fares', he stated as I left the room.

Henrietta's appearance brought a flood of relief to me for I had not been in England now for eight years and knew no more than he how things fared there. It would not be easy for me to have to spend the winter months under his roof whilst concealing my secret from Samuel Slater.

After eating a delicious meal and having had a friendly chat with Henrietta in the kitchen I finally made up my mind. I was going to tell my host, and only him, the truth.

It did me no harm to tell Samuel Slater my story, and my real name, for I think he realised the courage it took for me to do so. He recognised also that I need not have told him anything. What reason was there to invent such a story if it were not true? The brand on my shoulder confirmed that

I had been a convict so I reassured him that I had served my time by showing him my final ticket. By the time my confession was complete I believe we were almost friends.

He kept his word and found me employment with an acquaintance in Providence so each day I walked to the dockyards, did the heavy manual work which the job demanded and returned to my small room in his house. On many of those days the journey was hampered by deep snow but I pressed on and was always grateful on my return for the meal provided by Henrietta, in the kitchen. The long dark winter evenings found me resting or reading, for I did not force myself upon the kind hospitality of my host. On Sundays I spent a little time with him and felt obliged in return for his goodness to attend his place of worship.

My short visits to the kitchen became the highlights of my time in Pawtuckett, for Henrietta mothered me constantly. Little did I realise then, that she would eventually become my wife, and your mother, Luke! Anyway to continue. As the severity of winter held us in its grip I needed companionship, and Henrietta's happy face drew me back to the kitchen more often perhaps than it should have done. She must have thought me to have the appetite of a horse, so often did I make hunger my excuse to visit her domain.

My long hours alone in the bush had left its mark. I was still a man of few words and soon tired of lengthy discussions, more from my inability to express myself competently than laziness or disinterest. It was different being with Henrietta; her mothering of me helped me to overcome my reticence and she gently drew out of me all the bitterness and resentfulness of the past.

One particular morning, I rose early so that we might chat a while before I set off for work, and as I arrived at the kitchen door, I realised with quite a jolt, that I had begun to feel very much attached to her. As it happens, there was a musical recital in the settlement that night and I decided to invite Henrietta to it.

Watching her from where I stood in the doorway was a pleasant occupation. She looked up startled from her sewing, then lowered her eyes shyly when she realised that I was observing her, but not before I had seen the welcome on her face. I spoke first, 'Good morning! You look very busy,' I said brightly.

Henrietta nodded, 'I've been mending for an hour already, and my fingers are quite tired. Would you like something to eat before you go out?' she offered.

'Please!' I replied, although I was far from hungry, I had other things on my mind. As she placed the cold turkey and bread before me I noticed that her hand trembled. Had someone not entered the kitchen at that moment I think I would have taken it in mine, but I was not able to do so. I ate the meal without saying more than a few words and as I left, dared to ask, 'Would you liked to go with me to the recital at the Chapel tonight?'

She nodded, flushing deeply, 'Thank you. I would like that.'

'Then I'll call for you at half past six, so that we can watch the river for a while first.' She was not beautiful, your mother, but the smile she gave me brought her face to life and I was pleased that I had invited her to go with me.

With great care that evening I washed and attired myself, feeling as a youth might who had no experience of women at all. I think we were shy of each other for we did not speak at great length at anytime during the entire evening. Henrietta was content to listen first to me and then to the concert. She was wide-eyed with wonder when later I told her of some of my adventures; she made me feel like the old mariner of New Bedford with whom I stayed.

I allowed her to take me to Church—me of all people, who had never believed, and I suppose by the time spring was over we were 'walking out' together. On Sundays, after Church, we would walk along the river bank, or through the meadows at the north of the mill where cloth and yarn were bleached and stretched. As the weather improved and the grass dried out we would sit in the quiet stillness of the fields and I would tell her of my dreams. Your mother would sit beside me gathering the exquisite tiny flowers which grew in abundance on the grassy slope, and I would playfully rest my head in her lap, as I would have done on a cushion.'

Adam paused. He had done it several times during his narration and Luke suspected that his father was continuing the story in his head. There were parts of the story which Adam felt would be imprudent to relate but he could not wipe them from his mind. Luke, however, realised that to break into Adam's reverie would also break the spell and he was content to wait until his father resumed his tale. But Adam was remembering with clarity that day in the meadow and did not realise that he had ceased speaking.

Adam's thoughts went on then, to remember with such nostalgia the heady perfume of the flowers which filled his head that day with wild imagining, reminding him of Fanny. Until this time he had done no more than hold Henrietta's hand and playfully tease her, being unsure of his feelings and thinking it unfair to dally with her. But now, as he felt the gentle rise and fall of her soft body as she breathed in and out his desire to draw her closer overcame him. He realised that although she appeared to be looking into the distance, the soft flush on her cheeks told him that she was not unaware of his closeness, and he allowed himself to enjoy her warmth. How he savoured those moments, and the nearness of another tender human being within his grasp. The harshness of the past years rolled away and he took her hand which lay across his body, and squeezed it gently. She did not withdraw it as he feared she might, but left it there encouragingly. Drawing her closer, he pressed his head against her soft breasts and sensed no rejection; instead she dropped her head and kissed his hair affectionately. Perhaps she had acted instinctively because the hand which he held had trembled before stiffening apprehensively. He knew then that he must allay her fears and nestled his head closer into her softness. He lay there in her protective arms, like a child, fighting off the growing feeling of desire which was slowly overtaking him. In the years of his loneliness he had never dreamt that he would receive such wonderful comfort again.

Drawing up his knees, he eased himself round until their faces were only inches apart. She had waited patiently, her face filled with shyness, her eyes concealing her fears. Touching her cheek gently with the palm of his hand he knew that he could not hurt her, nor did he want to refuse the love which she so innocently offered. Pulling her closer still, he kissed her. Her kisses were warm, not as exciting as Fanny's had been, nor as demanding, but they were full of love and affection. She had also aroused in him longings which he had suppressed for years and he found himself caressing the soft breasts concealed beneath her modest, homespun bodice. He wanted her, craved to lose himself completely in union with her, but he felt her tremble and draw back a little. There was love as well as fear in her eyes and her trust in him made him ashamed of his desires.

Henrietta was not to know the anguish of his needs, nor did she deserve the passion which his body had wanted to unleash. It had been with utmost difficulty that he had held himself in check, for he was suddenly afraid of his inner feelings, and of losing her. Instead he knelt before her and cradled her against his breast. He was glad then that he had not harmed the gentle creature, nor disgraced himself in her eyes. He had need of her in more ways than she could ever have imagined, yet he was not deeply in love with her; she was, unfortunately, not Fanny. Kissing her again with genuine affection this time, he took her hand protectively in his and led her back to the house.

He felt no guilt over withholding one small part of his heart from her—that which would always be Fanny's, as he knew that he had made her happy, but nevertheless, he was in a dilemma. He had hoped to stay with Samuel Slater until financially more secure, then to move on and find employment as a printer in the State of New York. Now he realised that to stay longer would increase her expectation of him, and he was hardly ready for lasting commitments.

His bed, when he finally reached it, comfortable though it was, was a lonely one and the events of the day had stirred him more than he realised, preventing him from sleeping. The warmth of Henrietta's body had brought his very soul to life and he was tired of being alone. He knew that Henrietta's sweet disposition would make her a dutiful wife and loving mother, and God alone knew how tired he was of striving alone through life's battles. Pulling his spare pillow into his arms as though it were her, he resolved to propose to her on the morrow and ask her to accompany him in his search for work in nearby New York State.

Next morning, as he sat in the kitchen observing Henrietta busying herself more than usual about her tasks, he knew that he himself was being unusually quiet. A deep understanding had developed between himself and Henrietta so that they could be in each other's company for some time without needing to talk, but he knew that if he didn't speak up soon she would believe that he regretted his actions of the previous evening.

He went up to her and gently placed his hands around her waist as she worked, laying his head on her hair. He felt her soften, and squeezed her teasingly before turning her round to face him. Her face tinged with shyness as she looked at him from beneath her modestly lowered lashes and he realised then that any promises he made to her that day had to be kept. Taking her hand, he said, 'You know that I do not want to stay here in Pawtuckett forever, don't you? And that I want to move eventually, further west, building up a business!' She nodded. 'I still want to do that', he continued, 'but I would like more than anything for you to come with me—as my wife!'

For one moment her eyes went blank and he thought that she was going to refuse him. However, her amazement turned to joy and in that moment she appeared almost beautiful to him. He felt a twinge of conscience then for he knew that he ought to love her more than he did. 'It won't be easy at first', he said softly. 'I have to find work and a house, but I have been told that there is employment to be had if I am willing to look for it. I would want to go ahead and find both these things, and then come back for you! What do you say?' He waited nervously, allowing her time to think about what he had said.

Henrietta had tears in her eyes as she lifted her hands to his face and pulled him down to her level, for she was considerably smaller than he was. Tenderly she kissed his lips, his nose, his eyes, shyly, adoringly, before speaking. 'I will come, if you really want me to?' There was a hint of doubt in her voice. 'I don't mind waiting here, but please don't make promises you may not be able to keep.' She lowered her head, shielding her eyes from him, 'I'm not beautiful, or bright, but I love you too much to hold you to a promise rashly made. Go away and then come back for me, if you still want me.' She did not raise her head and he suspected that she understood him far better than he understood himself. He made to protest, but she placed her fingers over his lips. 'Hush!' she whispered. 'Do as I ask and I will wait for you!' She left no room for argument and he saw a strength and determination within her which made him feel almost ashamed of his lack of deep love.

Adam shuddered at the thought of what he had done to Henrietta, and lifted his eyes to his son's. Luke waited patiently still, seeing only deep pain in his father's eyes.

Stealing himself, Adam continued his story, out loud. 'I asked Henrietta to marry me, then I went to the State of New York where I found employment and a tiny house to rent, leaving her to wait for me. She was overjoyed to see me when I returned to Pawtuckett after a few weeks. I think she had half-expected a letter from me full of excuses why I would not be returning, but I am at least a man of my word. Before we wed I did tell her a little about my past history, but not all of it.

We had hard times your mother and I, but we were happy, and she bore me seven children. I worked very hard for other people over the following two years before branching out on my own and in all those years she never once complained. I wish now that she had, perhaps then I would have shown her more gratitude; instead I seem to have taken her love for granted.'

Adam paused again; Luke looked so much like his mother. 'Your mother is a saint. Without her love and loyalty I would not be the success that I am today. As you know, four years ago we became involved, through business, with the Latter Day Saints and our lives took on a deeper, happier meaning than before. Once again your mother has made a sacrifice by allowing me to come here to do God's work.' Adam was tired now and said softly, 'Son, I have no other secrets. You have it all. I feel now that I want to be alone for a while, then I shall write home to your mother'.

'But why didn't you tell anyone all this before?' Luke begged.

'Would they have understood? Perhaps it was just too painful for me and it was coming back here that has made me face it all. Sometimes it is almost as if it has been a dream, or that it happened to a stranger. However, when I left Sydney I changed my name, hoping perhaps that it would change my luck, but also to hide my shame. I didn't really intend to deceive anyone!' He shrugged his shoulders. His eyes were troubled but a wry smile crossed his face. 'I seem not to have changed things, for trouble seems still to have a liking for me. I have never knowingly done wrong in my life—that's the rub of it, but I've paid for what little mistakes I have made, the Lord knows I have.'

Later, his emotions spent and having rested, Adam returned to the Rockingham Street premises in search of Tom Linley. This time there was a more sober reunion with his old friend, who told him about the fire and the trip he had made with Gervase to London to buy a 'new-fangled' machine. That particular machine was getting old now but there were many other splendid machines and accessories in the building which Adam admired and envied quite openly.

'Of course, Miss Fanny ran things until Master George was old enough to take over. She was a genius for making money was Miss Fanny', Tom stated proudly.

Adam laughed out loud, 'Did you call her Miss Fanny up to the end, Tom?' Tom nodded. 'So you stayed all these years?' Adam shook his head in disbelief. 'Who would have thought it? Do you remember when you met me off the coach that day? I could see resentment in your every movement. How was I to know that my coming would make you homeless? None of us knew. Still, you have done well for yourself to be foreman over all this.' Adam turned, his outstretched hand sweeping to encompass the room. 'And I finally finished up in America after all, but my business is small compared to this.'

'Your lad was it, this morning?' Tom asked, 'What upset him so much?'

'Well, Tom, I never told anyone all that happened to me, especially that I changed my name once I left Australia. I'm Adam Johnson now, not John Andrews. It was a blow to him, he probably thought that if he stood there any longer I would turn into a monster before his eyes. I've told him the truth and left him to his own thoughts for a while. Do you have a family, yourself?'

'Four sons and a daughter', Tom smiled. 'Married a girl called Emily, from the Blue Bell, you remember that little maid they had? We live in one of those houses in the yard there. You must come and meet them, bring the lad too.'

'Indeed I will, but I'd better get back before he thinks I've met with an accident. Mr Webster insisted on inviting me over. I should have told him I was coming. Is he in?'

'Not today, he's gone to Derby on business, but he'll be back tomorrow. I'll tell him you've been but don't forget to come and meet my family. We've got a lot to talk about, you and I.'

Taking a pencil from his pocket, Adam scribbled his address on a scrap of paper torn from his pocket book. 'Here, Tom, give him this will you, he can find me there.' He placed the note in Tom's hand before bidding him farewell.

After all these years, Tom reflected sadly, as he watched Adam leave the yard, and Miss Fanny not cold in her grave more than three months past. Such a pity that was.

The following day when George Webster returned from Derby and made his usual early morning start at the Works, he was disappointed to find that he had missed his visitor. Tom handed over the paper which Adam had given him, saying, 'He was a grand chap when he worked for your father. It was tragic to have gone through what he did, and nearly broke your mother's heart, it did!'

'What do you mean, Tom? He went to America, what's wrong with that? He didn't tell us of any tragedy.'

Tom hesitated. 'He's not told you the full story then?'

'What story, Tom? Is there some mystery about him?'

'His names not Johnson you know, Mr Webster, it's John Andrews. Your mother must have mentioned him surely! It was partly his money which helped get us back on our feet after the fire!'

'What!' cried George Webster, looking up anxiously from the paper in his hand, 'You'd better close that door, Tom, and tell me exactly what is going on. He told us nothing about this.' He placed his hands on his hips, pushing back his frock coat, and waited impatiently for Tom to explain.

Seeing signs of anger in his employer's face, Tom was reluctant to begin. 'It's difficult then, have you not heard of John Andrews, Mr Webster? Didn't your father or Miss Fanny tell you anything at all?'

'All I know is that through some misfortune or other John Andrews left Sheffield and never returned. Apparently he left some money which father invested in the firm. You mean after all these years he's come back for it?' He was extremely angry now. 'So he was merely sizing up what we were worth, then! That's about as under-handed as anything I know!' He kicked out in disgust at a screwed-up piece of paper on the floor.

Bewildered by the angry outburst, Tom spoke up. 'It's not like that at all Mr Webster, don't take on. I think I'd better tell you all I know. He probably doesn't even know about the money. Please sit down, Sir.' Both men sat facing each other across the desk, which was piled high with papers and ledgers. 'He was a good man, and I suspect your mother was in love with him.' He ignored the gasp of disbelief from his employer and continued, 'Someone framed him and he was transported to New South Wales for seven years, that was in 1818. Your father said he was innocent and tried everything he could to get him off but he failed. I believe he was innocent too. Then, after the fire, Miss Fanny suggested investing the money which he thought the Militia had taken when he was arrested and it saved your father from ruin. Surely there is something in writing somewhere?'

'I haven't sorted out all the paperwork yet, Tom, and the solicitors are still working on the will. It's a damned mess! I thought there was something odd about that man when he first arrived.' He sighed. 'You know, Tom, these past three months have been bad enough without all this upset' he said, walking slowly away.

On returning to Bank House, George Webster immediately summoned his sisters to the parlour. The obvious signs of displeasure on his face warned them that all was not well. He had contained his feeling long enough and held his hands up to prevent any questions being asked before he began. 'I have come across some unfortunate news which leads me to think that we have been deceived.' Strains of annoyance entered his voice. 'Our friends,' he said scornfully, 'Mr Johnson and his son, are not what they claim to be.' Once more he raised his hand forbidding interruption. 'He called at the yard yesterday in my absence—though that is not the problem, and it would appear that he is well known to Tom. His real name is John Andrews, not Adam Johnson!'

His elder sister Becky had been listening with keen interest while Sarah stared in astonishment. She made to question George but he ignored her and pressed on with his accusations. 'He came here under a false name, partook of our hospitality knowing full well that he had the advantage of us all and then continued the deception. The man actually owns part of our business and certainly didn't wait long after mother's death before coming forward to stake his claim! Like a vulture!'

Speaking out defensively, Sarah said, 'But he didn't know of mother's death—you saw how ill he became on hearing the news'.

'You assume that was the reason for his illness. Why did he not tell us of his true identity when he came again? There is no possible excuse for anyone giving a false name unless it is to deceive someone.' Sarah fell silent, saddened at the soundness of her brother's reasoning.

Becky sniffed scornfully, 'I am not entirely surprised, for where there is religion then trouble is usually not far behind. Have you challenged him yet, George?'

'No! I have not even seen the man but he must be aware by now that I shall find out the truth.'

Now Becky took a firm line. 'Surely we must contact Mr Grayson immediately to find out where we stand.'

Nodding, George agreed, 'Yes, and in future I wish only to deal with Mr Johnson through Mr Grayson. I never want him to enter this house again. Is that understood!'

'But why does he own part of our business?' Sarah asked in bewilderment. 'I don't understand.'

Shaking his head George endeavoured to soften his voice, 'There is no need for you to be distressed, we are not in financial trouble'.

'I'm not a child', she retorted, hurt by his tone. 'I think you are very cruel not to listen to the man first before you stop his coming here!'

'I shall not change my mind. But there is nothing for you to worry about. We did know that one day a man named John Andrews could return and claim his share, but it is the deception which I don't appreciate. Tom insists that the man is not a thief, although he was sent away for stealing. He left some money behind which father used after the fire but after twenty-six years we thought him to be dead. This is a pretty kettle of fish, him turning up now! I have his address and will instruct Mr Grayson to send him a communication immediately. Let the two of them sort it out between themselves!'

In order that George should not see her distress, Sarah lowered her head. She could not believe that Adam had deliberately deceived them. She left the room and entered her own in a flood of tears.

Once behind the safety of her own bedroom door, Miss Becky Webster sat on a chair by her window, looking out. She saw nothing. Her left hand rested in her lap on the fullness of her brown, sober gown whilst the other held an envelope which had a wax seal.

Every so often she turned the envelope in all directions in an effort to find some clue as to its contents. What it contained she knew not, but she was certain that it must be important for her mother had insisted on her death bed that Becky alone should take charge of it. She could still hear her mother's voice ringing in her ears even now, urging her to tell no one of its existence. 'Let it fall into no other hands but to those of the person it is addressed to. This trust I am placing with you alone, and if that person never comes, then burn it, one day, for my sake!' It was almost as if her mother had been afraid to say the name out loud. 'There is no need for anyone else, not even you, to read it.' She had clasped Becky's hand in hers, pleading with her to promise.

Stirred both by curiosity and deep resentment, Becky fiddled with the letter, for it was addressed to none other than the man whom she and George distrusted—John Andrews. As Adam Johnson she had merely tolerated him as a religious crank, but now that he was also a business partner, it was disturbing the memory of her mother for her. She was, however, neither spiteful nor without principles, and knew that she must not open the letter or deprive John Andrews of it. She would have to deliver it in person and by doing so deceive George, and act which she resented having to do. Resolving to go into town as soon as possible, she replaced the letter in the little wooden box that had been her mother's and joined the others in the parlour below.

It wasn't easy to prise Adam's address from George without arousing his suspicions and she began to despair at her failure to do so. Eventually she asked casually, as if it were of no consequence, 'George, when will you be seeing Grayson?'

'First thing tomorrow, I shall call on the way to work. Don't you worry about it—Grayson's good at his job.'

'Yes, I know,' she replied calmly, whilst folding away the daily newspaper, 'I'll leave it to you.' She said no more but quietly formulated a plan in the back of her mind. Rising slowly from the sofa in order to retire for the night, she announced, 'I think I will go to town early tomorrow and would be obliged if you could drop me off on your way. I shall walk back if the weather is agreeable.'

George nodded and smiled, 'I feel a little happier myself, now. I shall be happier still, however, when we have resolved the situation'.

True to her vow, Becky rose early, dressed, and accompanied George in the carriage to High Street. 'I shall browse amongst the books in Mr Taylor's lending library before taking a peep at the new gowns which Mrs Warburton has taken delivery of,' she confessed, feeling the need to offer some explanation for the early journey, 'she always gets a consignment of gowns from London on Wednesday and I haven't bought a new one since before mother's illness began.'

Pulling the carriage to a halt, George handed his sister down. 'Treat yourself, life has been a trifle dull lately for all of us and I must remember to tell Sarah to do the same. I shall go round to Grayson's office straight away and get this business over with.'

She watched George until he had indeed rounded the corner leading towards Paradise Square, then stepped into Mr Taylor's shop. She was an avid reader and also a frequent caller to the shop but today the books held little attention for her.

'Morning, Miss Webster!' The quiet voice of John Taylor interrupted her thoughts, 'and it's a good one at that.' Becky nodded in polite response, not wishing to become involved in conversation and pretended to be engrossed in the novelette which she held. She would give George half an hour before following him into the Square, and if the carriage was gone would presume that he had departed.

Finally, gathering sufficient courage to set her plan in motion, she left the shop and crossed the street towards the graveyard so as to pass through it to reach the square rather than take the longer route round its perimeter. The carriage was nowhere to be seen when she reached the square, and she peered around gingerly before approaching the solicitor's office. The dingy hallway into which she stepped did nothing to calm her nervousness as she approached a young man at his desk. 'Could I possibly see Mr Grayson, Senior,' she asked politely. 'I believe my brother George Webster has just left the office?'

After several minutes she was ushered in to meet Mr Grayson, who was an elderly man of great charm and courtesy. He bent his head graciously as he held his hand out to greet her. 'Do sit down Miss Webster—you have just missed your brother. I don't remember him saying that you were calling too but it is of no consequence, I have a few minutes to spare. What can I do to help, or is it the same matter?'

He was a long-standing friend of the family yet Becky chose her words carefully, trying not to reveal too much. 'Mr Grayson, it is kind of you to see me without an appointment but George forgot to give me the address of Mr Andrews, or Mr Johnson as he prefers to call himself. I have a letter addressed to him which I need to deliver in person. Would you be kind enough to let me have his address?'

'I am about to contact him myself, could I not give it to him and save you the bother?' he offered.

She shook her head, 'I thank you for your kindness but I wish to deliver it personally!' The elderly gentleman accepted her answer without question.

'Your brother is not happy at the man's deception, but he has no need to worry, your parents left everything in order. I have promised to sort the matter out immediately for you all.' He wrote the address on a piece of paper as he spoke then escorted Becky to the door. 'If I can be of any further service you know where I am, my dear.'

Suddenly Becky had a twinge of conscience. What if Mr Grayson let slip to George about her visit to his office? Was it so very wrong, she wondered, to ask the man to keep her call a secret? If George found out he would not only be hurt but disappointed in her, yet she had to keep her promise to her mother. She stepped back into the office, much to John Grayson's surprise. 'May I take you into my confidence?' She begged.

Intrigue never surprised him these days. Over the years he had dealt with many a bizarre case and the extremes to which some clients went in their eccentricities served only to amuse him. 'My dear, everything in this office is strictly confidential, you have no need to fear on that score.'

Speaking softly, Becky explained, 'Mother left the letter for Mr Andrews and begged that only he and I know of its existence. I hate deceiving George but I am torn between my obedience to mother and loyalty to George'.

Smiling reassuringly, John Grayson touched her on the forearm. 'Your secret is safe with me—but if as a result of the letter there are any complications then I feel you should consult me immediately. Have you no idea of its content?'

'None, but mother was very insistent that I be the one to give it to him. It may be about his share in the business, or perhaps it is personal and we shall never know its message, that will be up to him. I am most grateful for your confidence.'

Leaving Paradise Square by the lower gate, Becky headed for Shalesmoor, then on towards Infirmary Lane. Several large houses now stood where there were once open fields, and rows of small terraced houses and shops were springing up on the lower side of the lane, opposite the sturdy iron gates of the elegant hospital. On enquiring, it was to a small road behind the shops that Becky found herself directed. Queen's Street had amongst its tiny dwellings a couple of family workshops and a corner ale-house which was adjacent to a carter's yard. This yard presumably belonged to the proprietor of the 'Grapes Inn', for the name John Thomas Sanderson was painted on both display boards.

It was now mid-morning and Becky began to wonder if she would be in time to catch Adam before he left to go about his business. She had no fancy to enter the 'Grapes' by the main door, believing that ladies should not frequent such places. Instead, she knocked on the door situated between the yard and the Inn. A slip of a girl, buried almost by a large apron and mop cap, opened the door. 'Yes, Miss?' she asked politely, 'Can I help you?'

'You take lodgers I understand?' Becky asked, looking beyond into the house.

'Why yes! But we're full right up at the moment, Miss. Try Mrs Williams down Infirmary Lane, she takes in boarders too.' She made to close the door without giving Becky a chance even to reply.

'I don't want lodgings at all!' Becky called out hastily. 'I'm here to find a Mr Johnson and his son. They do board here I believe?'

'Oh, dear,' the girl giggled in response, 'I thought you was after lodgings Miss.' Then, as if remembering her position, fell silent.

'Could you please tell Mr Johnson that Miss Webster needs to see him?' Becky replied, relieved to find her journey successful.

'I'll go and see if he's still in his room. Everyone wants to see him today. A man has just visited him, came in a carriage he did!' Her voice held a note of pride. 'He brought a message!' She promptly closed the door, leaving Becky out in the street pondering on this event.

The door was opened again several minutes later by Luke, who greeted her and explained. 'I'm afraid pa's gone out, Miss Webster, to see your brother's solicitor. The man offered to take him back with him in the carriage to save time and I have no idea when he will be back.' He seemed to be at a loss for words, then added shyly. 'I would invite you in but I don't think it's proper to invite a lady to my room, Miss Webster!'

He was obviously embarrassed and she felt a little sorry for him. 'It is your father I wish to see. Perhaps we could take a walk whilst waiting for him to return and you could leave him a message explaining what we are doing. It is rather a long way for me to come back again!' She waited patiently while Luke went back to the room and wrote out a message for his father, then together they walked along the lane towards Hill Bridge chatting amiably as they went.

'It's a mess, isn't it?' Luke spoke out suddenly. "I mean, Pa's name and all that. I think he really wishes that he hadn't been sent here, or called at your home. It has been a shock to me, too, you know!'

'You mean you didn't know that he had changed his name either?' she gasped.

'I knew a little of his story, but not much. I don't think Ma knows all of it either. You think you know someone but you don't really.' He seemed almost as bewildered as she was.

Sensing Luke's dilemma Becky encouraged him to talk. She could not dislike this pleasant young man who seemed to need someone to confide in. 'Did the man say why my brother's solicitor wanted to see him?' He shook his head. 'Has your father no idea at all?' she persisted.

'No! I don't see how he could. He would never have come to this place at all if he hadn't been sent. He did say that while he was here he would look up a couple of old friends, to see if they were well—as it turns out things seem to be getting out of hand. To tell the truth I have never seen him so put out before—after we had been to your workshop he told me a little more about what he had been through, I don't think I could have survived half of what he experienced.'

They strolled on slowly for almost half a mile until they reached the site where the solid sandstone footings of the new Barracks were rising from the ground. On reaching the bridge further on they turned to retrace their steps. Later, as they passed the old Barracks nearer the town, they watched the men parading on the cobbled yard and Becky was forced to raise her voice above the din of marching feet. 'I think perhaps we should go back now, Mr Johnson. It is almost dinner time and I must confess that I am becoming rather thirsty.' Luke was more relaxed now and beginning to lose his shyness of the formidable Miss Webster as he unburdened himself.

On returning to the 'Grapes' they found Adam waiting impatiently on the doorstep for the pair of them to return. 'Good afternoon, Miss Webster,' he greeted Becky politely. 'I'm sorry not to have been here earlier but I think you know the reason why I was out, don't you?'

Becky resumed her earlier haughty posture as she faced the stocky, bearded man before her. He had no right to have secrets that affected so many other people, and she found it impossible to find any sympathy for him.

Sensing the hostility which she held for him, Adam informed her, 'I have asked Mrs Sanderson for permission to use her sitting room for a few minutes while we talk things over. It will be better done there than out here on the street, don't you think?' He led the party into the house. 'There is a certain amount of ill-feeling on your brother's part, yours too I can see. But as I explained to Mr Grayson, your solicitor, I have used my new name for so long now that I almost forget the other ever existed. I did not intend to deceive anyone nor did I believe that it would lead to so much complication. Under the circumstances I think that I should meet with you all and offer some explanation for my conduct. Mr Grayson approves of this idea. Will you ask your brother if he would be kind enough to consider this?' He was weary and a note of resignation crept into his voice.

'I will, Mr Johnson,' Becky replied, accepting that it was possibly the best solution. 'Although it has nothing to do with the matter about which I came. My mother, before she died, entrusted me with a letter for you.' She noted the widening if his eyes coupled with the strangest of looks. What was it, fear or disbelief? He did not speak. 'She told me that I was to give it to you alone, should you return, or if you did not, then to burn it!'

Adam took the letter reluctantly, almost dropping it as his hand trembled. There was for an unguarded moment a haunted look on his face which passed so quickly that Becky wondered if she had imagined it. When he did speak his voice was soft and husky, 'It was most kind of your mother to remember me. I thank you for bringing it all this way in person'. He placed the letter in his pocket, 'I will read it at a suitable moment, when I am alone. This morning has been wearing enough and has brought back many memories which have distressed me', he said apologetically.

Luke interrupted, 'Father, Miss Webster has not had any refreshments since early morning. Do you think Mrs Sanderson would be able to provide her with some? It may not be easy to find a carriage at this time of day!'

'How thoughtless of me, Miss Webster. I'm sure it will be possible, humble though it might be. I'll go and ask but if you will then excuse me I will refrain from joining you; the thought of food at this moment does not appeal to me. Luke will help you find a carriage afterwards and if you will allow me I will take my leave of you!' Adam then went in search of Mrs Sanderson before leaving the house in search of solitude.

Making his way down to the lower meadow behind the house and crossing to where the river wound its way towards the town, Adam had the strangest feeling. The route was the one he and Fanny had taken on that fateful day when they had discovered the boy being beaten at the mill. It was ironic that at the moment when he was to read Fanny's last words he would not be five minutes from the spot where he had first kissed her. On reaching the grassy bank, Adam sat down and looked across the water to the hill beyond. There was no one about to see him and he was sheltered from behind by a clump of small bushes. He was afraid to break open the seal but he knew that if he didn't he would never know its contents. It was dated just three months previous.

Dear John,

Perhaps you may never read this letter, and if not then it will eventually be destroyed. I write because my dearest Gervase has already gone before me, and I too am sick and dying. If you are still alive then I feel that there are things which it is right and proper for you to know.

Neither Gervase nor I ever forgot you, you were a part of us. You will wonder why we married within the year of your leaving, but you must understand that I was greatly distressed at losing you, and as you know it was difficult for any of us not to love Gervase, with his kind, gentle ways. We were all lost without you, even Tom Linley walked about with a hang-dog expression all day. However, we were never allowed to forget you for I found amidst all my troubles and despair that I was with child, your child.

Adam gasped! The shock was almost too much to bear and it was several minutes before he could bring himself to continue reading the letter.

Becky does not know, for Gervase and I never told anyone, except my mother, that she was not his child. Whatever people must have thought of Gervase I do not know. Nevertheless, he protected and loved me. It was many months before I came to realise just how kind and generous a man he was, and I gradually grew to love him. Becky, however, is your daughter, do what you must, but do it kindly, for my sake. I realise this knowledge will grieve you, but I feel that you deserve the truth after all the hardships you have endured.

This letter is for you only, and unless circumstances demand, share it with no-one, not even Becky. Mr Grayson in Paradise Square is our solicitor and he will tell you what I did with your money, for the Militia did not get their hands on it. I have other possessions of yours at the house in the same basket which I used that dreadful day when you were arrested. I will ask Becky not to open this letter herself but to burn it if you do not return before she too passes on. I know she will keep her word for she always does.

Do not be too distressed my dear, we have prospered and have been loved. The world has been kinder to us than it has to you.

Farewell, my dear and lost friend. Perhaps we will all meet again in Heaven.

Your Fanny.

Adam sat numbed, staring at the grass at his feet. He read it twice before he was able to absorb its contents fully and knew that he had never been more stricken than he was at this moment. He was relieved that he had chosen this quiet spot, away from prying eyes, for he could no longer control his emotions. The back of his throat burned as sobs rose from the depths of his being and he could no longer hold back the pain which for years had been locked away inside his heart. He felt almost like a child and would that he could lay his head on a loving shoulder, or be allowed to die. He sobbed uncontrollably as he rested his head on his drawn-up knees, until there was no tears left, leaving him cold and shivery. The barrier which he had built around himself had finally collapsed and exposed all the emotions which for years he had suppressed.

Slowly, in the midst of his confusion, he took the letter and read it again, without haste, without guilt, absorbing its contents with eyes which were swollen and red. Then with a heavy heart he took up his Bible, his companion and soulmate, and read a well-thumbed passage which he had previously underlined in red ink:

> *If any of you lack wisdom, let him ask of God, that giveth to*
> *all men liberally, and unbraideth not; and it shall be given.*
> *James 1.*

He whispered the words softly to himself and with a final sob sank humbly to his knees in the meadow and prayed, unselfconsciously, as he had never done before.

There was no biblical flash of awareness, no Heavenly voice, but a gentle peace flowed through his mind, calming his senses. The anguish was past and he rose from his knees and looked towards the hills once more. The burden seemed lighter now, as though he had finally relieved his soul of its oppression.

He remained on that grassy bank for many hours, deep in thought and examining each step of his life, endeavouring to see the good that had come out of each one. Had he been favoured, he wondered, and allowed to tread the threshing mill of life and yet emerge complete? He had indeed experienced many things, seen many places which few others had, and he was here now a free man doing that which he chose to do. So many men were merely workhorses, trodden down by poverty and bondage. His heart swelled. Oh! He could do so much in this world! He could be an inspiration to others, needing no other reward except the satisfaction of knowing that he had improved someone else's life. He could help them find their true destiny, and return to God. He was overcome by a burning desire to embrace the ills of all humanity.

He resolved first to write to Henrietta, a long letter full of love and praise, but he would never spoil her happiness by telling her of Fanny, or Becky. That would be his secret and no one else's.

He marvelled at the thought that the formidable Becky Webster was his own flesh and blood. So different from his other children, who, he realised, were now her half-brothers and sisters. It was up to him to try and understand her more, and steel himself against any desire to call her daughter.

By the time Adam returned to the 'Grapes' his eyes were no longer red and swollen. He was confronted by an angry Luke as he entered the house. 'Where have you been?' Luke reproached him. 'I've been waiting here all afternoon for you! What's going on now? You could have been murdered for all I knew!' Adam had never seen Luke so distressed before, nor had he seen him so assertive. 'Well?' Luke demanded.

If the circumstances had not been quite so tragic Adam would have been amused at the fire in Luke's passion. However, he recognised the urgency and anguish in his question. Gathering his thoughts whilst placing his hat and Bible on the table beside him, he said hesitantly, 'Luke, I had no desire to cause you distress but I have been beset by matters that I did not know even existed. Until we came here I had few real problems, now it would appear that I am surrounded by them. To put it bluntly, some money which I left behind here was invested for me by George Webster's father. Now I am part owner of his business—and he's none too pleased!'

'I'm not surprised,' Luke rejoined, 'but what was in the letter that caused you to take off for so long that you forgot why we came here in the first place?'

'Oh, dear!' Adam sighed, ignoring Luke's unusual abruptness. 'It was just a letter written by a dying friend, telling me of all the happenings in the years whilst I've been away. It explains about the money, and says farewell.' He really wanted to tell Luke to mind his own business, to leave him alone, but his guilty feelings humbled him and he added, wisely, 'I'm sorry, my boy. I'll keep you involved in everything else which transpires. In fact I think we should go and call at the Webster's place as soon as possible to try and sort things out.'

'I don't think we shall be all that welcome.' Luke said. 'Apparently George Webster thinks, like me, that there is something strange going on.'

'It's not like that at all, Luke. You should know me better than that and I resent the implication that I am untrustworthy. If you remember correctly, I was the one who was wronged in the first place and deprived of my freedom and loved ones.' He fell silent, afraid that he had said too much already. 'Let's eat and then we'll call on Mr Webster and explain everything. Whatever happens, Luke, believe me—I have never harmed anyone deliberately or tried to take advantage of them.'

Although George Webster wanted no personal contact with Adam and Luke he had no option when they arrived on his doorstep, and he received them coldly, but politely. This immediately left Adam feeling at a disadvantage in the younger man's house. Leading them to the study in which Adam had been first introduced to the Websters, George invited them to sit on high-backed chairs facing him. The stern features which faced Adam, saddened him. Neither Gervase nor Fanny had ever appeared so formal and he found such hostility in their son disturbing. The whole affair was preposterous and embarrassing. He had to resolve the misunderstanding and bad feelings quickly, before rumours spread, and it reflected badly on the Church. He was well aware that people were only too ready to attach blame for anything on the members, and this often led to persecution and heartbreak.

As the more mature man, Adam felt that he should also be the wiser of the two, and having learned in the past that anger can inflame any situation, decided to forestall further hostilities before they began. 'I think,' he stated calmly, 'that these misunderstandings have gone on long enough. I would like to call your sisters here now so that we can sort out this matter one way or another.'

Taken aback by Adam's forthright manner, George Webster opened his mouth to speak but closed it again almost as quickly, as though realising that Adam's suggestion had merit. He nodded, then excused himself before leaving the room.

Neither Adam nor Luke spoke in George Webster's absence but sat in silence, each absorbed with his own thoughts. It was Becky who entered the room first and, as both men rose, Adam found himself examining her closely. Yes, he could see it now, how different she was to the other two, yet so like Fanny. He could even see why no-one had suspected that she was anything other than Gervase's daughter. In the old days Adam and Fanny had looked almost like brother and sister, with the same colouring, and similar eyes, but Becky was smaller and not so slender as Sarah and George. As she walked towards him he noticed the slight incline of her head—exactly the same, he remembered, as his own mother's had when she walked across a room.

Holding out her hand she came towards him, bringing him back to reality. 'I welcome this opportunity to hear your story Mr Johnson. Rumours tend to distort the truth, don't you think?'

'I am grateful to hear you say that', Adam acknowledged.

She shook hands with Luke, 'The others won't be a moment. I'm afraid Sarah takes a little finding on a pleasant evening such as this. She loves to wander around the garden, often sketching the birds.' The open animosity which had been present in Becky at their earlier meetings had softened, yet she seemed confident and in control of herself. 'My brother is not aware of the existence of the letter from our mother to you, Mr Johnson. I do not want him to know about it.'

'I had no intentions of telling him, Miss Webster. I see no reason to alienate him further.' It seemed strange to Adam that the letter invoked no visible curiosity in her and he wondered what her reaction would be if she knew the truth. 'We will consider the matter closed', he concluded quickly, hearing footsteps approaching.

George Webster entered brusquely, leaving Sarah to follow in his wake. She was flushed from hurrying when she appeared and Adam suspected that when she saw Luke her colour deepened and her eyes sparkled. Her lively spirit brought a freshness to the gloom of the room, and with it a warmth for which he was grateful. 'Good evening' she gasped excitedly. 'It is so nice out there this evening, and a shame for us all to be indoors.' She hesitated, lowering her eyes as if suddenly realising that there was an atmosphere in the room.

'Right!' George Webster stated, bringing them back to the matter in hand. 'Perhaps you will be good enough to tell us the truth, Mr Johnson, about your interest in this family and what plans you have for the future now that you seem to own part of this firm. You must see that I am placed in a very difficult position, one which has come as a great shock to me. We have just lost our mother, and now I discover that I am no longer in sole charge of the business. I give you the benefit of the doubt but it does seem a strange coincidence that you arrive so soon after mother's death to claim your share. Neither did you reveal that fact on your first visit, or since. It is twenty-six years since you were last here—why choose now to return? Your timing does seem a little hard to swallow!'

'Now just a minute, young man!' Adam could not remain silent any longer. 'You might do me the courtesy of letting me explain. This whole affair has been as much of a shock to me as it has to you!' He waited, allowing George to calm himself before continuing quietly. 'I did not choose to come to Sheffield but was sent by the Elders of my Church. The memories of the injustices I met in this town nearly made me refuse to come. However, I believe in the higher motive of my Church Elders in sending me here, to spread the word of God. I accepted the challenge. When I left this hovel of a town I left behind three very good friends. Two of them are dead, the other I bumped into unexpectedly in your own workshop—he is your chargehand. The first I knew of any monetary involvement was when your Mr Grayson sent for me.' As George remained silent Adam asked, 'Well, what do you want me to do?'

George stiffened. 'We can't keep the money, it isn't ours to keep. I didn't know when mother was ill that the money she recently set on one side for you would be required so quickly. I invested most of it in new machinery and in order to pay you out now I would have to raise that capital. A pretty mess that leaves me in!'

Adam raised his hand. 'Listen to me, please! I never knew what had happened to the money or my papers and possessions. I'm not here to demand them now, or see your family suffer because of me.'

'Apparently mother was most insistent in the documents which she left that if ever you should return you were to receive the original money with appropriate interest—she was insistent.' There was a finality to George's tone.

Accepting the decision rather than forcing a confrontation, Adam asked with a resigned sigh, 'Well, in that case, where does it leave us? As far as I am concerned the money can remain as an investment to be paid when you feel you are able to do so, without harming your business. Or, you could pay me an annual sum into an English Bank, to be disposed of as I instruct'. The money was the least of Adam's concerns. He was already modestly successful in his own right, although he didn't doubt that Henrietta would find a use for the extra luxuries it could provide. Dear Fanny and Gervase, all these years they had safeguarded his interests, why should he want to spoil their good intentions by being greedy? 'Although,' he added, 'I much prefer the latter method.'

A look of relief came over George Webster's face. 'That's decent of you. It takes the pressure off', he admitted somewhat reluctantly. 'I will contact Mr Grayson and get him to prepare an agreement, if that suits you? However, what about the day to day running of the business, and the decisions? I'd rather resent any interference after all I have done over the years—but if it has to be, then I accept it. When I say this it is on condition that my sisters are also in agreement.'

Adam forestalled any problems. 'I have no intention of becoming involved with your business affairs. You seem to have done very well so far. Just bank the annual payments and I will be satisfied.' Adam glanced at the two young women who had been listening intently to the proceedings and noted with satisfaction, the relief on Becky's face. Sarah beamed as though a boring but crucial game of cards had been concluded and dispensed with.

Not wanting to appear churlish at the outcome of the meeting, although he bitterly resented his dependence on the American's good will, George offered his hand in agreement, much to Adam's relief.

Adam felt sorry for George Webster. He would probably have felt the same resentment had the boot been on the other foot, but he concluded that under the circumstances he had proposed a sensible solution. He asked cautiously, 'Do you know where your mother kept the rest of my belongings? Mr Grayson says they were not handed to him'.

Becky spoke up, 'We haven't been through all mother's belongings yet, Mr Johnson. I will go and search her room now, if you don't mind waiting. Perhaps Sarah could take Luke into the garden whilst you and my brother discuss all the details of this business. I will try to be as quick as I can'.

'Thank you, my dear, that is kind of you.' Adam smiled wistfully. He had acquired a daughter who didn't care for him and whom he daren't acknowledge. How nice it would have been to talk to her alone, to learn more about her without arousing her suspicions.

'Yes, do come into the garden, Luke,' Sarah coaxed, 'the roses are beautiful.' The two older men eyed them suspiciously, and would have stopped the pair from leaving, but it was too late, Luke and Sarah had made their escape from the room.

It was Sarah who spoke first, 'They're all so stuffy in there. I can't understand why there is so much fuss, surely all businessmen can't be so dull'.

Luke laughed, 'George is still young, Sarah, and he has many worries right now!' He too was pleased to be out of the sober atmosphere. 'My father has been very upset by the whole thing. We didn't come here to make trouble.' He had to lengthen his stride to keep up with Sarah's scampering feet. 'Don't go so fast' he implored, laughingly, watching her golden ringlets bob up and down. He tugged at his necktie, aching to free himself from its inhibiting encumbrance. Before leaving America he had only ever worn a suit on Sundays and he still felt restricted by the formality of his present attire, which made him appear older than his eighteen years.

She breathed deeply of the sweet air. 'My mother laid out this garden, as I told you.' She took up the paper and pencil from a stone on which she had been sitting earlier and showed her sketch to Luke. 'I'm not very good,' she excused herself, 'not like mother was.' There were tears in her eyes. 'I do miss her! Becky is so strict and George so serious these days. He wasn't always like that, not before mother became sick.' She turned to face him, 'Is your mother still alive?'

Luke nodded, 'Yes, and I miss her too. It is the first time I've been away from home for more than a week. I suppose she will find me altered when I return. She certainly will find Pa changed. Even I find it difficult to understand him these days. Being here has had a strange affect on him, and not for the better either, he is like a stranger sometimes.'

She looked up at him mischievously and whispered, 'Do you think they were in love?'

'Who?' Luke asked, completely mystified by her question and endeavouring to keep up with Sarah's constant change of conversation.

'My mother and your father!' she giggled.

Luke's face became a picture of incredulous amazement. The idea had never occurred to him and he was stunned by her childlike suggestion.

'What ever made you say that! What reason have you for even thinking such a terrible thing?'

'Love isn't terrible!' she chided. 'And he was very disturbed when he heard that mother was dead. Tom Linley says that mother was heartbroken when he went away.'

Luke's startled surprise turned to annoyance. 'Really! I'm shocked Sarah, that you should even suggest such a thing. You are too romantic by far.' He gestured towards the house. 'If they hear you it will only make things worse for Pa!'

He scolded her with such seriousness that Sarah stamped her foot defiantly. 'You are as dull as they are' she fired at him. 'People do fall in love and do strange things. It is no wonder you are all so gloomy when all you do is preach about love. Becky spurns men who pay her attention and George pretends to be too busy, but I know he takes walks with a certain lady whom he doesn't bring to the house. When I fall in love I shall tell everyone about it!'

'You are still a child, Sarah! What do you know about love that is not in a novel?' He was annoyed to find himself drawn into this silly game of hers, and by her preposterous suggestions.

'I'm seventeen!' Sarah cried. 'Even George treats me like a child, but I am not!' She tossed her head, and marched towards the house calling back, 'Go home and read your precious Bible!'

'Sarah!' Luke called after her exasperatedly, but she ignored him and left him alone in the garden.

Becky was startled when Sarah brushed passed her on the stairs, almost knocking the basket which she carried from her hand. 'Sarah! Do be careful!' she called out. 'It is most unbecoming of you to dash about so.' She sighed, shaking her head. Sarah was becoming a handful these days. Since her mother's death there appeared to be a spirit of rebellion in her which neither she, nor George could understand. And where was Luke? She had sent the pair into the garden away from the atmosphere in the study but now, somehow Sarah had created an atmosphere of her own.

Entering the study, she noticed that Luke was not in the room and wondered where he could be. 'Mr Johnson,' she said, 'I think I have found your belongings, though strangely enough they were in this old wicker basket in the wardrobe. I presume they are yours because there is an Indenture for John Andrews amongst them.' She held out the basket for Adam to inspect.

The old wicker basket stirred Adam's memories more than the news of the money had done. Why had Fanny kept everything intact for so long? She had fled from the old barn with the basket still on her arm when the soldiers began to approach. He knew they hadn't caught her but he hadn't

135

realised that she had hung on to the basket, and its contents. She must have thought it unwise to bring them to him in prison.

Taking it gently from Becky's arm he ran his fingers through the papers. Some were yellowing with age. He turned to George and said sharply, 'I was not a thief!' Realising that he had raised his voice, he flushed with embarrassment and stammered uncomfortably, 'I do apologise. It was not of your doing. Forgive me, but no one except your father and mother believed me!' He gathered up his precious belongings and placed them in his pockets. 'I think it would be best if we left you in peace. If you sort the arrangements out with Mr Grayson, I will sign the papers.' Adam made his way towards the door. 'Could you please find Luke for me?'

As they wound their way back down the hill, Luke glanced sideways at his father. Who was this stranger walking beside him? Was Sarah's little hypothesis really so preposterous after all, and why had he been so rude to her? Nothing that was happening or anything they were doing seemed to make sense anymore and Luke began to wonder if there would ever be a satisfactory outcome to it all.

The atmosphere was tense at Bank House after Adam and Luke had departed, putting George into a foul mood. Although on the surface it seemed that a reasonable conclusion had been reached with Adam, nevertheless George could not banish his resentment of the other man's involvement in his business. It was four years now since he had been encouraged by his sick mother to look upon the business as his own, and he had tackled those responsibilities, and those of the house, successfully and without hesitation or failure. Webster's was his life, and apart from the occasional flirtation with the daughter of a colleague he had few other interests. He liked things as they were and saw no reason why he should accept changes. He slept badly that night and rose the following morning in a morose frame of mind.

Conversation was strained between George and the girls at breakfast and he could see even now, subtle changes within the family which he did not like. Sarah was becoming a stranger before his eyes, caused, he was convinced, by the influence of Adam and Luke. She sat, pale faced and moody, and he suspected that this might be connected with her sudden disappearance before Luke left.

He had never considered himself to be a man capable of violent dislikes, yet the tightening in his stomach and the anger which reared its head when he thought of those two men made him wonder. Wonder too how long Adam's desire to conquer souls would last before he asked for more control in the business. The more he pondered on the matter the greater became his fears. Never again would he permit either man to enter his house, and in future he would conduct any business through Grayson. He knew also that enforcing this rule would make him unpopular in his own household. 'Now that we have established a working relationship with Mr Johnson,' George ventured, breaking the gloomy silence. 'I intend to see him only at work or with Mr Grayson. I would appreciate it if you would not invite him into this house again, or Luke. There is little point in befriending either of them, as involvement would only complicate matters.' His voice was firm, almost overbearing, so that it was a shock when Sarah spoke out.

'I agree', she pouted. 'They really are a couple of weird characters, and I think the past is best left alone.' Her nose was held high, with an air of defiance, making George suspect her motives. 'Luke is a most quarrelsome young man' she added stubbornly.

'Well I think you are both being very narrow-minded!' Becky interrupted, taking him completely unawares. 'His offer is a fair one under the circumstances and I really do believe him to be sincere.'

Anger welled up inside George. Becky had been his constant ally in the past and whereas he had expected rebellion from Sarah he found this about-turn in the two girls bewildering and very annoying. 'You've changed your tune a bit haven't you? We know nothing about the man except that he is willing to stand on street corners and make a complete fool of himself. He's the talk of the town!' George's voice was full of ridicule. 'Don't get involved with that mob—you will bitterly regret it!'

'He is at least of strong conviction and not afraid to stand by his ideas', Becky retorted. 'I will not be told who I can and cannot have in my home. Our home! This is our home as well as yours.' She too was angry now, perhaps more with herself for allowing the discussion to get out of hand. 'I shall invite whoever I want, George!' she added firmly before leaving the table to busy herself furiously with the needlework stretched out on the frame by the sofa.

George tapped his fingers irritably on the smooth surface of the table, at a loss for words.

'Do stop that drumming, George!' Becky snapped. 'You are causing me to misjudge my stitches.'

Rising from the chair, George stared at the hands which drew the threads of wool so skilfully through the canvas. To argue more would merely add to the disagreement, so George stormed from the room without speaking.

Sarah also watched her sister's fingers at work without daring to speak. She was no longer sure whose side she was on, but the whole affair was taking a most unpleasant turn. Her own outburst had been borne out of indignation because Luke had scolded her and she was now in a deep state of misery. Leaving the room, she went out into the garden to seek comfort amongst the things she loved.

The lawn was damp with dew which sparkled as the sun's rays touched the blades of grass. Sarah skirted the edge of the lawn so as not to soil the hem of her freshly laundered gown, and reached the pond, where, beneath its surface in the darkness under the water lilies, she saw the occasional movement of fish. The sun was warm and gathering in strength as the morning progressed, soothing Sarah as she stood a while watching the changing shadows caused by the darting fish. Bulrushes, tall and proud, flanked the far edge of the pond, allowing a moorhen to conceal itself within. She loved this peaceful place where everything was so still and beautiful but she could find little peace within her mind. It had been so easy to fall out with Luke, and yet she had not intended to nor did she quite know why she had done so. Perhaps she was too fanciful and it had been rude of her to suggest that Adam might have been in love with her mother. She just hoped that George did not hear of her indiscretion. She liked Luke, with his shy, unassuming ways, unlike most young men with whom she came into contact. They were brash and pretentious.

From inside the house Becky watched Sarah with great fondness. She had never begrudged her younger sister her beauty nor her liveliness; perhaps she envied her a little, and wished that she too were a little more attractive, yet she had never done anything but love Sarah. She could tell by the droop of Sarah's head that all was not well and longed to lift the burden from her young shoulders. Sighing, she left the breakfast room and made her way outside.

'Is the world so bad that it bends your shoulders?' she asked softly, approaching Sarah quietly.

'Not really' Sarah sighed without conviction. 'I was just thinking about mother and why we were all quarrelling so much. She wouldn't have liked it if she knew that we were falling out. And George is so very angry these days!'

'He has been badly shaken by these events—he will get used to it.' Becky waited, hoping that Sarah would open her heart and tell her what really disturbed her, for she suspected that Luke might be at the bottom of it. Eventually she dared to broach the subject herself. 'Why were you so angry with Luke last night? You can't know him well enough to quarrel with him, and he doesn't strike me as an argumentative young man.'

Sarah shook her head, 'I didn't mean to upset him. It was something I said and he scolded me for it. I felt so small that I'm afraid I shouted at him, and stormed indoors.'

'What on earth could you have said to make him scold you? Perhaps he was only teasing you.'

'No, he wasn't! It was rather rude of me I suppose—but I didn't mean any harm, really I didn't.' She was near to tears now and turned away so that Becky could not see her face.

'Well, come on then, what did you say? Perhaps I am a better judge than two shy young people. Often things are not as bad when seen through someone else's eyes!'

'Oh, Becky. I know you will think me stupid, but I suddenly asked him if he thought that Adam might have been in love with mother. He was so shocked that it made me feel foolish!' She held her breath expecting the sharp edge of Becky's tongue, but it didn't come. She turned to find out why the silence was lasting so long. 'Oh, Becky,' she pleaded, 'was it so wicked of me that I have shocked you too? Please tell me!'

'It does seem to be a strange affair, Sarah.' Becky said thoughtfully. She had spent many hours wondering about the letter which had been entrusted to her. 'Tom Linley seems to think so too. How sad it would be—if it were true.'

'You're not angry with me then?'

Shaking her head, Becky smiled understandingly, 'You are sometimes too romantic and don't think before speaking out, but I have wondered myself if there was something else which we didn't know. However, we must keep our thought to ourselves, speculating will only make things worse. I certainly suspect that there has been more sorrow in it all than we know and maybe we have been a little too hard on Mr Johnson'.

'Do you think that if he had come back earlier, before mother died, we would have found out?' There was a childish curiosity in her voice.

'I think we would have known less than we do now, but here we are speculating like idle gossips.' She touched Sarah gently on the shoulder encouragingly. 'Let's try to forget the whole incident. There is a musical evening at the Assembly Hall next week. Shall we spoil ourselves and buy a new gown each? I didn't buy one myself yesterday when I was in town.'

Once the ordeal of the visit to the Webster's was behind him, Adam was able to turn his thoughts to the real purpose of his mission in England. He was free at last of all complications and began to relax, throwing himself into his work with such vigour that he was totally unaware of Luke's unhappiness.

For Luke, still disturbed by his tiff with Sarah, appearing before the robust crowds was no easy task. His delivery was hesitant and he lacked confidence, much to the delight of his audience who, sensing his shyness, took great advantage of the situation. Each meeting was an ordeal which left him thoroughly disturbed and despondent. It was not his faith that was weak, that was as strong as it had ever been, but he lived in fear of the crowds and that Sarah might see him standing there, an object of derision. He was also aware that his preoccupation with Sarah was not what was expected of him and he knew that his whole attention was not on his work. After one particularly gruelling meeting he was startled to hear a voice behind him call out his name. Turning, he found himself face to face with Becky Webster.

'Is it always this bad, Luke?' she asked sympathetically.

'Miss Webster!' he stammered, relieved to see a friendly face. 'I think we are merely a source of amusement for most of them.' He found himself looking round. 'Is Sarah here too?' he asked, half reluctantly and half with anticipation.

'No! I shouldn't be here either, but I stayed too long at the shops with a friend. What on earth gives you the courage to stand there and speak out like that? I marvel, I really do, even though I have no time for religion.'

'I don't enjoy standing there but I do believe in the message which I bring', Luke confessed. 'Why are you so against religion when there is so much good in God's teachings? If the world obeyed his word there would be no strife—you have to admit that!'

He was becoming more confident now and Becky searched to find an answer. 'Because, Luke, every religion condemns the beliefs of those who disagree with them, and here you are bringing yet another way of thinking. It does nothing but confuse simple-minded people.'

'It is people who complicate matters; only the Bible is true—not men's own ideas.' His eyes shone with conviction. 'Miss Webster, it is when I feel that someone like you really cares to speak sensibly on the matter that I know what I am doing is right. Won't you let me tell you why I feel there is hope in the message that I bring? All I ask is that you come just once to our Meeting House and see for yourself that we don't have two heads.'

This outburst amused her and yet on the other hand she found his sincerity rather touching. His optimism and youthful fire mellowed her. 'Alright, Luke, you win!' she conceded, 'But I warn you, I have no intention of visiting more than once. Nothing but a miracle will make me repeat the gesture.' She turned to leave and he let her go, not daring to ask her to bring Sarah along too; instead he contented himself with the knowledge that at least there was a mutual contact between them. All he could do was hope.

Adam detached himself from the clutches of two youths who playfully harangued and pestered him. 'Has Miss Webster gone?' he asked in surprise.

'Yes! I'm afraid so—she was in a hurry.' There was a glint of mischief in Luke's eyes which tantalised Adam.

'Come on Luke, you're keeping something from me, what is it?' Adam begged.

'Guess who is coming to Church on Sunday—only *the* Miss Webster!' Luke was puzzled by Adam's lack of reaction. 'I thought you would be pleased, it is an achievement don't you think?'

Adam frowned. 'It might have been wiser under the circumstances not to involve the Websters in any more of our affairs, there is enough bad feeling between us already. George Webster is not going to appreciate any further intrusion into his family life.' The news did not give him the pleasure it once would have done. He did not welcome the thought of being thrown constantly into the company of his new-found daughter. He was living a lie, one which did not sit easily on his conscience and, knowing that he would never be able to reveal the truth, would have preferred to refrain from repeated contact with any of the Websters.

'I would have thought that it was a cause for celebration, not regret' Luke lamented, completely at a loss to understand his father's reluctance. 'Perhaps it would be better if we told the Elders the truth and asked for a transfer somewhere else.' Immediately the words left his lips he regretted his haste, for that would mean leaving Sarah.

Adam sighed in resignation. 'All right, I spoke out of turn and I'm sorry. We'll make Miss Webster welcome and face any consequences that may arise.'

There was a dampness in the Sunday morning air and Becky rose reluctantly from her bed. What on earth had possessed her to make such a wild promise to Luke she did not know, but she had done and she was not in the habit of breaking promises. Somehow she had to keep her word whilst at the same time keeping her visit a secret from George. She was not normally in the habit of going to Church on Sundays but rather took her pleasure in strolling across the fields or tending to the garden. She knew however, that any change of routine would arouse his suspicions so decided to be frank about the visit. She was quite unprepared though for the strength of his objection.

'What!' he exploded, his face deepening in colour. 'You're going to THAT Church! You don't even go to ours so what's the attraction?' He was almost beside himself with fury. 'That's even worse than bringing him here. I don't want you to go!'

Becky stood firm. Once roused she could be as stubborn as any man and she clasped her hands firmly together. 'I'm sorry, George but you do not own me. If I wished to, I would join his Church without any regard to you. It would be for me to decide, not you! I have run this household for two years now and we have never clashed before. That arrangement suited us well but times have changed. One day you may wish to bring a wife home and then I would cease to be mistress here. I am twenty-six years old and it is time I led my own life. If Mr Johnson had not come onto the scene, then something else would have done, things were bound to change. Mother has gone and that in itself has altered our lives. We are no longer her dependants but are independent individuals.'

George swallowed hard, unable to speak, and turned to look out of the window. He hated Adam and Luke, yet Becky was right, things could not remain the same forever. It was their mother who had kept the family so closely knitted together, quietening Becky's stubborn streak, so he knew full well that continuing with his present stand would only drive a wedge permanently between them. Albeit reluctantly he gave in. 'Alright, Sis, you win! But don't ever expect me to meet either of them socially again.'

It was with a certain amount of trepidation that Becky approached the Meeting House. She was still smarting from the confrontation with George and she had very little desire to meet Adam again. It had been Luke's enthusiasm and her sheer defiance at George's pig-headedness which had caused her to make the journey into town. The sooner the visit were over the happier she would be.

She had barely entered the Mission Hall when she found Luke springing at her from nowhere, as if he had been lying in wait for her arrival. 'Miss Webster!' he cried jubilantly, seizing her hand in friendly greeting. 'You came! I wasn't sure that you would. Let me introduce you to a few friends.' He was charmingly relaxed on his own ground and led her to a group of men and women gathered round a small organ. Before she knew it they had all shaken her hand with a warmth which quite overwhelmed her. She did not feel like a stranger in their midst although judging from their attire she suspected that most were working class craftsmen of some sort or another. She was relieved that she had dressed simply and would blend in easily amongst them.

A feeling of contentment gradually replaced the reticence which she felt and, listening to the simple service, she was impressed by the sincerity of those gathered in the hall. Adam had been occupied on her arrival and now from the rostrum he smiled encouragingly down at her in a friendly fashion. She smiled back unaware of what it did to his emotions.

He saw eyes that were beautiful like Fanny's and, as the sun's rays touched her hair, he felt a swelling of pride in the knowledge that she really was his daughter.

What, she wondered, did the townsfolk fear in these simple people? She saw no evil here, only companionship and a peace which she had not experienced in months, and as the meeting drew to a close she found herself regretting the fact. She could not explain why she was loath to leave as quickly as she had planned, yet she had no desire to discuss religion. As she wavered, looking round for Adam and Luke in order to say that she was leaving, an elderly man limped towards her holding out his hand. 'I do hope you will come again, my dear' he said sincerely. 'This Church is always open to strangers. I'm Tom Smith by the way!'

'Thank you, Mr Smith. I have just spent a pleasant hour here but I only came because I made a promise to Luke Johnson,' Becky smiled at him, 'I'm not sure that I will be returning.'

His wrinkled face beamed knowingly. 'We won't eat you here—and we like to share our happiness with others. How about making and old man happy and coming next week to sit with me. That would make my day!'

'You make it hard for me to refuse' Becky smiled. 'I will have to think about it.'

There was a look of obvious disappointment on his face which made her relent. She was touched by his open friendliness and before she had really thought about it she heard herself reply, 'Alright then—just for you!'

His tired old eyes lit up, 'Then I shall keep a seat for you beside me next Sunday. Now don't let me down or I shall end up sitting all by myself!'

By this time Adam had reached her side. 'I'm glad you've met Brother Smith,' he said, placing an arm around the old man. 'He's a real old rogue, aren't you?' There was a fondness in his voice which surprised her. 'Brother Smith, do you think you can persuade her to come again?'

'It is too late,' Becky retorted. 'He's already done so!'

Old Tom Smith laughed at the look of amazement on Adam's face. 'An old man's charm is worth more than all your Bible thumping, and I'm too old to waste time.' There was a wicked glint in his eye and he winked at Becky before turning to Adam once more, 'I've put all the hymn sheets away but you'll have to excuse me as I have promised to be somewhere else in an hour. You will come next week won't you?' he asked finally before taking his leave of her.

Once he had gone Adam laughed, 'He really is a grand old chap'. Then, in a more serious tone asked, 'Did you find us as strange as you'd expected?'

Becky shook her head. 'No,' she admitted. I was very impressed, Mr Johnson, and I will keep my promise to the old gentleman but then that will be that.' She was relaxed now, and Adam could see beneath the formidable exterior signs of a much softer woman. 'I must go,' she concluded, 'George does not approve of me being here, so I don't want to upset him further by being late back. Please tell Luke that I was in a hurry—I don't seem to see him anywhere. Tell him that I was pleased that I promised to come.' She hastened from the room, almost embarrassed by her enthusiastic outburst and once outside paused to steady herself. It was strangely quiet in the street and she walked briskly, deep in thought, back towards Bank House.

Fortunately George was out on her return, much to her relief as she had no wish for another confrontation. Instead she was greeted by an irate Sarah. 'Where have you been?' she demanded. 'George said that you had gone to Church. You've not been there for years apart from mother's funeral, whatever made you go?' She was about to start again when Becky interrupted.

'Sarah, I didn't go to our Church, I went to Mr Johnson's.' She said calmly, waiting for Sarah's reaction.

'You!' she exclaimed, in a strangled voice. 'But why didn't you take me? I thought you didn't want anything to do with religion?'

'I didn't want any more trouble with George, there was enough when I told him that I was going. I went because, foolishly, and perhaps rashly, I promised Luke that I would. It was quite pleasant and I will go once more but that will be the last time.'

'Was Luke there?' Sarah begged. 'I don't care about George, so will you take me with you next time?'

'Alright!' She said with a smile. 'But on one condition—that you do not tell George. We must find a way of going without him finding out.' That, she concluded to herself, would not be a simple task as Sarah did not keep secrets easily.

Throughout the week which followed, Sarah struggled to contain her excitement and had George not been so pre-occupied with his business affairs he would have realised that she was in a state. She could not sit for any length of time without fidgeting, nor was she in the least bit interested in her meals. Her main concern was with the image which peered back at her from the mirror in which she glanced constantly, seeking reassurance that all was well with her appearance.

George had not questioned Becky about her Sunday outing, indeed hardly a word that wasn't necessary had passed his lips all week. However, the longer he continued his stubborn silence the more Becky was determined to stand up to him and keep him in the dark. She considered that it was no more than he deserved.

Sunday arrived at last, much to Becky's relief. 'Oh, Becky!' Sarah pleaded for the third time in as many minutes,' Do I look fine enough?'

'Oh, stop fussing, Sarah! We are only going to Church and Adam's service is a simple one. You don't want to look out of place do you? No one will mind how we dress!' Becky replied, well aware of the real reason behind Sarah's incessant chatter and nervous fidgeting. 'I am beginning to regret ever having promised to allow you to come with me—if George finds out that I've taken you, there will be ructions over my deception.' She watched her sister's eyes sparkle with excitement and felt that she should offer a word of caution. 'Be careful, now. You know that nothing can ever come from this feeling which you have for Luke. One day he will have to return home and you will be most unhappy.' She softened her tone. 'Just try to be sensible and don't let yourself get carried away—I don't want to see you get hurt.' What was the point? Ruefully she suspected that it was already too late to offer a warning and knew that she should not be aiding and abetting by taking Sarah with her. Shrugging her shoulders as if to shed her doubts, she pulled on her gloves, donned her pelisse and hat and then led the way out of the house.

The hollow sound of their footsteps on the bare wooden floor caused heads to turn as they entered the Mission Hall. Instead of the bright warmth that had greeted Becky the previous week there was now a sombre stillness that was disquieting. Obviously something was drastically wrong; this was not the lively place which she remembered. She was at a loss to know what to do, but to her relief Adam came forward with his face and manner grave, but not unfriendly. Only an occasional hushed murmur disturbed the silence as though they all shared a common grief. For a moment she wondered why she had come.

Adam took Becky's hand, then Sarah's, 'So you did return, my dear. You are both welcome,' his voice was subdued and barely a whisper. 'You will find us a little sad today, I'm afraid. We have had devastating news from America, about our leader. He was murdered by a mob in June and the news has only just reached us here'. His eyes were deeply troubled. 'We will understand if you don't wish to stay, but we are not quite our usual cheery selves—most of us are too deeply shocked.'

She was moved by the depths of his sadness and realised that it would seem churlish to leave now. 'We will stay with you' she said. 'It must be terrible for you, please don't let us interfere. We will remain at the back.'

Adam indicated to Luke that he should join them and the meeting commenced. Sitting between Adam and Luke gave Becky the strangest feeling of comradeship, and the genuine sense of loss in the room drew her closer to Adam. She wondered just how close he had been to her mother and what he had been like as a young man. It was when he stood to close the meeting with a prayer that she saw him for what he was. He hesitatingly uttered his hopes and prayers for his family and the Church members left behind where their leader had been killed. Adam gave way to his emotions, and tears ran down his face. She had never seen a man cry before, his soul was bared before his friends and she realised how worried he must be for the safety of his wife and children back home. His sacrifice in leaving them was evident in his voice and Becky found herself weeping too. There was no sensible reason for men to murder each other, or persecute them for their beliefs, and the more she listened the greater was her desire to understand him.

It was some time before the congregation felt inclined to leave their seats, and by the time they slowly began to disperse Adam had regained control of himself. He seemed not to mind that they had witnessed his distress for he could tell that both Becky and Sarah had been deeply moved by the whole affair.

At that moment she realised that in the upheaval she had not noticed the absence of the old man. 'Where is Mr Smith?' she asked Adam.

'As a matter of fact, Luke and I are going to visit him when we leave here. His legs are troubling him today and he couldn't walk this far. Would you both like to come with us? I'm sure he would be delighted to see you. He lives on Porter Street, so it's not far out of your way.

Becky thought quickly—there was no reason why they shouldn't. George didn't know that they hadn't just gone for a walk. 'Will it be inconvenient to him? I mean, we hardly know him!'

Adam smiled, 'I'm sure he would be charmed to have two young ladies call on him. I told him that Luke and I would call anyway, so it won't be a total surprise. He's a lonely widower who misses his wife and he's not in very good health.' With that he excused himself and passed Becky into the hands of a woman who was struggling to contain the activities of a young child.

It was then that Becky became aware of Sarah who seemed to have overcome her differences with Luke as both were deep in conversation at the far side of the hall.

At first, Sarah was at a loss to know how to begin to heal the rift with Luke, and she watched him fiddle with a sheaf of paper which he clutched in his hand. Then, unable to bear the silence any longer she finally whispered, 'I'm truly sorry for my rudeness the other day. It was unforgivable of me but my silly notions were not intended to offend you. I'm sure that my imagination is my very worst failing' she said, not daring to look at him. She stared down at her feet and waited desperately for a word of forgiveness from him.

Luke, his head bent, stared at the same pair of shoes, painfully aware that he should apologise for his sharpness that evening. He was also conscious of the fact that Sarah made a striking picture which was having a disturbing effect on him. Plucking up courage, he stuttered, 'Sarah, it is I who should apologise, for my harsh tone. Although I did think your notions to be rather romantic, I realised afterwards that you had meant no harm'. He paused for breath, and asked hopefully, 'Can we still be friends?'

'I would like that' she replied demurely. 'I would like that very much!'

On impulse Luke took her hand in his, then, as if becoming aware of his action, shook it in greeting whilst looking round anxiously hoping that he had not been observed. At that moment Becky waved, indicating that they were to go to her. 'Oh dear,' Sarah sighed, 'I think that we are about to leave.' The look of disappointment on Luke's face pleased her and she found herself saying softly, 'I really would like to be your friend'. By this time they had reached Becky and stood in self-conscious silence before her.

'We're going with Adam' she announced, 'to visit an old man who is sick. It isn't far out of our way but he was so kind to me last week that I really should like to go and see him.' She had not anticipated any objections from Sarah but was a little startled by the eagerness with which her statement was received. Nor did she miss the fleeting glance of pleasure which passed between Luke and her sister.

The anticipated five minute walk to the old man's house took almost ten, as the conversation between Becky and Adam was so intense that their walk became a leisurely stroll. Becky was hardly aware of the steps which they took, as Adam was easy to talk to and his voice gentle, yet he revealed little of his inner self no matter how hard she tried to coax him. It was obvious that he had other things on his mind. As for Luke and Sarah, they were equally absorbed in each other, but for different reasons.

Finally, she came straight out and asked, 'Why did a mob kill your Church Leader—what had he done?'

Seizing on the topic which so preoccupied him, Adam explained. 'Joseph Smith, that was his name, did nothing more than express his beliefs and defend his people. He and three companions did not resist arrest on trumped up charges in order to avoid being dragged humiliatingly to the gaol like common criminals. They knew that they ran a great risk of persecution but they trusted in the law. The mob, however, took things into their own hands and attacked the gaol, where Joseph, his brother and a friend were brutally murdered. He died for his faith!' Suddenly his voice dropped and became strained. 'My wife and family are in that same community over there without me to protect them and although other members of the Church will take care of them I cannot help but worry about them. Mobs do not think clearly nor do they care if the innocent get caught up in their ravings. I cannot return home yet so I just have to trust in God!' He was visibly shaken, and she admired his strength of faith.

'Why do you stay in such a place where men hate you so much? Wouldn't it be easier to move somewhere else?' she asked.

'Why should we have to move? All we want is to be allowed to live our lives in peace and worship as we please. We have already moved for these same reasons—and to a mosquito-ridden swampland which nobody else wanted. Yet the moment we flourish and prosper the resentment begins all over again. America is so vast that you would think there was enough room

for everyone, but it looks as though we may be forced to move once again.'
He fell silent for a moment, alone with his thoughts, whilst Becky
contemplated his story. Then he added, with some bitterness, 'I always
wanted to go to America, where I thought there would be tolerance, but it
seems that I was wrong. Wherever there is success then greed and jealousy
seem to follow. Wouldn't you think mankind would learn to live in peace?'
His voice got angrier. 'The Church is growing so rapidly that other
denominations are becoming fearful at their own losses. They are
beginning to realise that what they have to offer is not fulfilling the needs
of their own members.'

For all that there was no arrogance in his voice, Becky found the
statement rather annoying. She was of the firm belief that religion was the
root of most of the troubles in the world and here he was coolly assuming
that his beliefs were infallible. She could not stop herself retaliating.
'Whenever people become too religious they become intolerant of other
ideas. You believe that you alone are right—is that not presumptuous?
What gives you that right?'

'My dear Miss Webster,' Adam protested, speaking out defensively, 'I
am sorry if I have offended you by voicing my inner thoughts, but do you
not have any beliefs at all?'

She thought for a moment, unable to answer him directly.

'Your mother was not a disbeliever!' he stated bluntly, then immediately
wished he had left Fanny out of it.

'No, I agree, but she rarely attended Church. I refuse to get involved
with the squabbling which goes on in the name of God. None of the
religions seem able to stem the cruelty and avarice in this world.'

His voice was softer as he replied, 'May I tell you why we believe as we
do, so that you may understand our cause better, and my motives?'

They had now reached Tom Smith's house and further discussion was
impossible. Adam turned to Sarah and apologised, 'I do beg your pardon
for my inattention, I hope we have not bored you too much'.

'Not at all, Mr Johnson,' Sarah replied, 'but you will find my sister to be
a formidable challenger, I warn you!' Then, seizing the opportunity to meet
Luke again, added, 'But I, too, would like to hear what you have to say'.

Adam did not miss the frown on Becky's face at this juncture, nor the
quick glance which Sarah gave Luke, but before he could give the matter
further thought Luke had knocked on the shabby wooden door.

Although Tom Smith had been expecting visitors the sharp noise still
took him by surprise as it echoed through the room. He levered himself
slowly out of his old armchair just as the knock was repeated. 'I'm
coming!' he called out, afraid that the visitors would go away before he

reached the door, 'I'm coming!' The pain increased with each step, causing him to groan out. 'Who is it?' he asked cautiously before sliding back the bolts.

'Adam and Luke Johnson, Brother Smith! With two visitors. Take your time, we can wait!'

On recognising the voice, Thomas Smith immediately turned the key and opened the door. His age-lined face shone with pleasure when he saw them. 'Come in, come in!' he insisted warmly, before struggling valiantly back to his well-worn chair.

The room was tiny and seemed to be littered with books. It was as if each pile was on hand to be ready at any moment, saving him the task of rising. 'Move a few books and sit down', he chuckled, seeing Sarah's astonishment at the disarray. 'An old man needs his belongings where he can get at them my dear. Life is too short and painful to be constantly moving about.' It was also apparent that Tom lived and slept in the same room for there was a bed in one corner and a stone sink in the other. He was obviously a very independent-minded old man and Becky wondered how he managed to carry the heavy water bucket from the well in his state of health. She fought down the desire to help tidy up because it would only draw attention to his inabilities but asked out of concern, 'Do you get many visitors to help you?'

'Not very often and certainly not so many at one time. None are ever as charming as you two ladies, though.' His eyes were twinkling now, teasing her and she could see why Adam had called him an old rogue.

'We have bad news, Tom.' Adam said when the old man had finished speaking. 'We have received a letter from America—Joseph Smith and his brother have been murdered, and all the antagonists are out in force again. I really fear that we shall never find peace anywhere and will be hounded forever.'

Shaking his head sadly, Tom said wistfully, 'I've been expecting something like this—I knew the situation was getting worse for our leaders. Once our enemies get their teeth into something they rarely let go.' He sighed deeply. 'I've seen it all before in my long life span, but I think they have made the biggest mistake of their lives—it will rebound on them, mark my words. They've made Joseph into a martyr and it will draw the 'Saints' together, and make other men curious. It will give us more publicity and help than they ever dreamed possible'.

'You're an old sage, Tom—what a pity you're not well enough to travel, we could do with the likes of you over there to help us build Zion.'

Tom smiled. 'I'm content enough, there is work to do here,' he indicated to Becky and Sarah, 'welcoming these charming young ladies for instance!' Sarah blushed. 'You haven't introduced us yet, Adam', he pointed out.

'I do beg your pardon. I think it must be the bad news which is affecting my manners. This is Miss Webster's sister, Sarah. I'm afraid things were a bit subdued at Church today, for her.'

'Oh, no!' Sarah protested spiritedly. 'I quite understood the reason and I'm sorry that people are so cruel to each other. I'm very happy to meet you, Mr Smith.'

There was no physical weakness in his handshake and Sarah began to think that she would never get her hand back so vigorous was the ardour of it. 'He always does that, Sarah,' Adam laughed, seeing her flex her crushed fingers. 'There's still a lot of life left in this old rascal. He's an inspiration to us all.' His voice was filled with love and respect.

'Sit down everyone, find something to sit on!' Old Tom said, pointing to the edge of the bed as he turned to Becky. 'So you kept your promise to an old man to attend Church, my dear. I almost wish that I had struggled on my two sticks to get there.' Becky tried to avoid leaving her hand too long in his by quickly releasing her fingers but his grip was firm and vigorous. 'It's no good,' he laughed, 'ask Luke. Even he has given up trying to out-shake me!' A ripple of laughter filled the small crowded room and it wasn't long before almost an hour had passed without their realising it.

'Oh dear!' Becky exclaimed on hearing the clock chime. 'It is getting late and George will be getting suspicious by now. I'm afraid we must go, we've stayed rather too long already.'

'Please,' pleaded Tom, looking at Becky, 'can I save you both a seat by me next Sunday? It will give me a great deal of pleasure to look forward to.'

Adam interrupted, 'Tom, I wanted to tell Becky what we believe in but we are not welcome in George Webster's house. Could we come here occasionally to talk instead of going up there?'

The old eyes lit up. 'Why, Elder! You know that my home is yours. I can think of nothing that would give me more pleasure! You young people are always welcome.' His face was filled with joy and once more Becky had not the heart to refuse him. They left him seated comfortably amongst his possessions, with the promise that they would all meet at his home the following Wednesday afternoon.

Standing by a window, George observed the little group winding its way up the hill. At first he wasn't sure if he was imagining things but as the figures became more discernible his worst fears were confirmed. His sense of indignation intensified the closer they came. He had asked the girls not to bring the Johnson's to the house and here they were half way up the hill! He fumed. So, they had defied him, first by going to Adam's Church and now this! He had guessed where they were going the moment they left the house earlier in the day, and had followed them at a distance until they disappeared into the Mission Hall on Rockingham Street. Sarah had never been able to disguise her feelings well, or hide her secrets, but he had bided his time, waiting proof of his suspicions. He had spent a week seeking out information on the Mormon sect and was disturbed by rumours of strange goings on at the Hall and by the river. Now he was well-armed in his fight to protect the Webster family and their good name.

To his enormous relief the four parted company at the gate thus preventing an outright confrontation. He drew back from the window and escaped into his study, leaving instructions with Henry that he was not to be disturbed for the rest of the day. Although sad at heart over the situation he was resolute in his decision to enlist support in preventing further intrusion and discord into his family life. On the morrow he would invite a couple of friendly Church Ministers of his acquaintance to dine later in the week at the house.

The news of George's seclusion in his locked study came as a relief to Becky; she suspected the reasoning behind it but concluded that it was for the best. She did not want a confrontation with him, as she loved him dearly, but could not allow him to dominate her life. For too long now she had staved off her discontent for her mother's sake but now that she was gone, her future seemed empty. Before long she would be cast in a role which she neither admired nor aspired to, that of a spinster. She had always been interested in the world of commerce but knew full well that a woman of her status could never enter that male-dominated society. How she envied George his activities, but what could she do, she was trained for nothing. She did not intend to allow herself to become an unpaid servant by marrying the first man who proposed, as many of her friends had done already. She had despatched more than one fond suitor from the house because she felt nothing more for them than friendly affection. That left only one alternative, a 'doer of good works'. That she could not abide, yet the thought of being permanently dependent on George was objectionable to her.

As arranged, on the Wednesday she and Sarah met with Adam at old Tom's house. It was a pleasant interlude and would most probably have ended there had George not taken the action he did.

Standing by his decision, George pleaded his case before his two friends who were only too pleased to defend their doctrines against those of the charlatan. He merely informed Becky that he had two gentlemen coming to supper and would be pleased if she and Sarah could join them. It never entered her head to question the gathering even though George seldom entertained on his own account; in fact she welcomed the diversion if only to ease the atmosphere which prevailed in the house.

With supper neatly laid, and George in affable spirit, it was almost as though the past two months had never transpired. The two guests arrived punctually and were ushered into the drawing room. 'My dears,' George said, smiling, 'may I introduce James Palmer and Richard Wallace. Gentlemen, my two sisters, Becky and Sarah!'

The men appeared pleasant enough and revealed nothing of the real reason for their visit. 'What a pleasure it is to meet you both,' James Palmer exclaimed as the two ladies entered the room. 'We have been remiss in not making your acquaintance before. I must say that you have most impressive views from the house; I had no idea you would be able to see so far.'

'We can often see the heather up on the moors, when the weather is right!' Becky replied proudly.

'And the smoke over the town,' mused George who seemed to be in excellent spirits.

'What I wouldn't give to live away from the grime and soot,' Mr Palmer joined in again, 'but then I would have further to go to feed my sheep,' he concluded.

'You are a farmer?' asked Becky innocently.

James Palmer laughed affably, 'Goodness me, no! I'm a teacher and part-time preacher. My sheep are my congregation. I like to count myself as their shepherd'.

Blushing with embarrassment at her mistake, Becky mumbled, 'I seem to have made a silly blunder. Do forgive me, only George hasn't told me anything about you at all'.

George smiled uncomfortably and asked if anyone would like a glass of Madeira, adding, 'I didn't get much chance to tell you anything Becky'. He turned, 'My sisters have been rather pre-occupied of late, gentlemen, and I doubt if they will remember what I did say!'

Becky thought this a rather strange remark to make, especially as, at that point, Mr Wallace informed them that he too was a man of the Church. She eyed George with suspicion, 'We have all been rather pre-occupied since our mother's death,' she informed the two guests. 'and have been trying to adjust to a very changed way of life here!'

Taking a glass of Madeira from the offered tray James Palmer raised his glass, saying 'To us all then, let us hope the future will be better for you than it has been in the immediate past'. Sipping the contents of his glass he turned again to Becky, 'Your brother tells me that you have had the misfortune to be confronted by two American Mormons. I would be very interested to know what your opinions are of these people?' His eyes were lowered casually, as if the topic was only of passing interest yet she suspected his motive.

She answered cautiously, refusing to be drawn. 'They seem, under the surface, to be no more strange than we are, perhaps a little more dedicated, but sincere enough. I can see no harm in them.' She sensed his indignation at the slur but continued, changing the subject, 'You are not from these parts, I gather from your accent. From where do you originate?' She smiled disarmingly, hoping to dissuade him from returning to religious matters. 'I am most interested in travel but have unfortunately not done as much as I would like.'

'I am Lincolnshire born and bred although my forebears are from Norfolk. I was born in Gainsborough—though it is many years since I lived there. I do visit the area from time to time however.'

'What a coincidence,' Becky gasped excitedly, 'I have a small property near the village of Pilling, just outside Gainsborough! I was born there but the house is leased out to a farming family now, and I simply receive an annual rent via my solicitor.' The memory of those idyllic days of her childhood came flooding back as she spoke. How strange it was to think of the house now after all these years. She must go back one day. A voice cut into her thoughts.

'Then we are country cousins, Miss Webster!' James Palmer mused, his cold grey eyes softening behind his spectacles, and Becky had the irresistible urge to remove those same items which sat precariously on the bridge of his nose.

'We are indeed, Mr Palmer,' she agreed. 'And now I think it is time to dine. Will you excuse me whilst I check that all is prepared?' Leaving him to join the others, Becky slipped into the dining room and quickly made out seating cards for all the party. She intended having James Palmer where she could keep her eye firmly upon him, and not seated by her side.

Sitting down finally with George to her right and Mr Wallace to her left Becky felt in complete control of her situation. There was a nudge at her right elbow and she turned to see the bewildered look on her brother's face. He whispered quickly, beneath his breath, 'What's the idea of seating cards—what are you playing at?'

Turning calmly, Becky hissed back at him between clenched teeth. 'Nothing, George dear. I just wanted to see his ridiculous little glasses wobble on his nose.' She felt George stiffen and quickly suppressed the giggle which she knew was rising to the surface.

For a while at least conversation was simple and James Palmer seemed content enough to chat to Sarah, leaving George to pick irritably at his food.

'Miss Webster!' James Palmer finally called out across the table, 'Your sister tell me that you have indeed had discussions with these Mormon Elders. What pray is your opinion of them?'

So! Things were much as she had suspected, George had staged the visit, most probably with the intention of discrediting Adam. She had, of course, forgotten that by seating him next to the voluble Sarah she had given him the very opportunity he had been seeking. 'They are correctly titled Latter Day Saints, Mr Palmer, and it is mainly the ignorant and antagonistic who nickname them otherwise!' She knew she was being impolite but she enjoyed watching him strive to keep calm. 'I have been met with nothing but kindness and consideration from them,' she concluded.

'But they are advocates of the devil, my dear!' Mr Wallace interceded. 'With their wild doctrines and talk of visions. I am surprised to hear a level-headed and educated young woman such as yourself, speak out on their behalf. What is it about them that you find so defensible?'

Becky found his arrogance and condescension annoying. 'I find the fact that they are willing to make such sacrifices in order to tell other people about their beliefs, very commendable. I know of few other people who are willing to give up so much in the service of their religion, and fewer still in this town willing to leave a comfortable living to do so!'

'Ah, but what is their real motive? Is it not in order to entice simple men and woman to leave behind all they own and go to America to work as nothing more than slaves?' He smiled, yet his eyes were cold and hard. 'What kind of future do these people expect?'

'Most of them have very little here to leave behind or to look forward to. As a man of the cloth are you not as concerned about their spiritual welfare as their physical well-being? They hope to find work in America, but at the same time they seek spiritual fulfilment, which is just as important as worldly things, is it not?' Her annoyance was increasing with each defensive word. 'I thought that was the main concern of all religions!'

'You misunderstand me, Miss Webster.' His face was flushed with indignation. 'I too am concerned for their souls but these people are taken from established churches and tempted by wild stories to what they think is a better way of life. What right have these foreigners to steal my congregation?'

'But they are not your congregation, Mr Wallace, but God's. They must be very dissatisfied with what they find in the established churches to be tempted to seek answers elsewhere.' She realised that she had unintentionally walked straight into George's trap and was becoming deeply committed to an argument over something which she had never previously considered herself to be interested in. Was it merely to thwart George and these two conceited Ministers? At least she had some satisfaction in knowing that they were obviously discomforted by her forthrightness. If they thought that they had come to see her beaten then they were very much mistaken!

'But you must admit,' James Palmer joined in, 'that their story is nothing but a fabricated invention to dazzle the poor and down-trodden, a way of getting cheap labour.' There was a look of challenge in his serious grey eyes.

'Perhaps if you were all to stick to the principles given in the Bible then you might keep your own congregations, Mr Palmer,' she said, raising her voice to the brink of rudeness. There was a gasp of horror from George, and the others fell silent.

George was furious. 'Becky!' he snapped, 'Your manners are deplorable! These Reverend Gentlemen are our guests and I think you owe them an apology!' He turned. 'Now you see, gentlemen, why I invited you here tonight. You see the influence these people exert over my sisters in only a few short weeks, and now they think they know more than men of God!'

Becky's eyes flashed and she was about to retaliate when James Palmer raised his hand, and spoke up. 'Please! I am not offended, but it is true they do have an effect on ordinary decent people. Their heads are turned by stories of 'visions'. I am here to help fight such heresy.' He could not have missed Becky's growing agitation, nor the animosity in her eyes but his next words took her by surprise. 'I must confess however, that I have never heard such forthrightness from a woman before and I find it most refreshing—although it should be curbed.'

Had Becky not exercised iron control over her temper at the moment, she would have screamed at him for his near-insufferable audacity. Instead she replied calmly enough, 'I have no axe to grind. I have not embraced their beliefs but I do find a lot of what they say makes good sense. Let me ask you this, why do you not practise baptism by immersion as written in the Bible? Did Jesus not find it necessary to go into the waters of baptism physically, rather than just sprinkle his followers?'

'What do you know of the Bible?' George retorted angrily.

'More than you think, brother dear, and I want the Reverend Palmer to answer my question!' She faced the Minister, watching the nervous throbbing in his cheek as he gathered his thoughts,—'Can you not answer truthfully—why you do not obey the Bible?'

'Please!' James Palmer cried out, 'I will answer your question, but on condition that when I have done so we may leave the table and calm down. I have to admit that I have indeed pondered on this subject for many hours in the past and many religions do accept that principle of immersion, but I accept sprinkling as being symbolic.'

Becky clapped her hands together, 'Then Jesus went to an awful lot of trouble when he too might have used a symbol in its stead. Adam Johnson says one is literally born anew when coming out of the water.'

Here Mr Wallace quickly intervened before his friend could answer. 'And what does Mr Johnson say about these visions and angels that seem to appear only in America? Does that not make you sceptical?' He smiled now, as if confident that she was out of her depth.

However, she no longer felt intimidated by his pompous air of authority and replied, 'Does it not happen in your Church? It happened all through the Old and New Testaments, when there were Prophets and Apostles. Has God ceased to appear to his children? I would have thought if anything the world needs guidance now more than ever!'

As if waking suddenly from a deep shock, Mr Wallace opened his mouth and cried out fervently, 'This is heresy!' He was seething now. 'You would do well, young woman, to humble yourself and study the scriptures before confronting men of God. Nor is it a woman's place to know all things!' There was scorn in his voice and his face was red with anger. 'I suggest we adjourn this conversation and that you attend our Bible study classes. Bring your Mormon friends—I'm sure we'll set them straight too.'

'Wait a moment,' James Palmer interrupted. 'I see no point in falling out on such a pleasant evening, or in losing our tempers. I think Miss Webster is under a very strong influence but to give her credit she has the ability to reason, and deserves fair answers. May I suggest that we meet again at a more convenient time and place to examine these ideas?'

Becky nodded. 'I accept your proposal, Mr Palmer, indeed I shall look forward to the discussion.' She folded her table napkin neatly, as if ending the matter. 'Perhaps we can all retire to the drawing room and enjoy ourselves in a lighter vein.'

'I think,' Mr Wallace dissented, 'that the hour is late and it is time for me to go, if you will excuse me? Thank you for a delicious meal.'

Catching Becky by the arm as they all rose from their chairs, George hissed, 'That was the most embarrassing meal of my life, I hope you are as ashamed as I am'. Then he ushered Mr Wallace to the cloakroom, all the while muttering apologies as they went.

Becky would have followed but James Palmer approached, towering above her. He was taller than she had realised and she suspected that beneath the spectacles he was almost handsome. 'Miss Webster,' his voice was calm and although flushed from the confrontation his face held no sign of resentment. 'May I escort you?' he offered, holding forth his arm. Sarah was already on the other arm. 'Perhaps we can talk about Gainsborough?'

'Oh, dear! I fear that I have been rather rude—whatever must you think of me?' she said, lowering her eyes with embarrassment. 'George will never forgive me.'

He smiled, 'Perhaps not, but I can say in all honesty that I am not offended, and in spite of our differences I found the female point of view very revealing. However, we agreed not to discuss the matter further this evening and I look forward to our next meeting. I trust you will keep your promise and perhaps bring Mr Johnson with you?'

The remainder of the evening passed pleasantly enough, and after Mr Palmer had taken his leave, Becky scribbled a brief note to Adam asking him to meet her at old Tom's house later the following day.

Making her way down the darkened staircase, Becky was careful not to disturb George who had gone to bed immediately James Palmer departed, without saying a word. His glowering face had been sufficient to warn her to keep out of his way as long as possible. She made her way to where a shaft of light came from beneath the kitchen door and knocked softly before entering. 'Hello, Mary. Is Henry about still?' she asked the startled maid. 'It is important that I see him before he takes George to work in the morning. See if you can find him for me, please!'

It wasn't long before Henry appeared, surprised by the late summons. 'Yes, Miss, what can I do for you?'

Keeping her voice low, and handing Henry a sealed letter, she said, 'I want you to take this letter to the Grapes Inn near the Infirmary, and give it to Mr Johnson tomorrow after you have dropped off Mr George, but don't tell him anything about it, he is angry with me enough already.'

Taking the letter reluctantly, Henry placed it in his pocket, saying, 'Yes, Miss, I'll deliver it sometime before lunch, providing Mr George doesn't make me take him out of town'.

'Oh, I don't think he will tomorrow. I know his plans, but it is most important that he doesn't find out about it!' Henry shook his head as she left, a look of disapproval written plainly on his face.

Chapter 10

*L*uke and *Adam* were already at old Tom's the following evening when Becky arrived and Luke answered the door. 'Why, Becky, you're all flustered,' he commented as she endeavoured to catch her breath. 'We thought you weren't coming.'

'I'm sorry,' she gasped, 'but I had difficulty avoiding George and began to think you might not have waited for me. Is Adam in?' He nodded.

Old Tom welcomed her with a smile as she bent over and gently kissed him on the cheek. 'It's good to see you, Tom, and I'm grateful to you for letting me meet Adam here. I need to see him urgently.' She turned to Adam. 'I've created a problem with George and alienated him completely. I'm not sure what to do now!'

'Then perhaps you had better tell me about it,' Adam said, searching her face for some indication of the cause of her distress.

'George invited two non-conformist Ministers to the house for supper last night and I think the idea was to turn me against you and your Church. I'm afraid I argued in your defence so well that it wasn't long before we ended up in a heated discussion which became quite unpleasant!' She covered her mouth with her hand in horror at the memory of her conduct. 'Oh, Adam! My behaviour was disgraceful! I also agreed to meet them again and promised one that I would bring you too, for a discussion. What shall I do?'

'Then we shall meet them as promised, as soon as you like!' He wasn't angry, and continued, 'Did you really believe what you said to them or were you merely repeating my words?' He was curious as to just what she might have said to cause such turmoil.

She paused a moment, having asked herself the same question. Why indeed had she defended Adam's beliefs so fiercely? 'I'm not really sure,' she confessed. 'I truly don't know. Maybe it was the way George deceived me or the fact that they did not approve of a woman holding such strong views. Yet, I think I believed in my argument or I would not have said what I did.' She paused, then said sadly, 'Mother would have been ashamed of my behaviour!'

Adam closed his eyes for a moment seeking to rid himself of the memory she had invoked. 'Your mother was a rebel, too, you know!' His voice was tender and as she looked into his eyes she was stirred by the certain knowledge that he had loved her mother, she was sure of it now. Her heart went out to him and she wanted to weep.

His voice when he spoke again was husky, 'Would you like to talk about your mother—would it help?' he offered. She nodded. 'Perhaps we could go for a walk. I'm sure Luke won't mind keeping Tom company for a while, will you my boy?'

There was a cool wind blowing dust down the cobbled street as they left the house, and Becky drew her cloak tightly round her small frame. It was several minutes before she finally broke the silence and dared to ask, 'Adam, did you love my mother?' She looked at his bent head, tinged here and there with grey, 'I really would like to know!'

His face was deadly white as he struggled to find the words to tell her what he had never told another human, except Fanny. Words which would not distress Becky or spoil the memory of his lost love. He battled too with the scars in his soul that he knew would never completely heal. 'Yes!' he said simply, relieved to be able, finally, to share his thoughts with someone, someone who cared. 'Yes, I loved her very much. Her memory was the only thing which gave me the strength to survive throughout my ordeals. Perhaps I should start at the beginning. It isn't easy for me to talk of the past and I would not like Luke or his mother to find out the truth, it is best that they should never know.'

'I would never hurt Luke or break your confidence.' She wanted to say, 'I respect you too much for that'. She merely said, 'I hope you trust me!'

There was a growing closeness with Becky that he had never really experienced with anyone before, which released him from any embarrassment as he told her his story. They were oblivious to the crowds as they walked, and Adam dredged his soul to tell her everything about his life. She was not conscious of the fact, but she had led him towards St Paul's graveyard. Suddenly finding themselves at its wrought-iron gates, Becky took him through into the peace and stillness within. Softly the words came from his lips, 'Is she here—is your mother in here?'

For many minutes they stood together in silence before Fanny's grave, each alone with their memories until, deeply moved, Becky laid her hand gently on his arm to comfort him, and said tenderly, 'I'll be back in a minute'. Then she left him to be alone with Fanny.

They were not aware of the figure watching them through the railings, nor of the trick fate had played by bringing them all together at this moment. Mr Richard Wallace had observed them for some time in their deep and intimate discussion, seen the tender touch on Adam's arm, and had entirely misconstrued its intention.

Leaving the railings, he slipped away. The secret of Miss Webster's passionate defence of the persuasive American was his! He had work to do.

By the time Becky returned to the graveside Adam was waiting patiently, his face calm and composed. A smile had replaced the sadness in his eyes and Becky could quite see why her mother had loved him.

'Come,' he said, 'we had better return before they send a search party out for us.' They wandered slowly back to rejoin Luke. 'Were your mother and Gervase really happy?' he dared to ask. 'I do hope so, they are all I have of the past.'

'Yes, I think they were. They seemed to love each other very much.' She hoped the answer did not pain him too much, but she could not lie to him.

He smiled, relieved, a kindly smile that was tinged with the wisdom of age. 'I'm glad, so very glad. I would not have wished it to have been otherwise.' They walked on companionably until they were just short of Tom's house when Adam stopped and suggested, 'If we are to meet your Mr Palmer it would be better if I taught you a little more about what we believe. Then you can argue from strength and they will not be able to ridicule or humiliate you!'

'I'm not much of a believer, you know,' she replied, truthfully. 'I may even disagree with you!'

He laughed delightedly, 'Oh, yes! You're Fanny's daughter alright! Don't ever change, will you? Your strength of mind does you credit and is a valuable gift which will see you through rough times, and shield you from temptation'.

The revelations of the day gave her much to think about as she returned slowly to Bank House, where, on arrival, she was confronted by none other than Mr Wallace. She had not known of any intention on his part to visit and was quite surprised to see him standing in the hallway in earnest conversation with George. Almost immediately the two men drew apart, conveying the impression that she had been the topic of their discussion.

Aware that both men were now eyeing her intently, she drew herself up to her full height and walked forward to greet the Minister. His eyes were cold and unfriendly as he took her hand, and she could sense the animosity in him. He gave her a stiff, patronising smile which caused her to shudder. Noticing her reaction he commented, 'It is quite cool outside for the time of the year is it not, Miss Webster?'

'Mr Wallace has come to see if you managed to arrange a meeting', George spoke out, unaware of the ill-feeling in the hall. 'But now that you have arrived you can deal with it yourself. Would you care to come through, Richard? Becky will tell you her plans, Don't let my sister get above herself!' He laughed but it had a hollow ring which she knew hid the anger he still felt towards her. There was also a familiarity between Richard Wallace and George which did not ring true and for the first time in her life she did not trust her own brother.

Once the door had closed behind her and Richard Wallace, there was no need for pretence. She was not really interested in what his opinions were, she would have preferred it had he been James Palmer. Mr Wallace addressed her now directly for the first time, his manner formal. 'Miss Webster, I have come here today because I feel that it is my duty to make you see the errors of your ways.' Becky frowned but managed to conceal her disdain as he continued, 'You are a very silly woman and easily impressed, I can see that, yet you have certain qualities which I could admire and which should be put to proper use. Therefore I do not wish to be blamed for not giving you sound advice.'

How dare he! 'Mr Wallace,' she replied with slow deliberation to the pompous figure before her, 'you have no duty towards me whatsoever, and you are mistaken in thinking that I even care what your opinions are!' His jaw dropped and he seemed thunderstruck at her words. 'If you wish to discuss religion then I prefer that we meet again in the presence of Adam Johnson. Please leave your address, Mr Johnson will contact you to arrange matters accordingly.'

Richard Wallace was not used to being spoken to with anything but respect and he had certainly never been so rebuffed before by a woman. He was seething inwardly, as she could see from his angry expression. 'James Palmer and I came here at the request of your brother, to save you from yourself, and I can well see how right he was. James may admire your spirit but like me he abhors your attitude.'

'Then it would be better if you left this house, Mr Wallace, before I spoil my reputation altogether.' She opened the door and stood impatiently, waiting for him to leave.

Taking his hat from the hall stand as he passed, he glared at her and spoke menacingly. 'Pride will be your downfall, Miss Webster, and you will rue the day you spurned my advice.' At that, he clamped his hat firmly on his head and marched out of the house without shaking hands.

The encounter left her shaking with fury, and she could hardly believe that such arrogance existed, especially in a man of the Church. So James Palmer agreed with him did he? Well, let Mr Palmer try confronting her and he would receive short shrift too. Spirit indeed! Power to think for herself more like and she was not short of that, but she would not be beaten by them, next time she would give them a good run for their money.

It was a full three weeks before the meeting could be arranged to suit all parties and then Adam became ill, delaying it still further. In the meantime James Palmer made his own effort to 'save' Becky but she was ready for him when he arrived at the house. His reception was cool and unfriendly, her manner that of a very determined young woman. 'I suppose you have come on the same errand as Mr Wallace did last week?' she challenged impatiently. 'Well, I am in no mood for pious speeches. Mr Wallace was despatched with a flea in his ear!' She saw the look of amazement on his face and felt a little ashamed of herself. 'If you only come to upbraid me then you are most unwelcome.'

James realised he would need to proceed with caution, and replied calmly, 'I have no wish to quarrel with you—I have come on my own behalf. I have not seen Mr Wallace in days and as I had not heard from you regarding a meeting with Mr Johnson I thought I had better call and enquire if arrangements had been made'. He had not the arrogance of Mr Wallace and, feeling somewhat guilty about her verbal attack, she invited him into the house.

'You are a friend of Mr Wallace are you not?' she questioned, 'and of similar opinions too?' He nodded, watching, bemused by her haughty manner. 'Then unless we can agree on some topic of conversation other than religion, Mr Palmer, your time will be wasted here!'

'Must we talk about Gainsborough again then, Miss Webster?' he said, smiling, trying to break the ice.

'Don't mock me, Mr Palmer—I am not a fool!' she snapped.

'No! That you are not, but you are without common courtesy at times.' He was becoming annoyed by her persistent disdain of him. 'I came because of my concern for your welfare and nothing else!'

'Mr Wallace came about my welfare, or so he said, but he and my brother are conspiring against me and would like to discredit Mr Johnson in my eyes.' She had softened her tone a little now, which pleased him better.

'That I would not wish to do, but I do know something of the reputation of these people and their effect of splitting families by encouraging them to leave the country. Women in particular are vulnerable to their silken tongues, and there is a growing resentment in England at the number of young women who are being taken to America.' He was aware of the fire which came into her eyes but not prepared for the venom in her voice.

'Good God, Mr Palmer, what do you think we women are, creatures without brains?' Her eyes flashed again. 'Perhaps it is the gentleness of their ways and their respect for women that attracts us to them. Threats from pompous men are not a solution, I'm afraid. I am not likely to allow myself to be dragged off unwillingly, I assure you!'

She stood before him proudly, with her head raised in defiance, and he had a desire to shake her. She was the first woman ever to have aroused such strong emotion in him, and he was quite taken aback. Controlling himself with difficulty, he faced her and with some emphasis replied, 'So, my dear Miss Webster, you find me pompous do you?' His angular jaw was determinedly set and his stern grey eyes searched her face, seeking to penetrate her animosity. He almost enjoyed the challenge and took a step closer without knowing why, but the flicker of alarm on her face held him back and when he did speak his voice was hoarse. 'Don't be hasty—you may regret it!'

His plea seemed genuine enough, and she was almost sorry that her treatment of him was as if it had been for Mr Wallace, but he had come on the same mission, of that there was no doubt.

'It is already too late, Mr Palmer,' she said adamantly. 'I have studied much in the past two weeks and I am to be baptised into their faith within the week!'

'Then you are a bigger fool than I gave you credit for!' He was angry now, with her and himself for allowing her to rile him so much. 'Does your brother know of this folly?'

'Not yet, and I'll thank you not to inform him. I will do that after the event.' She stood her ground, angered in her turn by his effrontery and wishing that she had not revealed her intentions.

'Do you realise that you will be turning your back on everything that you hold dear? Your brother told Mr Wallace and me in the first instance that he would have none if it in his house. I fear you will destroy this family with your stubbornness!'

'George can do what he likes, as he has no understanding of my feelings, and unless he is willing to listen to both sides of the argument then he has no right to complain about my actions.' She paused for breath, and, realising that he was watching her and listening quietly, she spoke again, softly and patiently. 'Mormons believe that the truth has been lost and fragmented between so many religions, and that God's wishes are no longer observed. That the power of authority to act in God's name was lost also, and now God has seen fit to restore it in our times. Why can't you listen fairly to their reasoning, without prejudice?'

Having regained his self-control, James Palmer spoke firmly but with authority. 'What right have they to claim to be the sole intermediary with God, when so many good men in the past have given their lives for His sake, and yet have never spoken with Him? All this talk of descending angels seems highly unlikely after all these centuries!'

Becky no longer felt threatened by him. Her confidence had returned, and she pressed him for an answer to his own theory. 'Why does it? I thought God to be all-powerful. Is it not up to him to decide if and when it is time for him to speak to men? You are a man of God—do you not think he has the power to appear, and have you no explanation as to why there has been no heavenly intervention since Christ's time?'

Removing his spectacles, he rubbed his eyes wearily, 'You now argue cleverly,' he said, with admiration in his voice. 'It would appear that I will have my work cut out if I am to convince you of your mistake.' He replaced the glasses and his eyes became serious and cool again. 'Think carefully before you take the final step', he pleaded.

Becky, however, was not to be thwarted. 'You have not answered my question! Is it so impossible for God to speak to men? And why is it so wrong, as Mr Wallace and others think, for people to question in order to better understand the ways of God? Or do they think people will find fault with their explanations?'

'Unfortunately, Mr Wallace is only one of many who believe in blind obedience, and to challenge them and the Church is considered blasphemous. I am perhaps more open-minded than some Ministers, but understanding how they think makes me fear for your good reputation.' The sound of carriage wheels filtered through the window, bringing their discussion to an abrupt end. 'I'm afraid I've overstayed my welcome, Miss Webster, but I would be obliged if you could let me know when you have arranged a meeting with Mr Johnson. Withdrawing a visiting card from his pocket and handing it to her he added, 'Please don't hesitate to contact me if you need me. Remember that in spite of our differences my help will always be available'. He took her hand fleetingly in his own slim fingers, shook hands, and was gone.

It was several minutes before George and Sarah reached the room, sufficient time for Becky to arrange her thoughts but, try as she might, she could not erase the feel of his touch from her fingers.

Chapter 11

In spite of Becky's stated intention to James Palmer, Adam was not sufficiently well for several weeks to conduct the meeting or go down to the river for her baptism. Becky particularly wanted Adam to perform the ceremony and so it was late September before he could do so. This delay gave James Palmer fresh hope that it had merely been a defiant threat. It was really none of his business and he was powerless to do anything but await further developments, yet he was disturbed in his mind about the whole affair. Mr Wallace, however, was only too eager to keep him informed of any activity taking place down by the river and it came as a shock one afternoon to hear from him that Miss Webster had taken it upon herself to submit to fanciful doctrines.

The afternoon sun had been warm as it fell on the scene, enhancing the glorious autumn tints of the leaves, but Becky was cold as she was escorted carefully over the stones and rocks in the river to where Adam and Luke were already waiting waist deep in the cold, murky water. She did not feel well but Adam beckoned her forward and she knew that there was little point in postponing the ceremony still further. She hesitated, fearing the depth of the water, but two men held her arms to steady her as she caught her foot on a stone. Holding down the gown against the billowing current she could feel the material getting heavier as it absorbed water and she shivered as it clung to her body.

'Take courage—it will only take a minute, and will be a day to remember all your life', Luke said encouragingly as they went deeper. She was passed by strong gentle hands to Adam, and his smile was serene as he took her fingers and placed them on her nose.

'Hold your breath when we lower you down into the water and don't let your legs come up. I will lower you backwards and if we do the job properly first time we won't have to dip you twice.' He was thrilled. No one knew the joy he was feeling to be baptising his own daughter, but it was his secret and one he would never be able to share.

She smiled weakly, 'I'm scared!'

'Trust me.' he said. 'Don't think of the cold but of what it will mean. A new beginning in your life.' Placing one hand over hers as she held her nose and the other in the small of her back he lowered her quickly backwards beneath the surface of the river. His voice rang out loud and clear, 'I baptise thee in the name of The Father, The Son and The Holy Ghost, Amen!'

The shock of the cold water stunned her, but as she sank beneath the surface all fear left her. Her mind became suddenly clear, and void of everything except the strange feeling of peace which blotted out all thought. Then it was over and the water parted, revealing the clear sky above and Adam's encouraging smile. 'Let's get you to the bank quickly,' he said, breaking her trance. 'The sisters have blankets ready, and your dry clothes.' They helped her back to the water's edge and Becky shivered violently as she was shielded from the crowd which had gathered to watch the spectacle. With her huddled beneath a blanket they hurried towards a rough screen where she endeavoured to dry and dress herself with numbed fingers.

She was grateful when two of the Sisters with rough linen towelling massaged her cold limbs and she sipped thankfully at the hot gruel handed to her by one of the women, she wondered if she would ever feel warm again.

Concealed amongst the curious crowds, the pious Mr Wallace watched the whole proceedings contemptuously , as he had done many times over the past year. Like many other Ministers he found every new conversion to the American sect harder to bear, but it was becoming difficult to disregard its swelling ranks, especially those who had dissented from his own order. With furious haste he left the scene and arrived at Bank House, breathless, with the news.

'You want to disown her', he remonstrated with George, who fumed at the news. 'She made a spectacle of herself in the river with those men, dripping wet she was with her clothes clinging to her body like a woman with no morals. Get rid of her before she bewitches the other girl—that's my advice!' He promptly departed, leaving George beside himself with rage, and set off to find James Palmer at the school where he worked. Not that James could do anything, the deed was done.

The house was strangely quiet as Becky approached and the door refused to open to her touch. It was locked! She knocked hard but there was no reply, so she walked round to the back, but no door or window would yield itself to her touch. Returning to the front door she found a large valise together with an envelope addressed to herself. It had not been there on her arrival, and someone must have placed it there whilst she had been round the back of the house.

She tore open the letter, intrigued by the fact that it was in George's handwriting. The message was bold and clear enough:

> *You went against my wishes today. You are no longer*
> *welcome here and your influence on Sarah is undesirable.*
> *Here are some of your things—let your new friends take*
> *care of you now.*
>
> *George*

166

Gasping, she clutched the letter and leaned against the portal of the door. The walk up the hill had tired her and her head ached. As the afternoon had worn on she had slowly been overcome by a feeling of weakness, and the shivering which she had experienced in the water had returned. They had gone to old Tom's from the river and although her dishevelled hair had now dried, she longed to wash the filthy river water from it. She had imagined that a soak in a hot tub would take away the weakness but even that comfort was to be denied her.

How dare he do this? What right had he to bar her from their house? She banged hard on the door but all she heard was the echoing sound of her knock ringing through the hall. She knew her brother's stubborn ways by now, knew too that further knocking would be futile and would only give him satisfaction, and she certainly wouldn't give him that.

Lifting the valise she turned, angry and dispirited, and headed back down the hill to find Adam. She would fight George another day when she felt less dizzy, less feverish.

A carriage approached, heading in the direction of the house and she stepped aside to let it pass, almost dropping the valise as she did so.

'Whoa, there!' A voice boomed and the horse's hooves clattered sharply to a halt, sending sparks flying into the air.

'Miss Webster, wait a minute!' A voice rang out from within the carriage itself. 'Please, don't go any further!' She turned to find James Palmer leaning out of the carriage window. He opened the door and climbed down but by this time Becky was hurrying down the lane with no intention of stopping. Striding after her he soon caught up, 'You stubborn young woman,' he hissed, catching her arm. 'I know the trouble you're in—that is why I came.'

'To gloat!' she retorted, angrily, but almost in tears.

He stepped in front of her, forcing her to stop. Her face was pale and her eyes distressed. 'Where will you go—do you have relatives?'

'I will go to my new-found friends, as George puts it!' She thrust the note angrily into his hand. 'Did you have a hand in this? Someone must have told George, and so quickly too!' Her voice was accusing and full of scorn, but there were tears in her eyes and his heart went out to her.

'No, I did not!' James Palmer assured her, 'Mr Wallace saw the whole event and went directly to your brother. He then came to see me and told me all about it. I knew how your brother would react—he had intimated as much once before. I came immediately to see if I could smooth things over between the pair of you!'

'Well, you are too late, Mr Palmer. That stubborn brother of mine has thrown me out, without means of support. Neither do I have any money until I sort things out!'

'You must go back—I will see that he takes you back!'

'I will not go back there until he apologises!' Her voice was not as strong as it had been at first, and he suspected that she was far from well.

'You must not go to the Americans,' he blurted out. 'Your reputation would be ruined forever. People will say things about you that are not true but they will stick and you will be disgraced in the eyes of society.'

'Then where am I to go?' she demanded, irritably.

He hesitated, afraid that she would misunderstand his suggestion or reject it. 'I have a home,' he offered, 'in Glossop Road. May I offer you my hospitality, humble though it is?'

'You, Sir! And what makes it more respectable, sharing your house rather than Mr Johnson's?' Her laugh rang out hysterically across the adjacent fields.

He seized her arm. 'Be quiet young lady,' he snapped angrily, glancing anxiously towards the driver of the carriage. 'Do you want everyone to know your business? Is it not enough that you make an exhibition of yourself in the river, but now you let a town coachman hear your ungrateful tirade.' His grip tightened. 'You do not deserve my help nor that of my sister who keeps house for me!' he said with disdain.

She could feel his fingers biting into her flesh as he towered over her and she thought him angry enough to strike her. 'You owe me an apology, Miss Webster,' he said, his eyes as dark as thunder.

Unable to answer she stood gripping the valise which was becoming increasingly heavy the longer she held it, but she could not bring herself to give him his apology.

'I'm waiting!' he hissed, as though talking to a naughty child. 'I will not let go until I get one!'

'Then you shall wait all night,' she snapped, petulantly stamping her foot.

With that he lost his patience, released her and strode back to the carriage, determined to wash his hands of her.

She looked around at the gathering gloom of dusk. Weakness was replacing the anger which had consumed her and she knew she was being extremely foolish. To go on alone was both unsafe and unwise. She raised her hand to her forehead, aware of the clamminess there.

'Take me back to town!' James ordered the driver as he slammed the carriage door. He had done his best, and short of bundling her into the carriage he was powerless to help the obstinate woman. He sat back in his seat knowing that she would be at the mercy of every footpad and villain, yet he could not bring himself to plead with her to see sense.

Becky pressed on aware that she would have to walk through the dark streets of the town alone; she was tired and cold, and as the carriage passed her, gathering speed, she panicked and ran after it, shouting frantically, 'Mr Palmer! Mr Palmer! Please wait!'

The coach came to a halt but James Palmer remained within the shadows, unapproachable and unbending, waiting for her to come to him.

'I'm sorry,' she stammered. 'Please could I make use of your carriage in order to get to town?'

Saying nothing, he threw open the door and returned to the shadows, allowing her to struggle aboard with her valise. In the gloom of the carriage his face was stern and he said nothing. She knew that he was angry with her, and that she had been foolish, as searching for lodgings alone at night invited trouble. Her wretchedness increased the nearer they got to town and the silent man in the shadows watched her, aware of the dilemma she was in. 'Where do you wish to be dropped?' he asked, his voice cold and unfeeling.

She did not answer immediately, though she knew he had the upper hand, and that he alone could help her. 'Mr Palmer,' she begged 'I am truly sorry for my behaviour. Will you forgive me and take me with you to your home?'

'Why not?' he answered with cold indifference, 'If that is what you wish me to do.'

Sitting in the dark she reflected on the strange events that had led to her present predicament. James Palmer had deliberately come out of his way in order to help her, had offered her sanctuary, yet she had been extremely ungrateful to the man. Something about him made her want to rebel, perhaps it was because he watched her in the gloom from behind those spectacles, hiding behind them like a shield. There were moments, just fleeting moments when she saw something beyond the mask, an unguarded sign that perhaps he was human after all.

The jolting of the carriage made her senses reel, and in her misery as they came to a halt before his house, she whispered weakly, 'Mr Palmer, I feel most unwell. Would you be kind enough to carry my bag for me into the house?'

Picking up the bag he descended from the coach, leaving her to fend for herself and to follow him up the short path to the large Georgian door. She waited behind him, humiliated and wretched, until he had unlocked the door, then she obediently followed his stern, silent figure into the house.

No word had passed his lips since the moment when she had begged him to let her stay in his house, yet there was no sign of anger on his face. Finally, when he did speak it was without emotion and coldly polite. 'I will find Elizabeth. If you would kindly wait in here I will see that you receive a hot meal and a bath.' He opened a door and ushered her into a small sitting room where a fire glowed comfortably in the iron gate. Then he was gone.

Exhaustion and the heat from the fire made Becky sleepy as she sat awaiting his return. In the end she could no longer fight off the drowsiness, and when James Palmer returned with his sister he found her asleep in the uncomfortable hard-backed chair. She looked forlorn, helpless, and he knew that without his help she was in danger of becoming a waif, lost and alone. 'She's asleep, Elizabeth,' he said quietly, 'Leave her for now and get something hot for her to eat when she wakes. She has need of a bath too, you can almost smell the river on her from here.'

The small woman at his side replied kindly, 'She looks all in, poor girl. Leave her to me.' She went to reassure herself that Becky was not about to fall from the chair. 'She is unusually flushed, James. I would not be surprised if she is ill!'

Some time later a clatter within the house woke Becky with a start and she stared round in bewilderment at the unfamiliar room. As the misty haze of sleep began to clear she remembered where she was. The heat from the fire had made her hot but she could not find the strength to lift herself from the chair in order to remove her cloak. She had not lied to Mr Palmer; she really did not feel well at all.

Within minutes of her waking, the door opened quietly and a homely lady entered the room. 'Oh, my dear! You are awake!' The friendly voice continued, 'It seemed a pity to wake you. I am Elizabeth Palmer. My brother has told me of your plight—such a shame, but you are safe with us!'

Managing to smile weakly in return, Becky summoned sufficient strength to answer, 'I'm sorry to be such a nuisance, really I am!'

'Nonsense! You are not to worry about anything, I am only too pleased to help. You look exhausted, but I have a meal ready for you and will bring it in here on a tray. However, first you must get that heavy cloak off.' Helping Becky to rise from the chair to remove the garment, she realised the extent of Becky's fatigue. 'You are very hot my dear—I do hope you didn't get a chill in the river today. Never mind, a hot bath will do you the world of good, and I am boiling up the water now.'

Becky settled gratefully back in the chair and waited as Elizabeth Palmer left the room to return later with a tray, but in spite of the well-prepared meal, Becky found that she had little appetite.

'Do try to eat something.' Elizabeth coaxed, although by this time she was becoming quite alarmed at the flushed face of her brother's guest. 'Even a little will give you strength.'

How Becky got through the meal and walked, even with support, to the kitchen where they had prepared the bath tub, she hardly knew. 'Let me wash your hair first,' Elizabeth said kindly, 'it smells of the river. Bend over the tub while I pour the pitcher of water over your head.' Even the clean fresh water did nothing to improve Becky's feeling of weakness and when eventually she climbed into the tub of water her body shook uncontrollably. 'I'll leave you alone to your toilet,' Elizabeth offered. 'Give me a call when you have finished.'

She left Becky and went directly to confront her brother in his study. 'I really am concerned, James. I think Miss Webster is ill. Can you imagine, bathing in that river at this time of year? The weather has been quite chilly of late. I suspect she has the start of a fever and I have heated the bed to help her sweat it out.'

'The woman is impossible, Elizabeth, but I could not see her thrown out on the street like that. I shall go to her brother in the morning and attempt to smooth things over.'

Becky sat in the water caring little if she was dirty or not, but in spite of the warmth of the kitchen she was still cold and unable to control her shivering. Her forehead burned as she endeavoured to wash but the room swam before her eyes. Elizabeth returned at that moment, and hastened to aid her.

'James! James!' Elizabeth called out frantically from the kitchen. 'Come immediately, Miss Webster is ill.' She seized the bath sheet from the chair in an effort to shield Becky from the eyes of her brother. 'I left her alone for privacy but I think she must have fainted.' Her voice was anxious as she continued, 'I can't lift her. You will have to do it.'

His face was drawn with worry, 'But she's naked Elizabeth, I cannot touch her, it isn't right!'

'But you can't leave here there!' she remonstrated. 'She'll catch her death, if she hasn't done so already.' She was almost in tears, 'Don't be so proper, I'll wrap this sheet tightly round her then you must lift her.'

He bent low, plucking Becky from the tub, endeavouring to avert his eyes from her body. She was lighter than he had expected, and softer too. Her head fell wet against his shoulder and he could feel the heat of the burning, dripping body through his shirt. 'She certainly does have a fever,' he heard himself say. 'I must get her to bed with hot stones and if she is no better tomorrow we will have to fetch the doctor.' He was almost as wet as Becky now and he looked down, half afraid to find her uncovered. He could see her face, softly cradled beneath his chin. 'What shall I do with her now?' His voice was steady but it belied the tenderness which he felt. He did not want to put her down. He held her close, possessively, yet he was disturbed by his desire to keep her there. His face was flushed with embarrassment at his inner thoughts and he looked helplessly towards Elizabeth.

'Don't be so silly,' Elizabeth laughed at him. 'Lower her onto the chair, I will dry her and dress her. I'll call you when I have done.'

James Palmer was not himself as he left the room to wait in his study. Every nerve in his body seemed taut with unfamiliar desires. He placed his hands on the high mantel-shelf and stood over the fire to dry his clothes. He groaned, resting his head on his hands and stared into the embers of the fire. No other woman had ever disturbed him half as much as the rebellious Miss Webster did. She was the most infuriating creature he had ever set eyes on. His mind was in turmoil now and the memory of the softness of her body against him, gave him no peace. He bent to throw another log onto the fire, but could not blot out his desire to hold her again. Damn! What wickedness was this that made him lust after a helpless, unconscious woman, a man in his position? Anger welled up inside him at his own weakness and he resolved to harden his heart against her before he made a fool of himself. There was a noise behind him and he spun round. It was Elizabeth, but he had no idea how long she had been there.

'She is awake, but is delirious and burning up. I have put the stones back in the oven for a while. Will you take her upstairs, please?'

With stern purposeful strides he reached the kitchen and seized Becky's shivering body roughly in his arms. 'Oh! James! Do be more gentle', Elizabeth remonstrated. 'You are hopeless, you have no idea how to behave with a woman. It is time you found yourself a wife.'

'This is a pretty kettle of fish we're landed with, Elizabeth,' he replied sternly, ignoring her remarks, 'and not a situation in which I wish to find myself again!'

Step by careful step he worked his way up the stairs, holding Becky tightly against his body, all the while acutely aware of her murmurings and unconscious clinging. She was completely in his power at that moment, undefiant, dependent, and cradled in his arms. Nevertheless he sensed that the power which she now held over him was by far the greater. Elizabeth pulled back the bedclothes and he laid her down on the white cotton sheet and pillow. In that moment James came to the realisation that he was capable after all of great tenderness and passion. Elizabeth momentarily left the room and as he looked down on Becky's flushed face and tousled hair, he cried hoarsely to himself, 'I will wed you before long. You will be my wife or else I'll be destroyed by my desires!'

Elizabeth Palmer stayed by Becky's bedside watching faithfully as she tossed and turned continuously through the long hours of night. She mopped the girl's beaded brow and re-heated the stones with which to sweat out the fever, wondering who this 'Adam' was for whom the sick woman cried out so constantly in her delirium. At six, James entered the bedroom to find both women sleeping peacefully, one in bed and the other most uncomfortably in a chair. Becky's face was still flushed but she slept calmly now, a stirring picture before him, and he knew that the worst was over. He touched Elizabeth gently on the shoulder and woke her. 'You have done well,' he spoke gratefully in a low voice so as not to wake Becky. 'Go and get some proper sleep and I will attend to everything now.'

He closed the door behind them both, leaving Becky alone. 'She's sleeping peacefully now but I will listen in case she calls out.'

Elizabeth yawned, 'She'll be alright. I knew it an hour ago but could not trust myself to leave, just in case the fever returned!'

'You have done enough and I am grateful. Now go and get some sleep!' he ordered firmly.

Occasionally over the next two hours he quietly opened Becky's door and found her sleeping peacefully. When the creaking hinges eventually disturbed her she found herself facing James Palmer.

Pulling the bedcover closer to shield herself from his gaze, she looked around the room apprehensively, her eyes wide with anxiety. 'Where am I?' she begged in confusion. 'How did I get here?'

'Don't you remember anything at all?' He asked softly. 'You came in the carriage with me rather than search the town for lodgings. Do not distress yourself, you are safe here with my sister and me until you are fit to leave.'

'Yes, I remember, but what happened—why am I in bed and feeling so weak?'

'After arriving you became unconscious and have been feverish all night. My sister sat with you until two hours ago but now she is resting. You must have caught a chill yesterday but the worst is over, thank goodness. How do you feel?' There was genuine concern on his face.

'Quite weak, but I felt ill all day yesterday even before I went into the river. What time is it?'

'Gone eight, but there is no need to be alarmed; it is Saturday and I have few commitments today. Would you like something to eat?' He came closer, where she could see him more clearly, and waited for her to answer.

'I have been the cause of so much trouble,' she said sadly, 'and I am truly grateful to you both for your help. Yes, I would like something to eat, please. Then I must set about putting things to rights.' She tried to sit up but the room spun round. 'Oh, dear!' she cried, 'I do feel strange!'

'You are going nowhere, Madam!' His tone was firm, leaving no room for argument. 'You are to stay in bed all day. I will go to Bank House and consult your brother before any more of this nonsense takes place. You must remain under this roof until things are sorted out and you are completely restored to full health again, otherwise I shall have to answer to my sister for the consequences.' He left the room, considering the matter closed, and she realised that she was in no condition to protest.

Once he had gone she looked around the room again. How had she got upstairs, for surely his sister had not been able to carry her? He must have brought her here, for she could not have walked. She flushed, who had lifted her, bedraggled and uncovered as she must have been, from the bath tub? She closed her eyes to rid herself of the possibilities. How it must have pleased him to see her thus, finally humiliated and defeated. She decided not to question what had occurred, fearing the worst and refusing to give him the satisfaction of seeing her further humbled.

He re-appeared, almost relaxed, in his rolled-up shirt sleeves and carrying a wooden tray. 'I have coddled an egg, and there's a little buttered bread, as lunch will not be ready until one o'clock. I am preparing the meal whilst Elizabeth catches up on her sleep, but everything will be ready on time.' He seemed oblivious to her embarrassment, and when finally she met his gaze it was impersonal, almost withdrawn, that of a stranger again. In his shirt sleeves he looked younger than before, and master of his house. What a mess she must look! As if reading her thoughts he said, 'I will bring water for washing when you have eaten and there are toiletries on the dresser over there.'

By the time she had tidied herself, James Palmer had left the house to call upon George. He was right of course, she was too weak to stand and her head ached, making it impossible for her to do anything but remain in bed. She lay half-sleeping, half-waking, never quite sure where she was.

His visit to Bank House was not a success. At first George had welcomed James Palmer with open arms until he received the news that Becky was staying at his house in Glossop Road. 'You had no right to take her in when I had thrown her out!' George fumed. 'I asked for your help in the first place to stop her making a fool of herself, and much good it was. Your help came a bit too late. She has disgraced us all!'

'I think,' James Palmer protested, 'that you would do better to consider your part in the affair. I do not approve of what your sister has done but she is not beyond help nor become so changed overnight. She is ill from a chill she caught and must remain in bed a day or two. I suggest you reconsider the matter thoroughly for Monday and then make your peace. You should know your sister better than to think that she will come begging for forgiveness, although I presume that she has some legal rights in this house?' George bridled at this last remark and although he chose to ignore it, James Palmer knew that he had made his point.

'I do not want her here when Sarah returns from visiting friends in Rotherham', George stated flatly. 'Sarah has been influenced too much by the Johnson's already and the less she sees of them from now on the better. Now I'll thank you to leave my house!'

But James had more to say. 'I'll leave, but I think you are being foolish—and for what? She is just as stubborn as you and there are more subtle ways of resolving the matter.' He placed his hat angrily on his head. 'Give it careful thought for Monday and then if you wish to make amends you know where I live.' He turned and walked away, leaving George to consider the matter.

Becky slept for most of the day, unaware of James' futile visit to Bank House. Elizabeth Palmer was kindness itself, fussing, visiting and caring, until by Sunday lunchtime Becky was fit to sit up and read. In fact by the time James returned from Church in the evening she was dressed and downstairs, sitting by the fire.

He seemed genuinely pleased to see her. 'You look much better,' he said brightly, as he crossed the room and saw her rise to her feet. 'Do you feel better?'

She smiled weakly, conscious of the trouble she had put him to. 'Thank you, yes I do, Mr Palmer. I fear that if you had not been there that night things would have been very difficult for me, to say the least.'

'That is good, but Miss Webster, must you continue to call me Mister in my own house? My name is James and I would be quite happy if you could call me that.' There was a playful smile on his lips which made it difficult for her to do anything other than to agree. She was not very happy about being quite so informal but she was beholden to him and under the circumstances it was the least she could do, especially as she was calling his sister Elizabeth. She did not however, give him permission to call her Becky.

'Then it is settled, Miss Webster. Now I wonder if there is a meal ready for this hungry mortal, I did not excuse Elizabeth from Church just to take care of you!' There was even a touch of humour in his voice.

Why she had not allowed him the same privilege of calling her by her first name she did not know, but throughout supper she refrained from addressing him directly and avoided meeting his eyes.

Mistaking her reluctance for shyness he relaxed, and in order to retain her company a little longer, asked, 'Do you play chess, Miss Webster?'

'A little, but I'm not an expert,' she confessed. 'Are you?'

He chuckled, 'No! I certainly am not—but as Elizabeth rarely plays I wonder if you feel up to a game?'

Becky excused herself, promising a game as soon as she felt well enough; she was however, more concerned that he appeared reluctant to discuss his visit to Bank House, and asked, 'You did go to see George, I presume? Was he so difficult that you refrain from telling me what he said?'

'Do you feel well enough to discuss your affairs tonight?' He raised his eyebrow questioningly. 'I do not wish to pry but thought to allow you to forget your problems for a while. I'm afraid your brother was adamant about you not returning to the house, but as I pointed out to him you do have some rights, no matter what he says. I suggested that we should give him until tomorrow to reconsider the whole silly situation, and if he does not change his mind then I think you should seek legal advice.'

'Becky sighed, I cannot believe the change that has come over him these past few months. The problem is that the house is George's; as I have my Lincolnshire property and a share in the business, he, along with Sarah, has Bank House. I don't really know why that is, except that the farm was left to me before either of them were born. I am not really fitted to take any employment other than as a housekeeper, and if I sell my shares in the business I am without security. As things are at the moment with Mr Johnson's involvement, George would be hard pressed to raise enough capital to pay me out.'

'Oh, I didn't realise that Mr Johnson had any business connections with your family.' He seemed taken aback by the news. 'How does this come about? I thought it was purely a religious matter that disturbed your brother.'

'It goes deeper than that. Let me explain.' Taking a deep breath she continued, 'Mr Johnson left some money behind in Sheffield twenty-six years ago and my parents invested this in the business after the fire which destroyed their original premises. Mother left instructions that Mr Johnson was to be paid out with interest should he ever return, and now that he has returned George suspects his motives—yet Mr Johnson did not even know that the money still existed!'

James fell silent realising that there might not be a quick solution to the problem. Instead he could see that there were going to be even more difficulties ahead. After pondering for a few moments he suggested, 'Then George may have to adjust his thinking. You ought to work through a solicitor, but give him until tomorrow night to think things over. How is Sarah fixed? Could he throw her out as well if provoked sufficiently?'

Becky shook her head. 'Sarah's case is different. The old aunt who left me the farm had an unmarried daughter and the instructions in her will were that on the daughter's demise I was to have the property. Neither George nor Sarah were born when that will was drawn up. They, therefore, have bigger shares in the business than I, and George has to provide for Sarah. I have no legal share in the house—but why should he want to throw Sarah out? She is not as independent as I am.' She saw him smile to himself, and added, 'The matter would surely not arise, would it? She asked anxiously.

He waved his hand as if to dismiss the matter, and replied, 'I merely wondered what will happen when she returns to find you gone!'

'I think perhaps, knowing Sarah, she will cry and maybe pout a little at George, that is all. I will write her a note to say I am well, but it would help if she could visit me here to see for herself.'

'Of course, she will be welcome,' he agreed.

For a while they sat quietly in the cosy sitting room each deep in their own thoughts, feeling no need to converse. The mantel clock struck nine, bringing Becky back to the present. She would be sorry to leave this comfortable room, small though it was after the spaciousness of Bank House. She was growing fond of Elizabeth too and was even beginning to appreciate a warmer side to James Palmer's character than she had imagined he possessed. Once, she had caught his eye and was intrigued by the strange expression she saw on his face. However, the long day had taken its toll and she was quite beyond further discussion. She rose slowly from the chair to take her leave. 'Thank you for your help,' she said. 'Tomorrow evening, I will play chess with you, but now I am very tired and would like to retire.'

He rose too and opened the door for her, 'I shall look forward to our game, very much!' His voice was almost tender now. 'Good night', he called softly after her.

Chapter 12

*B*ecky waited all day Monday, impatient for a message from George, but this did not come and she knew that she would have to take steps to rearrange her life if she was not to bow to his demands. She resolved that on Tuesday morning she would see Mr Grayson on her own behalf, letting George know that she intended to make a stand.

James Palmer returned from work hoping the matter might have been settled during the day, and also, secretly hoping that Miss Webster's sickness still prevented her from leaving the house. He was almost in a jubilant mood by the time dinner was over and the promised game of chess was started.

With a stealthy cunning Becky moved her Queen to cover his King. 'Checkmate!' she cried excitedly, clasping her hands with glee. 'I have it and you owe me a shilling!' The triumph in her eyes made them sparkle and James Palmer found himself watching her with silent admiration.

Passing the coin across the exquisitely inlaid mahogany table on which the chess board stood, James conceded that she had won, fair and square. 'I admit defeat Miss Webster,' he laughed. 'Tomorrow night I shall challenge you to another game and take it back from you.' He lay back in his chair. During the game he had been content to watch her as she lost herself in concentration, enjoying her unselfconscious delight when she was winning and the good humour when she lost. She had captivated him. It was years since he had enjoyed himself so much, and he found her a delightful companion, capable of more than just idle chit-chat.

Moving to more comfortable chairs by the fire, they joined Elizabeth. 'I have a surprise,' he announced mysteriously, then bent over the drawer of a side table and like a magician withdrew, with a flourish, a small paper package which he tossed on the table. 'Marshmallows! We shall roast marshmallows by the fire.' His eyes twinkling, he demanded, 'Elizabeth, where is the fork?'

Seated between brother and sister in the light of the glowing embers of the fire, Becky waited eagerly as he toasted each delicately flavoured sweet. This warm companionship was soothing away the ills of the past few days, and she had no desire to retire to her bed. Instead, she lowered herself from her chair and sat on the rug in front of the fire, chatting amicably with Elizabeth, and leaving James to amuse himself.

He was content enough to sit watching the occasional flame highlight the colour of Becky's hair, and as he bent closer with the toasting fork he fought off the desire to caress it with his hand. It was perhaps as well that they were not alone, for the desire in him to touch her was growing. He had tried all evening to read her face, and her eyes, waiting for a sign of encouragement, but none came. She had not even addressed him directly by his Christian name, almost as though she had placed a screen between them behind which she could keep him at arm's length. He wanted so much to hold her and to touch her face gently with his fingers, to bury his face in her hair as he had done with no other woman.

She was unaware of his watchful eye and before long found herself again succumbing to the warmth and cosiness of the room. Nor was she aware that in dozing she had relaxed backwards and now rested against his legs. Elizabeth raised her eyes to his in amusement, but he shook his head and whispered softly, 'Leave her, she is at peace. You go to bed and I'll wake her when the fire goes low'.

He sat for some time, indulging himself in her closeness until in the end he laid his hand caressingly on her head and said, 'Miss Webster. It would be better if you went to bed. The fire is almost out and it is getting late. Elizabeth has already gone and I have much to do tomorrow.' He took her hand to help her rise.

Unsure of where she was, Becky stirred. Her face was barely inches away from him now and so pretty in sleepiness, but he knew he would be foolish to take advantage of her. She seemed unaware that he held her hand far longer than was necessary or that his head was so close. It was as well that she could not feel the desire within him, for she would have been horrified by the intensity of it.

In standing, she became awake. 'It has been a wonderful evening, and I am grateful to you both,' she said softly. 'And now I have to think about tomorrow.'

'Have you decided what to do?'

'You know, I am very fond of my brother, but he is as stubborn as I am, and when cornered will not take the easy way out. I would ask one more favour of you—could I stay a little while longer—it will give me time to organise things?'

'Aren't you going to tell me of your plans?' he asked, eyeing her cautiously.

'No! But I think it will work out amicably—if I can stay here?'

'To make him sweat it out?'

She smiled demurely. 'I must be wary of you Mr Palmer. You are beginning to read my thoughts.'

'You've done it again Miss Webster, and broken our agreement. My name is James—is that so difficult to bring yourself to say?' He wasn't angry but there was an intensity in his voice which disturbed her. 'You are in danger of hurting my feelings by treating me this way!' He was mocking her, his face stern. 'You tease me, I suspect!' His pale grey eyes searched her face and when she did not answer he grasped her wrist, preventing her from leaving. 'Say it!' He demanded more harshly than intended, not wanting to let her go.

Suddenly she was caught up in a game, his game, and it seemed he wanted to dominate her. It was only a game but his face was grave as though his life depended on her obeying him. The gentle man had disappeared and she was faced by a man consumed with a passion. The pressure of his grip on her wrist increased and with a desperate urgency he pulled her closer to him until his lips were almost touching hers, his breath warm on her face. 'Say it!' he begged fiercely.

This was a stranger before her, one whose persistence frightened and unnerved her. She heard her own voice cry out, 'Stop it, James! Stop it!' But he had held himself in check too long and the sweet scent of her now destroyed his reserve entirely. He no longer cared, and at the mention of his name he caught her to him, roughly, demanding, before his lips sought her protesting mouth. She could not breathe as she struggled for freedom, then his fingers entwined her hair and his mouth sought her throat. She was numbed but he must have sensed that she was about to scream, for suddenly he released her.

'How dare you!' she cried out angrily, 'How dare you!' How could he have done such a thing when she had just begun to like him?

He saw the anger in her eyes. 'Damn you!' he cried hoarsely. 'I did not intend to do that!' He stared at her ashen face. 'You will find that hard to believe, but it is true!'

Becky rested her hand on the back of the chair for support and stood staring at him in disbelief. 'Why?' she begged, half in tears.

'Because you drive me to distraction, Miss Webster!' he sighed. 'But you need not fear me again for the incident will not be repeated, and I will keep out of your way until you leave. Nor do you have to go away on my behalf—you have my word.' So saying, he bowed awkwardly and left the room.

Twice now within a few days she had suffered at the hands of men, and those who were supposed to care for her, but instead they cared for nothing other than their own ego. She was sad too with disappointment, and sorry that he had spoilt their growing friendship. Lifting her fingers to her lips she found herself unable to erase the burning passion of his mouth on hers and vowed never to be alone with him again. But to whom could she speak of her problems? She was alone. There was only Adam! With a start she realised that in the days which had just passed she had almost forgotten

Adam, with his gentle voice; he too had had many bitter disappointments. Only he would understand her problems, and tomorrow she would find him.

Next morning, Becky refused to go down to breakfast until she heard the door close behind James Palmer. She had begun to think that he would never leave the house, and that Elizabeth would come in search of her, giving her no option but to face him. However, on reaching the kitchen she realised that his sister had no idea that anything untoward had happened. Elizabeth seemed equally disgruntled by his behaviour. 'James was very annoying this morning,' she complained 'and behaving like a crusty old bachelor at that, I'm quite pleased to see the back of him!'

'All brothers are troublesome,' Becky replied, trying not to arouse his sister's suspicions, and pleased that at least he had remained silent about the incident. 'Did he tell you that I would not be staying much longer?'

'He said very little, but I gather from his mutterings that you may be staying a couple more days until you have sorted things out. I'm pleased for I shall miss your company when you leave—you have brought a touch of sunshine into this kitchen.' Her smile was warm and loving.

Poor Elizabeth, thought Becky, I shall be going much quicker than you expect, leaving you all alone with your intemperate brother! Gently she answered and with sincerity, 'I shall miss you too, but we can still remain friends when I am gone. You have come to mean much to me!' She was close to tears for she really had become quite fond of the motherly Elizabeth.

Shortly after eleven o'clock Becky resolutely entered Mr Grayson's office, having made her decision, and determined to see it through no matter what George or James Palmer thought, even if it left her with no option but to find somewhere else to live. Neither man was going to get the better of her!

'Mr Grayson,' Becky began, 'I wish you to write a letter as soon as possible on my behalf, and despatch it today to my brother George at his business address in Rockingham Street. Please will you inform him that if he does not apologise for his behaviour in throwing me out of the house, and allow me back in again, I will have no alternative but to realise my share in the business immediately. This is not an idle threat, I really have no other choice if I am to survive on my own.'

Mr Grayson groaned inwardly, he was distressed by the recent upheaval in the once happy home of his clients. Nevertheless, he complied with Becky's wishes.

Having completed her business she next intended seeing Adam, but he was unfortunately not at home, and reluctantly she returned to the Palmer's house with a great deal of trepidation. The thought of coming face to face with James Palmer did not bear thinking about, although with any luck he would not return before the evening. She need not have feared for, on entering the house, she was met by Elizabeth with the news that James had unexpectedly gone away for a few days.

Elizabeth was in a state of agitation, her hands and face both covered in soot and her hair dishevelled. 'Whatever has happened?' Becky asked in amazement.

'I have had a day of days!' Elizabeth exclaimed, 'James came home as bad-tempered as he left this morning, saying he was going away, and I had to help him pack. Shortly after he left, your sister arrived on the doorstep in tears, accompanied by Mr Johnson and his son, all asking for you. Then to top it all there has been a fall of soot in the kitchen.' She brushed wisps of unruly hair back from her face in exasperation.

Feeling responsible for half the morning's interruptions, Becky offered to help. 'Come on, I'll help you clean up, it's not perhaps as bad as it looks. Have you any old clothes that I can wear whilst I work?' Taking an old dress and cap from Elizabeth she asked casually, 'Where has James gone? It's rather sudden isn't it? He was going to play chess again tonight.'

'I found it rather strange, to say the least. He was quite snappy and secretive about his visit, and that's not like him at all. He did ask me to tell you that he hopes your efforts today will solve your problems and that you will be back home before he returns. I'm sure he didn't mean it quite the way it came out but he was in such a dreadful hurry. He has left no forwarding address either.'

Suspecting that he had left deliberately in order to avoid any contact with her, Becky wasn't sure of her feelings on the matter. If he had indeed kept his promise to keep out of her way rather than face her contempt, well, she would not disappoint him, she would be gone within twenty-four hours! She did, however, owe Elizabeth an explanation. 'I have taken steps this afternoon to resolve the problem Elizabeth. But what of Sarah, what did you tell her?'

'Oh dear, I should have told you that first, before pouring out all my troubles. She was very upset to find you out, especially when she learned that you had been ill. It appears that your brother omitted to tell her that. I reassured her that you were completely recovered and told her that you were expected here late this afternoon. Apparently Sarah returned home last night to be confronted with the news of your departure by your brother, who was still angry. This morning she went straight to Mr Johnson's to seek his help and brought him here. I think I managed to reassure them all that you were in good hands, but Sarah was still very unhappy about the circumstances and as James was going to be away I invited them all to supper this evening. But that was before the soot fell—and now look at the mess I'm in!'

'Oh, Elizabeth!' Becky cried, putting her arm round Elizabeth's shoulder, 'you are a good soul. Let's clean this mess up before they come.' So, she thought, that's how Adam had found out where she was. Sarah, dear Sarah, had known what to do! She worked on, scrubbing and cleaning with fresh spirit, knowing that she would see him again soon. She wasn't exactly used to domestic work and it wasn't long before she too was covered in soot. It was a relief to know that James would not return and see her in such a state. Standing back, a little weary, but proud of her efforts, she said, 'Now we had better clean ourselves up before anyone sees us.'

The sound of the door-bell ringing through the house caused Elizabeth to shriek, 'Oh, no! Not the door-bell again! Will you go and see who it is? I have too much to do.'

At first Henry did not recognise his mistress in her ill-fitting dress and mop-cap, but when the truth finally dawned on him, a look of consternation crossed his face. 'Miss Becky!' he gasped, his eyes wide in disbelief. 'Is it you?'

'Yes, Henry! Of course it is.' She was resigned to the fact that she looked more like a charwoman than the Mistress of Bank House.

Recovering quickly, he replied tactfully, and referring to the cause of his visit. 'I beg your pardon, Miss, but I've come to collect you. Here's a letter from Mr George.'

So George was being presumptuous again was he? She took the letter, which was short and very much to the point:

> Becky,
> *I regret my haste of Friday evening and shall be obliged if you will return to the house in the carriage with Henry immediately.*
> *I apologise,*
> *George.*

Poor George. How difficult it must have been for him to write the letter and how damaging to his pride, as each word testified.

'Henry, you can see that I am in no fit state to return to the house now. We have had a fall of soot and I am helping Miss Palmer to clean up. Tell George that we have guests coming tonight and that I shall let him know if and when I intend to return.' Then as an afterthought she added, indicating her soiled garments, 'And be discreet, Henry! Just tell him that I am well—should he bother to ask!' Henry smiled knowingly and left.

Watching Henry disappear, she felt triumphant. She had won! Knowing George as she did, she knew that he would want to forget the matter as soon as possible, and for that reason alone she would make him suffer a little longer before returning home. As for James Palmer, she would depart before his return.

Four days later James Palmer arrived home, confident that Becky would by now have left his house. He knew that her pride would never permit her to stay a moment longer than necessary and although he could not face the contempt which would be on her face he was sorely depressed at the thought of her departure.

Having thought long and hard about his own behaviour, he had come to the conclusion that his only real regret in the matter was the haste with which he had declared himself. He was simply in love with the wretched woman, bewitched and possessed, and did not know how to rid himself of his desires. He was aware that he was not handsome or wealthy, in fact he had less to offer a woman in her position than many other men of her acquaintance. It was only when she had been dependent on him that he felt some sense of power over her, and he was in a thoroughly disagreeable frame of mind when he finally entered the house, still suffering from the malaise which had kept him from it for several days. He was being a fool, she had made that clear, yet he believed that their companionship could have flourished had he not been so impatient. Now he was left with a memory and a void which would be impossible to fill.

On entering the house he listened intently for the sound of voices. He could hear a clattering coming from the kitchen and nothing else. 'I'm back,' he called out to warn Elizabeth of his return and was grateful to find her alone. 'Miss Webster's gone, has she?' His voice concealed the true depth of his interest.

Elizabeth smiled, 'Yes, she went back yesterday and in happy spirits. But you look weary. Here, let me have your coat. Dare I ask where you went or is there some mystery to which I am not to be a party?'

Avoiding further comment about Miss Webster he merely informed her that he had been to Manchester to a college there, but that no great benefit had come out of the interview. Elizabeth was surprised. He had never expressed a desire to move before, but seeing his reluctance to enlighten her further she fell back to considering her own dilemma. Before long, however, he became aware of Elizabeth's pre-occupation and her reluctance to look him directly in the eye. She was avoiding facing him. Had Miss Webster revealed his misdemeanour? He hoped not! He had judged her to be incapable of spite or indiscreet comment.

He began to sense a tension in the house and as the afternoon wore on he became more and more irritated by Elizabeth's obvious agitation. It was not in his sister's nature to be devious and in the past he had often been perturbed by her soft-heartedness when put upon. As the atmosphere worsened he found that he could not stand the strain any longer, and in the end he was forced to bring the matter to a head, fearing that she had learned of his actions.

'Elizabeth,' he began cautiously, 'you are not displeased with me I hope?'

Raising startled eyes to his she stammered, 'I with you? It is I who have disappointed you!' Realising what she had said she raised her hand instinctively to her lips.

He stared, bewildered. 'I'm sorry, I don't understand. Is it about Miss Webster? How can you have disappointed me?'

'No! No!' she cried anxiously, 'It is not her fault, I assure you! It was my own doing.' He had never seen her in such a state before. 'I know that you did not approve of what she did, James, but you did not let it spoil your friendship, like her brother did.'

James Palmer shook his head, being completely at a loss as to what she was rambling about. 'I am very fond of Miss Webster,' he said lamely, 'but how does that effect you?' His bewilderment was now complete.

'I don't know where to begin!' Her voice was low as if anticipating an angry response from him. 'I have become very interested in the theory of her religion!' she confessed.

'What!' he exploded, slamming his hand down on the table. 'What did you say?' He was seething—so, Miss Webster had taken her revenge had she? By enticing Elizabeth away from him! 'How can you know anything about their beliefs? I have only been away four days. Has that woman whom I sought to help turned your head too?' He stared in disbelief. 'You can't be serious, Elizabeth. Not knowing what you do about the world.'

She nodded meekly, but was unwilling to be brow-beaten. 'It is no good your being angry—I find it all very plausible!' She had not intended to tell him this way but now that the truth was out she was not inclined to back down.

He sat glaring, half tempted to rage at her, but the irony of the situation struck him. Thankfully he was not like George Webster, who was inexperienced at dealing with human failings; there were other more subtle methods open to him and being hasty was not one of them. He had made that mistake before—to his regret.

'How much do you know? Miss Webster is hardly an expert on religion just because she took a dip in chilly, murky waters!'

'I have another confession to make,' she said sheepishly, trying to conceal her nervousness. 'I have been entertaining Mr Johnson and his son, together with Becky and Sarah. We have talked at length of things which have never really been clear to me before. I did not think that you would be home until tomorrow, you didn't inform me as you usually do, and they are all coming here again this evening!' She held her breath and said a silent prayer, waiting for an eruption of anger from him.

He said nothing, but the white knuckles of his clenched fists said it all. He realised he would need to tread warily, and he strove to calm himself down. Grim-faced, he sat staring at the table, as much disturbed by the change in Elizabeth as the blatant cheek of the Johnson's and Miss Webster. So this is how she had repaid his kindness, by destroying his life completely.

'If you don't wish to meet them I can keep them in the kitchen,' she offered. 'You don't have to see them at all, but I would like you to, and Becky would think it rather strange and rude if you did not!'

So it was blackmail now, and so unlike Elizabeth. What choice had he got? It was his duty to show both women the error of their ways and not allow these usurpers to entice Elizabeth away from him. Had he not offered to meet the Americans and discuss religion in a civilised manner? He must handle the situation tactfully, so he chose his words carefully. 'No, I will not shirk my duties as host, but I owe it to you to show you the error in their teachings. Please, sit down and tell me what they have said to you already!'

Surprised by his self-control and comforted by his more amenable attitude she sat down. The biggest battle, she felt, was over, and she had told him the truth.

By seven o'clock he had prepared himself thoroughly and was confident of his ability to answer any challenge which might arise. He had gone to a great deal of effort in such a short period of time, to study those aspects which Elizabeth had told him of, and in one or two instances was disturbed by his own lack of conviction. But, he had to prove them wrong and he did not want to bring in re-inforcements in the shape of Richard Wallace.

James Palmer had never set eyes on Adam but he was immediately struck by the man's friendliness and his remarkable likeness to Becky. He accepted the other man's cordial handshake but appeared not to see Becky who stood behind Adam. However, as the party was being shown into the living room, James blocked her path, cornering her in the hall. She froze. 'Don't worry, Miss Webster,' he hissed at her, 'I shall not touch you, but is this how you repay my hospitality, by taking your revenge and turning my sister away from me?'

She flinched, a look of dismay crossing her face at the intensity of his feelings. He immediately regretted his outburst, not really intending to accost her in such a manner. He tried to mutter an apology but she edged around him and quickly rejoined her companions in the other room.

She could think of little else but his harsh words which ran through her mind all evening. If she had known of his return she would not have come.

When he had delayed her from joining the others she had half expected him to seize her again, and was startled by her own mixed emotions at his nearness. Her mind was now reeling from the shock of this experience and his rejection of her.

During most of the evening Adam and Luke were locked in deep discussion with James, whilst the three women listened intently, but all were oblivious to her discomfort. The painful episode earlier lingered in Becky's mind, and prevented her from taking in the details of the conversation. All evening she was conscious of his proud, arrogant face, partially averted from her.

Through hidden tears she watched, resenting him more with every minute. He spoke with confidence but, watching his lips, she recoiled. She had felt that mouth on hers, pressing hard, warm and demanding. She quivered, ashamed to be remembering with such clarity, the passion of his embrace, and shaken by the strange warmth which was creeping over her. Suddenly she found him watching her and quickly avoided his eyes.

He had watched her for several seconds, knowing that she did not see him, puzzled by the far-away look on her face and the rising colour in her cheeks. With a start she came back to reality and caught his look. Her colour deepened, and the tremble on her lips stirred him. He was forced to acknowledge that the only genuine reason for his rancour against her was due to his own great need of her.

The events of the evening left Becky so visibly shaken as to cause Adam to make the comment that she ought to rest for a day or two more, it was not, however, a physical sickness that ailed her now, more a despondency of spirit, a state of mental confusion, and she could not rid herself of the strange effect James Palmer had upon her. She was also growing closer to Adam in a way which she did not fully understand.

In addition to all this she knew that Sarah and Luke were in love, a situation which could only lead to more trouble. Elizabeth, too, seemed about to follow in her footsteps and accept baptism at Adam's hands. She was under no illusion. James Palmer would hold her responsible for the latter and George would accuse her of leading Sarah astray.

She had to get away from them all, away to think and to find herself again, for life had become so very complicated. She returned to Bank House pale and despondent, her life empty of purpose.

Chapter 13

The dark muddy river banks had never been less attractive than they were now as she watched the Gainsborough ferryboat tackle the swift-pulling current of the Trent. It was a dull, damp day and she was weary and sore from the long and uncomfortable journey over landscape which held little magic for her. They had passed through miles of soft, undulating land which to Becky compared adversely with the valleys and hills of home. Perhaps on brighter days, when the overcast skies did not conceal the autumn tints of the foliage, she would have appreciated the countryside more.

She had wanted solitude and had chosen well, for the mist shielded the isolated farms and blanketed the rich productive fields, but that was why she had come, to escape. During the journey she had merely stared blankly from the windows of the jolting coach, banishing her present troubles from her mind. It was easier that way, to think of nothing, rather than the mess from which she was escaping.

George had not even questioned her departure and she suspected that he would be relieved to have her go, but Sarah had begged her to stay, or take her with her. That idea had crossed her mind but she could think better if alone.

As there was sufficient light left to enable Becky to complete her journey in one day, she took a carriage from Gainsborough to Pilling, a small village which lay across the fields from Hawthorn Farm. She asked to be set down outside the 'Boars Head' but as it was almost dark by the time they reached the inn she became apprehensive lest she would be unable to secure a room there.

It was, therefore, with some relief that she entered the room which she had taken, and as there was nothing else for her to do until morning she did not rush to unpack. The small cosy room with its wood fire crackling in the grate pleased her, but she had heard tales of travellers being beset by fleas and bed bugs so, gingerly lifting the bedcovers, she peered amongst them, only to find the bed clean and free from pests. She recalled how once, as a child, she had heard her father tell of the time when he had piled all his clothes on a chair in the middle of a rented room, away from the bugs and fleas. In the morning he found that he had been bitten several times whilst he slept!

She longed to climb into the bed and rest but she was hungry and covered with the grime of travelling. After washing and tidying herself she dined on roast duck with currant jelly followed by a tasty plum pudding, then she climbed the stairs back to her room and went straight to bed. She tried to read the well-fingered book which she had brought from home, but instead found herself staring up at the low wooden beams above her head, contentedly savouring the warmth.

The day had been a long one yet she had achieved much by her own endeavours, starting from the moment she had boarded the train to Rotherham. That part of the journey had been no new experience for her, and once aboard the coach her sense of adventure took over, even if she had been shaken unendingly. Unfortunately there had been insufficient time to explore the thriving turnpike junction at Bawtry, only a half-hour halt being allowed. She did not miss, however, seeing the countless tempting baubles in the brightly-coloured shop windows. There were changes ahead even here, she observed, the railway being constructed outside the town would see to that, and many a traveller would by-pass the town instead of staying at the various hostelries.

The book fell from Becky's hand and when next she saw the old wooden beams it was daylight. In spite of the well-lit room she had drifted into a deep sleep such as she had not experienced in weeks. She was eager now to get to the farm.

So many changes had taken place in the intervening years since Becky, then a child, had been to Hawthorn Farm. Gone were the rambling ivy and hollyhocks which had climbed the walls, half covering the mullioned windows from which she had watched the men at work. Ramshackle farm implements now lay neglected in the overgrown grass, where once the tidy kitchen garden had been.

Today, in the October chill, the house hardly resembled that shown in the framed water colour which hung above her bed at Bank House. In that painting her mother had captured the romance of the scene for her husband all those years ago, whilst waiting for Becky to be born. The house, like the painting, was fading.

The once proud farm, cherished by Gervase and his ancestors, was suffering at the hands of the tenant who did not love it. They paid their rent on time, and by all accounts raised decent crops, but they felt no more emotion for it than her Gainsborough agent who took their rent. Perhaps as tenants they felt under no obligation to preserve its character, but were content provided that the walls and roof protected them from the weather. In many ways she too bore the guilt of years of neglect. What a pity she had not done her duty, by returning more often and taking a keener interest in the farm's welfare. Her father had taken an interest, but on his death it had been put in the hands of an agent.

She could never live here so far from Sheffield, so what good was the farm to her? It would be better off in the hands of someone who cared. She felt it deserved more than an absentee landlord and had her Gainsborough agent, who drew a handsome commission, kept a more watchful eye over it, the property would not be in such disrepair and might have fetched far more at auction than it probably would do.

It was too late to be sentimental about the place, and Becky refrained from knocking on the door to take one last sad look inside. Convinced that it would be wiser to sell than allow the decay to continue, she decided that she would issue instructions to the agent on her way home through Gainsborough.

Retracing her steps across the muddy field she savoured fond memories, distant though they were, of gentle evening walks, picnics in the fields and of times when nothing was important to her but childish dreams. Those times, so far away now as if in another age, could never be repeated unless through the eyes of her own children. But she was twenty-six years of age, unmarried and childless. Her life had been sheltered from all ills, with the certain knowledge that the future was secure, yet here she was, trying to find herself amongst the confusion of strange emotions. The decision to come to Pilling had been a good one, forcing her to come to terms with the future, free of any outside pressures. She had no desire to ignore Adam or the profound things which he had taught her, as to do that would be to deny her inner voice. She did, however, wish to avoid James Palmer, who seemed constantly to invade her every thought. As for George, she was in the process of sorting that problem out.

Turning into a lane, she headed towards the little church which stood cold and grim-looking, its low Norman tower and walls half concealed by ancient yews and oaks, lost in time. A movement near the lych gate caught her attention, and a tall figure came towards her who, for a moment, she mistook for James Palmer!

'Good morning!' The man said, raising his hat, 'I'm sorry if I startled you.'

'No, No!' she gasped. 'You caught me unawares, for a moment you reminded me of someone else.' He was in reality nothing like James Palmer, except for being tall, slim and in clerical garb. Yet the incident disturbed her more than she cared to admit.

'You're a stranger here, I see!' The man showed no signs of leaving.

She nodded, 'I own property in the district which I am thinking of selling. This visit is I suppose, a sad farewell to old memories, and a break from a few personal problems which I have.' It was obvious from the papers and keys in his hands that he was an incumbent of the church. 'I was thinking about coming into the churchyard to try to find the graves of my father's family. His forbears lived in this village for centuries—do you know of any Shearmans of Hawthorn Farm?'

'Not personally. I do, of course, know the present tenants. I've only been here for six years but I know of some Shearman graves along the path by the chancel door; they may be the ones you want? Come on, I'll show you!' He led her through the old churchyard where so many worn stones stood, half buried and nearly obliterated, amidst thorns and brambles which would have seized and torn her skirts had she been forced to search for her aunt Mary's grave by herself.

'There's one, but it is so old that you can hardly read it. And another! Is there one in particular which interests you?' He seemed almost as interested as Becky.

Struck by his helpfulness and grateful for someone to talk to, she answered, 'Thank you! Yes, Mary Shearman. But am I hindering you in your work?'

'No, my dear! I'm only too pleased to help—now I wonder which one it is?' He plunged amongst the gravestones like a child seeking treasure. 'Are you sure she has a stone?' He called out.

'Oh, dear, I really don't know—she died about eighteen years ago when I was a child. That would be about 1826.'

She read several inscriptions, fascinated by the knowledge that perhaps beneath them lay members of her family, long since dead. Which one, she wondered, held the rebellious Isabella about whom she had heard such stories?

The man moved from stone to stone and remarked, 'They're often buried in family groups you know. There can't be many more.' He pushed aside the ivy covering one, read a moment, then called out, 'Here we are!' He began reading, hesitating as he tried to decipher the words, 'Margaret Shearman, Oct 12th, 1819 aged 87'. Then continued, 'Mary Shearman, April 15th, 1825. John Andrews Webster...' he rubbed off the lichen which had started to fill the lower inscription, 'relict of the above Dec 14th, 1818 aged 1 day.'

'Yes, that's it,' Becky replied, stepping over the uneven mounds of earth to his side to read the stone. How she remembered Mary and her delicious rhubarb pies! 'I wonder who John Andrew Webster was,' she asked, puzzled. 'The Websters are Sheffield people. Do you know, that child was buried the day after I was born?' She sighed sadly, 'I suppose we shall never know now who he was!'

'Perhaps not, although if we look in the burial register we might find a clue or two. Let's go into the church. If the Vicar is still there we can get into the chest.' He paused as they reached the church and remarked. 'You'd best remove the mud from your shoes on that iron scraper over there before you go in, or he won't be too pleased!'

They passed through the ornate archway of the church to the heavy iron-studded oak door, which was unlocked. Their footsteps rang through the large old church and Becky felt the cold air strike her. 'Will he mind us looking, the Vicar I mean?'

'No,' he replied, shaking his head. 'You wait here while I go and find him.'

He left her staring up at the high vaulted roof of the church, wondering who the little boy was. No-one had mentioned his existence to her before. Almost immediately the man returned, followed by the Vicar, who shook her hand and introduced himself.

'Good morning! You've just caught me in time! Let's see what we can find, shall we?' He led her to an old heavy chest which was bound with iron and secured by two large locks.

'I really am most grateful,' Becky offered, eager to see what was in the chest. She watched as each man inserted a key to his own lock and then, together, raised the heavy lid. All she could see was a pile of papers and a few large books.

'Here we are,' the Vicar said, lifting a book from the chest and blowing the dust from its cover. 'Dusty, I'm afraid. This is the burial book; fortunately we don't have to use this one as frequently as the others.' He closed the lid and laid the book open on top of it, turning its pages. '1812...1817...1818. Here we are! John Andrews Webster, son of Gervase and Fanny Webster of Sheffield, one day old, December 14th, 1818 (Twin).'

'I don't understand!' she queried, 'Does that mean that he could have been my brother? He was born to my mother on the same day that I was born.' It was difficult to think straight. 'Please, could you read it again to make sure I heard you correctly?'

He re-read the entry, taking care, but the words merely confirmed his previous findings. 'Does that tell you anything else?'

'No! It doesn't and I can't understand why they never told me about him!' she whispered, hurt by the mystery of it all.

'Well, perhaps it hurt your mother to talk about it or you don't remember them mentioning it. It may not have been so important to you when you were very young; so many children die early you know, that quite frankly, people prefer to put death at the back of their minds.'

Curious she asked, 'Is Andrews a Christian name, I always thought it to be a surname?'

'It is less fashionable these days but often people used a mother's maiden name as a Christian name, to perpetuate a family name.'

'But my mother's name was Garnett!' she stated categorically.

'Yes!' he smiled, 'but sometimes it is the name of a patron or in acknowledgement of some gift or other from a friend. I can look in the Christening Register and see if it is the same spelling there but there is little else I can do.' He delved once more amongst the books in the chest until he found what he wanted and opened the page for December 1818. 'Yes, the name has an 's' here too. It was a private Christening, probably done at the farm if it looked though they knew the child was dying.' He ran his fingers further down the page, 'I don't see another baptism until January. You were not christened at the same time, nor even later at this Church.'

'No! That was done in Sheffield. Thank you for all your trouble and time, I suppose I shall never really know the facts now that my parents are both dead.' She shook hands with the Vicar and his Clerk and returned to the Inn in a pensive mood, endeavouring to recall any incident that she had forgotten which would explain her lack of knowledge about the child. There were twins in the Garnett family, she knew that, going back several generations, but to forget this one particularly seemed very strange.

Only later did she realise that she had not really looked at the grave properly and curiosity drew her back to the area. The second visit shed no more light on the matter than did the first yet it gave her a chance to pay her respects to a brother she had never known.

On the third day, having fulfilled her need to find relief from her problems, she began to realise that she did not altogether like being alone, a stranger in a strange place. In truth she missed the bustle of the old town with its outspoken people and all their faults. She even missed the noise and the shops, and she was ready to return home.

Breaking the journey in Gainsborough to instruct her agent about the sale of the farm, she then continued on to Bawtry where she spent one night at 'The Crown'. She would always remember that particular evening as she had mixed with many fine ladies and gentlemen who were breaking their journeys along this ancient route. Now she looked forward to her arrival back in Sheffield where she was to organise her future.

Chapter 14

*B*ecky *was somewhat surprised* on reaching home to find that George appeared to have mellowed. He was almost affable in his greeting. Choosing the most appropriate moment to reveal her plan and not knowing quite how he would react, she broached the subject cautiously. 'I have come to a decision, George. My life has become tedious and it is time I did something other than be mistress of this house. There will come a time when you may bring home a wife who will want to be her own mistress and the events of the past months have convinced me that it is not enough for me to just exist. I have health and strength in both mind and body, sufficient to make my existence on earth count for something. You have your work and the responsibility for the workers, to give you motivation. I have nothing.'

George listened in astonishment, realising that Becky was determined to have her say. 'I assume that you have some plan in mind?' he asked, patiently.

She was trying to explain without being strident, yet she wanted him to understand that she was not willing to deviate from her intentions. 'I am also fortunate in that I have a choice. Many people are in no position through lack of money and circumstances to do anything other than struggle, merely to survive. I do have a plan in mind, and I have instructed the agent in Gainsborough to sell Hawthorn Farm at auction as soon as possible. It will not realise as much as it would have done if there were no tenants in occupation, but the farm has been neglected and needs money spending on it, if not it will fall into ruin. I have no use for the farm now or in the future, and I am happy with my decision to get rid of it.'

'I am inclined to agree with you, it does seem to be a bit of a white elephant. Will you re-invest the money in the business?' He was alert now, ever the businessman.

She hesitated for a moment, pleased at his reaction, and then continued to explain. 'I want to create a business of my own!' There, she had said it!

He laughed. 'What? A woman, in business? What on earth for?'

It was a typical reaction which she had already anticipated. 'I've tried to explain. Because I need to be useful, to stretch myself and to find myself. To find some kind of fulfilment before too many years pass and I become an old maid!'

He shook his head. 'I will never understand you, Sis! It is as if we come from different moulds. You think more like a man at times, than a woman.' It was more of a statement than rudeness.

'It is, perhaps, that we are too much alike! Circumstances force women to be obedient and dependent, yet it is quite acceptable for a widow to run her dead husband's business successfully in his name. Some women open beer houses to support their families after they become widows; that's alright, but if she sets up in business in a man's world she is shunned. Why must we become seamstresses, school mistresses or lodging house keepers? She realised that she was straying from the point. 'No matter, I want to run a stationery and book shop.'

'You don't know enough about running a business,' he protested.

He was right of course. 'Not as much as I should do, but hear me out! I want to invest my money in stock that will be compatible with our present business. A showcase for the works—like father started out with. It would bring work your way as well as mine.' She knew that he was not convinced. 'Don't you see, now that mother has gone I am lost!' She pleaded for understanding.

'It's that religion of Adam's that has changed you!' He remonstrated. 'I told you that no good would come of it.'

'But don't you see? It has opened my eyes and I can see that my life will become dead unless I use the gifts that God has given me. The ability to work and think, and the opportunities, I mustn't waste them. I cannot turn away from this, it is impossible to do that, I have to move forwards!' She waited patiently, willing him to understand. 'It will cost Webster's nothing at all. I stand to lose the money from Hawthorn Farm admittedly, but I still have a home and a part of the business. At least I will have the satisfaction of knowing that I have tried.'

He sighed with resignation, 'We have grown apart of late. You are determined, I can see that, and I have no wish to fight you again. What makes you think you can succeed where others have failed?'

'How does anyone know for certain? I will succeed, I am convinced! I have a few ideas of my own and I have prayed about it. I feel good about the whole project.'

He shook his head again. 'You certainly have changed.' he conceded. 'I will do all I can to back you—if that is really what you want.'

The sincerity of his offer left her a little surprised. She smiled warmly, grateful for the opportunity to breach the gap which still existed between them. 'I would appreciate your advice, George, and I'll work hard to make sure you don't regret helping.'

His face relaxed, and he looked more like his old self. Then he smiled, 'I'm sorry Sis, for everything,' there was a catch in his voice, 'I seem to have messed things up of late, don't I?'

With that she agreed, but it was good to know that he was not going to oppose her; besides, she considered that her proposition was quite a good one. 'Let's start afresh,' she pleaded. 'Nothing is so bad that we can't live with it. Perhaps we relied on mother far too long and adjustments just had to be made after she died. My independence will, in the long run, prevent me from becoming a burden on the family and certainly will stop me from becoming a crusty old hag!'

George laughed, 'Of that I'm not so sure!' It was a mischievous laugh such as she had not heard from him in months. 'Alright, Sis, you win. Start looking for premises as soon as you like, but don't shut me out even if I don't always see things your way.'

Nothing went quite as easily as Becky had imagined it would; simply awaiting the sale of Hawthorn Farm strained her patience to the limit as her head buzzed with plans and ideas. She scoured every newspaper which came to hand in the hopes of finding premises, not too large, not too expensive and in the busiest part of the town. She set a limit at what she dared hope the farm would fetch, and, knowing that she could not afford to be extravagant, she diligently searched bankruptcy columns and auction room sales, looking for suitable stock. Nothing was left to chance. There was work to do and she did it.

It was Adam who encouraged her to think positively in her moments of doubt, always caring, seemingly proud of her efforts. This total absorption suited George too. In spite of the fact that no conversation these days was free from the impending venture, he saw the atmosphere in the house return to what it had previously been prior to Adam's arrival. He was content not to question her every movement, not even her Sunday visits to town with Sarah. He seemed oblivious too, at what went on in Sarah's pretty head, although it was obvious to most of the Sunday congregation in Adam's Church.

Almost four unbearably long weeks passed before the auction took place, the farm realising what was expected under the circumstances, and a further two weeks before Becky could make a positive move. All the agents in town were under instructions to notify Mr Grayson of any leases pending termination, or premises being vacated. Finally, on a bitterly cold day at the end of December, Becky was informed that there was a shop in the Haymarket available for leasing. She could contain her impatience no longer and compelled George to re-arrange his own affairs so that they could go and look at the building immediately.

As they entered the gloomy, empty shop, only Becky with her dreams could muster sufficient enthusiasm to prevent them from leaving straight away, locking the place behind them. She had heard her father tell of his excitement when he first opened the door of his own shop. It, too, had smelt abominably and been filled with litter but he had taken it all in his stride, seeing it as a challenge. Father had only wanted to be a printer but the shop had come along with the deal. After the fire he had been content to part with the shop to concentrate on his flourishing printing business. Now, after all these years, 'Webster's Stationers' would open up again. She did not mind the dust or dirty windows in the euphoria of seeing her dream become reality. George, on the one hand, could see only the hard work needed to make the shop succeed, while Becky could see nothing other than that which effort and determination could attain.

Running his hand over the dusty counter George said, 'Look! Everything is in a state, there are repairs to be done and it is so gloomy that it will all have to be decorated thoroughly. This surely isn't what you want, is it?'

'I think,' Becky replied thoughtfully, 'that I can do something with it. It is in an excellent position and its condition is reflected in the price of the lease. The place is dry enough, and if I get a cheap decorator in to do most of the work, and a woman to scrub down whilst I look for stock, then I can improve things as time goes on. We don't have to pay for good-will, just the lease and rent.'

George crossed the room to the grimy, many-paned windows and peered out into the thronged street beyond the glass. The position certainly was ideal and it was plain that she would not be dissuaded from her venture. It had also come to his notice that there was an alarming increase in the rumours and reports of large contingents of Mormons leaving the country for America. He wanted to keep Becky here in England, and one sure way of achieving that would be to keep her busy and successfully occupied. 'Well, the outlay is certainly going to be a lot less than we had imagined,' he conceded. 'Do you feel you can take the risk, and are you prepared to be disappointed if the shop fails?'

'Yes, I am!' There was no hesitation in her voice. 'It is small, but if I make a success of it I could eventually find larger premises. It would also give Sarah an outlet and an opportunity to meet more people, if she helped me sometimes. We could even arrange for your customers to collect the work orders from here, then they would see what else we stock and possibly buy other lines.'

He eyed her seriously. 'Is this going to be a partnership, Becky, or what? I can't give you commission on old orders without cutting my profits, yet if it does work out well you will need some remuneration for the service.' His forehead was furrowed as he pondered over the possibilities. 'Now that the idea is more of a reality than a dream, I think we should be very business-like in our approach. I could, of course, pay commission on new orders and, I agree, old customers would be tempted to buy other things. The outlay is obviously within your means, being mainly for decorating and stock, and there is no need for you to draw a wage for the time being.

You would need recompense in the long run, but it takes the pressure off to begin with.' Suddenly he had become the businessman again, his mind pondering on the intricacies of trade which were dear to his heart and she knew that he was warming to the idea. 'We have to do things legally,' he mused.

'Are you offering me a partnership, George?' she asked cautiously, surprised by his sudden keen interest.

'Well, yes! I suppose I am!'

She had no hesitation about opening the shop but the idea of a partnership had never entered her head. 'I honestly don't know, George. The idea sounds fine but I need time to think. I want to run this place myself, to make my own decisions about stock and staff, if needed. What guarantee do I have regarding that side of things?' There was no animosity in her thoughts, merely a reflection of cautious thinking.

'I'll not interfere, I give you my word, but it is cold in here, so let us adjourn to the agents and discuss this further at home tonight!'

Before locking the door carefully behind her, Becky took a final encompassing glance around to reassure herself on the feasibility of the project. Alright, it needed a lot of small repairs but there was no doubt in her mind that this could be her salvation.

George waited patiently, satisfied by the fact that she was thorough in her study of the venture, even down to such small details as heating and lighting. It served to convince him that this was more than a game to her.

She caught up with him and linked her arm through his as they had done when they were younger. 'I'm happy that we are friends again,' she said softly. 'We are alike you and I! I know that you can see my dream in your own head now and I do need your guidance. I feel that it is going to work out very well for both of us!'

'You mean that you've got your own way again, Sis,' he chided, conceding that she had won. 'You are a bossy female—did you know that?'

But there was strong affection in his voice.

Within three weeks, the drab, dingy shop had lost all trace of being abandoned. Gone were the bare walls whose only decoration had been an intricate pattern of spiders webs. Instead, those same walls, now a brilliant white, were lined with shelves groaning under the weight of the books, papers, inks and an array of desk-top furnishings. Sturdy wooden counters, freshly scrubbed and varnished, stood on equally well-scoured flagstones awaiting the arrival of her first customers. The chill of winter still persisted in spite of the pot-bellied stove in the corner of the room, and a chair, unwanted at Bank House, was thoughtfully placed for the use of weary patrons.

Becky stood that first morning, plainly dressed and wearing a large starched white apron over her olive-green gown, viewing the shop with pride before opening the doors for the first time.

In spite of the brightly-dressed window which attracted the curious, it was some time before anyone actually entered the shop to make a purchase, and she began to wonder if her efforts had been in vain. Many of the callers were well-wishers who had read of the opening in the local newspaper. Others who hovered around the window were ragamuffins attracted by the stuffed toys which she had lovingly made during the frustrating period before the farm auction. By the end of the day there was little more in the cash box than when she started.

Slowly, but very slowly as the week advanced she began to see results from her toil, especially when she obtained several new orders for George.

Since Becky had returned from Gainsborough, up to the present time, she had taken great care to avoid all contact with James Palmer, and never once did she mention his name to Elizabeth, who was now a regular companion on Becky's visits to Church. In order to placate James' displeasure, Elizabeth went along with him to his own Church as well, but her sense of dedication to the latter was declining fast. It was inevitable that eventually there would be a row over this; Becky accepted the fact but the longer Elizabeth took to declare a wish to formally change her beliefs, the more Becky put the problem to the back of her mind. She had butterflies in her stomach whenever she considered the possibility of Elizabeth taking to the waters of baptism, for she knew that James would place the blame squarely at her door. She did not relish facing his wrath, nor was her fear without foundation, for James Palmer was tiring of playing the waiting game.

Having taken a leaf out of George Webster's book, James Palmer had decided to play along with Elizabeth where her visits to Adam's Church were concerned, hoping that her first flush of enthusiasm would wane. To his consternation he began to realise that he had played the wrong card, and she was becoming more resolute than ever in her new beliefs. She even went so far as to challenge him! Beneath the surface he was beginning to simmer with rage. So much for his desire to rid himself of Miss Webster, for Elizabeth harped on constantly about the woman!

It was, therefore, as well that Becky remained in ignorance of his ill-feelings, and of his intended visit to the shop.

The tall figure studying the window intently did not immediately draw her attention, and it was only when he strode through the door that she realised he was there. His face was as black as thunder, his jaw set rigid with rage. His eyes were icy cold—and he had her at a disadvantage. She had no desire to speak with him, and studiously occupied herself with a pile of untidy samples left over from a previous customer, but she could not ignore him forever.

His voice was quiet and heavy with accusation when he finally broke the silence. 'Well, Madam! You have achieved the ultimate. You have done to me what you did to your brother, and have eroded the foundation of my family life. Elizabeth declares that she wants to leave my Church.'

Becky stammered, nervous yet defiant. 'What on earth have I to be blamed for? I merely offered friendship to your sister, and she responded. Besides, she has a mind of her own! I may also point out that it is not *your* Church anyway!'

'She was content until she was brainwashed by the likes of you! She had at least got a religion, unlike you! She knows the Gospels inside out without needing to be taught them!' He watched her colour rise with indignation, taking a delight in her discomfort as she fought to answer him. 'However,' there was a loftiness in his tone now, 'I have been able to talk some sense into her head. The river is freezing now and she remembers how you ailed after such foolishness. I have extracted a promise from her that if she will wait until spring, and if then her heart is still so engaged I will not stand in her way. She is sensible and I believe common-sense will prevail. Do not encourage her—she has not the rebellious streak that you have, Madam!' There was a cold finality in his voice which defied retort.

How could she let him win? With determination and scorn she retorted, 'You treat her, Sir, like a wife, a chattel, a mere housekeeper. She is a kind, loving creature, devoted to you, and you seek only to keep her by your side for your own sake!'

It was his turn to flush as he strove to control his mounting fury. He was incensed by her arrogance. She had gone too for this time, and he no longer cared what she thought of him. 'She does not flout the rules of womanhood trying to prove herself better than a man. She is content as she is—or was until you turned her head. I won't allow her to be dragged across the world by powerful persuasion, just to follow that rabble-rouser and his kind, like so many silly sheep.' His voice rose, like a fire and brimstone preacher. 'Be warned, it won't be long before Mr Johnson suggests that you and your sister follow him across the sea! I want no heartache for Elizabeth. Also, a word of caution. People are saying that many of these men are taking more than one wife at a time. Are you certain that you are not destined for a harem? He could not stop. 'Perhaps it would do you good, and bring you down off your high horse!'

The blood had drained from Becky's face, and her lips were white with anger. He knew he had gone beyond the limit, yet could not withdraw the words once spoken.

Her eyes flashed with contempt. 'How dare you! You evil man!' she raged, with disbelief in her voice and all air expelled from her lungs. 'How dare you even think such wickedness!' she gasped. 'Call yourself a man of God? You need to pray for humility and forgiveness for what you have just suggested. If such evil thoughts are prompted by your religion then I shall make it my duty to rescue Elizabeth from your clutches.' He recoiled from the passionate hatred in her eyes.

His fingers gripped the wooden stick which he held until they became numb. There was nothing he could say to repair the damage. She was right, he had overstepped the mark and as a man of the cloth he had proved his own fallibility. He was a hypocrite, a man driven by jealousy and desires, and he was ashamed of his outburst. Turning without speaking, he strode to the door, his face turned away from her and creased by the pain of remorse. On an impulse of repentance he turned to face her but the contempt on her face shook him to the depths of his being. An apology now would be a waste of time, and there was no alternative but to leave. He closed the door gently behind him and hastened from the scene.

His sudden departure left Becky reeling with shock and fury. She lowered herself onto the little chair from Bank house, grateful that there had been no-one to witness the disgraceful scene. She shuddered with disgust at the memory of her own violent outburst and had she not been in the shop she would have burst into tears, but the chances of someone entering made her suppress such emotion. This restraint served only to disturb her more. Poor Adam, such accusations of malice and spite! She would not, of course, repeat the foul allegation which James Palmer had lowered himself to utter, nor would she ever forgive him such wickedness of thought.

It was impossible to eradicate the incident from her mind and, as if to compound her miserable thoughts, the sky was darkening as the morning advanced, and by early afternoon the heavily-laden sky began to shed its burden. Fine powdery wisps of snow danced wildly, then, as if a feather pillow had been violently shaken on high, fierce flurries of driving snow blotted out her view of the shops across the street. Few customers entered the shop, relieving her of the necessity of being polite. By four o'clock in the afternoon there were several inches of soft snow covering the ground, leaving the normally congested pavements almost devoid of people. There was no let up in the precipitation, footprints were filled as quickly as they were made, and Becky became concerned as to how she would reach the house in the flimsy footwear which she had put on that morning.

As if in answer to her plight, a carriage pulled up before the shop and a figure alighted, stumbling its way across the pavement, to reach the doorway. In those few moments George was almost hidden beneath a mantle of white flakes.

'Come on, Sis!' he called out as he stamped the snow from his boots. 'It's no good remaining here now, everyone is going home and the snow is getting deeper by the minute. This bad weather is going to continue all night.' In spite of the look of relief on Becky's face, he was aware of the pallor of her cheeks and presumed that all was not well. 'You look starved through,' he said, thinking her to be cold. 'I'll bank down the stove and collect the money, and you gather your things together, as it may be several days before it's worth your while opening again. Henry is going to drop me off at the Works before he takes you home. I will stay there until seven and if Henry doesn't return I'll stay the night with Tom Linley. He won't mind.'

Moved by his obvious concern for her comfort while she was still smarting from the confrontation with James Palmer, she felt the old feeling of affection for her brother, 'I really do appreciate your concern, George. I was beginning to wonder what to do!' There was a catch of emotion in her voice which did not escape him. Thank you for coming,' she said quietly. She was weary and drained, yet she could not bring herself to tell him anything of her troubles. Not once since they had first visited the shop had he decried her plans or shown any lack of support and for that she was grateful. 'Do you think the shop will be safe if left for a few days?' she asked, her confidence having deserted her.

George laughed, 'Look, you can't sleep here or worry about it all the time. It'll be fine!' He lifted the shutters and moved to the door. To cheer her up, he said, 'One of those orders you acquired for us could end up being very lucrative in the long run. You did well there'. He peered intently at her face, 'Are you sure you're alright, Sis? You don't look at all well.'

Smiling weakly she waved the idea away, 'I think it is only the excitement of the past few weeks. I shall be alright with a hot meal inside me and a spell by the fire'.

He went out into the flurrying snow and put up the shutters before handing her protectively up into the carriage. 'Right, Henry, we're ready!' he called out through the soft top of the carriage, once he had taken his seat beside Becky. 'Are you sure you're alright?' he repeated gently.

'She nodded, 'Just tired, thank you.'

They sped through the quiet empty streets as though riding on velvet, and the sound of both wheels and horses' hooves muffled by the snow-covered cobbles, had a soothing effect on Becky. Though the blustery wind blew flakes of snow in through the gap above the door, she sat and enjoyed the welcome isolation, peering out at the beautiful scene. It was only when they had delivered George and were heading out of town that the going became difficult, as drifting snow slowed the journey almost to walking pace. Strangely, the prospect of becoming marooned within the walls of Bank House for a few days did not dismay her, indeed isolation from the outside world would, at this moment, be a welcome blessing.

On entering the house she was met by a relived Sarah who, on finding her sister to be safe, promptly offered her a letter addressed in unfamiliar handwriting. 'I shall open it the minute I have thawed out', Becky said, shaking the snow from the hem of her skirt and removing her shoes. 'Who brought it?' she asked, noticing the lack of a postal stamp.

'A youth left it at lunch time, so I have no idea. But come, you must get warm, it is so cold out there!'

Becky was intrigued to know of its content. Perhaps it was from Mr Grayson? Letters written by unknown hands seldom arrived at the house addressed to her, so normally she could tell immediately who the sender was. The characters were neatly and boldly formed, giving her the impression that they were the work of a man. As she entered her own room she broke open the seal with eager, still cold fingers, and quickly scanned the page.

It was several seconds before she realised that the letter was from James Palmer. She gasped out loud and looked round hastily, but to her relief Sarah had not followed. Nothing in it could be of the slightest interest to her, so she resolved, there and then, to reply. Sitting immediately to her desk she quickly wrote:

Dear Mr Palmer,

I have not read your letter, nor do I intend to. I dread to think what awful insinuations you make in it. Please do not send any more communications as I shall immediately burn them.

Miss Webster

By six o'clock Henry was ready to leave with the carriage to fetch George back and she knew that if he did not go soon it might be impossible for him to go at all. She hurried downstairs, handed him the letter and urged him to deliver it, on foot if necessary, to Reverend Palmer's house which was no more than 700 yards from the Works. It had to be delivered before the night was out, she insisted.

This being done she resolved to forget James Palmer, and put the letter out of reach and out of mind, in the little wooden box that had been her mother's.

She was confined indoors by the weather for three days before the sun's rays broke through the heavy clouds. Never before had she seen the sun glow white like a silver dish, nor seen the town in the valley below shrouded in a fine mist as though submerged in a lake. Later that day though, the weather broke again and a million more flakes of snow obliterated the view from the window, quickly burying the earlier deep falls with a fresh soft covering.

The Arctic conditions which had brought the town almost to a standstill, threatened further difficulties and chaos. It was impossible to keep warm even in the house, whether wrapped in blankets by the fire or in bed. There was no corner free from the icy draughts moaning under the doors and down the corridors, and when she rose each morning her warm breath froze in the cold air. Attempting to wash, she found ice in the water jug in her room and on peering through the curtains she saw a veil of long pointed icicles hanging from the eaves of the house.

No-one could remember a previous spell of cold weather like it and the large airy rooms of Bank House did nothing to ease her increasing boredom. She thought with envy of old Tom in his cramped, cosy little house, until she remembered that he too would be house bound, alone and unable to venture out, even to the pump. Tom had good friends, she knew that, but the weather conditions had made it impossible for many of them to work and as a consequence they would be on short-time, struggling to make ends meet themselves. Whatever the circumstances she must ask Henry to try and deliver to old Tom a gift of fuel and food. It was impossible for her to struggle there and see him herself.

But old Tom had not been abandoned; Adam and Luke had seen to that. It had not been an easy task for them, with the snow concealing everything on the ground worth burning, and coal in short supply, but they had managed well enough. By scrounging scraps of wood and broken furniture from anyone who had a little to spare they had kept him warm. Henry's arrival with some food and a load of logs also eased the situation so that by the time Becky and Sarah arrived a few days later, old Tom was quite comfortable.

He was more than grateful to see them, however, and for the opportunity to have a chat.

'There was a time,' he said, in reminiscent mood, 'when I would have been out there on Little London Dam, skating to impress the girls. Now I can't even stand upright in the snow!' He had a wry smile which did not quite conceal his lament.

'Have you still got your skates, Tom?' Sarah asked hopefully, a small tremor of excitement in her voice. 'I've never been skating in all my life!'

'My old pair are amongst the tools in that cupboard,' he said, pointing towards the chimney breast. 'They'll be a bit rusty but you can use them if you like.'

With childish enthusiasm, Sarah rummaged carefully amongst Tom's old tools as he continued, 'I was a shoemaker, you know, and those were my tools. I made many screw-on pairs of skates in my time, but mine tie on'.

'These are a bit ancient', laughed Sarah, holding his skates aloft by leather straps which were green with damp.

'Yes, and they need re-grinding, but I've got a stone in the backyard.'

Her eyes were excited now, 'Could we borrow them, Tom?'

'They're a bit too big for you, lass, but you're welcome to them. There's probably another pair in there somewhere. Why don't you get a group of youngsters together from Church to go skating with you, when the ice is right? You'll have a fine old time of it.'

'Oh! What a good idea!' Sarah's voice rang with glee. 'Can we, Becky?'

Sarah's delight and enthusiasm was contagious. 'Oh, why not?' Becky agreed without thinking. 'There are several pairs in our stable, if Tom will sharpen them for us. I haven't skated for ages myself but it is good fun.'

'Oh, that I could come with you young people!' Tom sighed, 'But I have good memories which will have to do.'

By the time Tom had prepared the skates, there had been several days of very hard frost, and the ice on the dam was deemed safe to use. Luke, who needed no urging from Sarah, soon rounded up a small group of young people willing to trudge the two miles to Little London Pond, and with six pairs of skates between them they set off.

Henry had scoured the outhouses and made several large bundles of wood with which to make a fire, whilst Becky filled a basket with small potatoes and biscuits for the outing.

'Oh Becky! This is such good fun,' Sarah cried, as the group wound its way in a crocodile through the snow. 'Why haven't we done this before?' Her eyes were alight and sparkling with happiness in the lantern light.

'You don't even know if you can stand up on the ice yet!' Becky cautioned, before Sarah scampered off enthusiastically to join the others, leaving Becky alone with Adam who had also joined the party.

'It seems to have been a good idea of Tom's,' she admitted as she watched the younger folk hurrying on ahead. She had not been completely alone with Adam for some time since opening the shop, and when they had met they had been surrounded by so many other people that conversation had remained impersonal.

'How has your business venture worked out?' he asked. 'Are you happy with your decision?'

'I found it difficult at first, and tiring, but I am beginning to find it easier now. It's a long time since I attended Miss Senior's Academy for young ladies, and I think George believed me incapable of hard work, but I know I have surprised him—and even your investment will benefit in the long run, if the new orders continue to come in.'

After a pause, Adam asked suddenly, 'When I return home with Luke, will you stay true to the faith?' The question was blunt, and concealed his sadness over today's news of his imminent departure from Sheffield. He did not want to spoil her happiness tonight.

Becky had quite forgotten that Adam would eventually be sent elsewhere, and with dismay, asked, 'You're going? When will you have to go? And does Luke go with you?' She was concerned for Sarah now, as well.

'Yes, he must. We will not be going home but have to move on to another district.' He avoided telling her when.

'Sarah won't be happy to hear of Luke's departure, nor will I be happy to see you go!' she lamented, and the thought of losing Adam began to fill her with dread. 'Part of me will go with you!'

He took her hand instinctively in his, when he saw the dismay on her face. He might never see her again, the daughter who still did not know who he really was. 'Will you come home with me?' he begged without thinking, 'I don't want to lose you!'

'But…why…?' she stammered, astounded by his question.

He was being rash now, forgetting that only he knew the truth. 'I have come to care for you. There is a future for everyone and a chance to build Zion amongst our people. I want you to consider coming to live with me, and my family. I want to take you home!' His voice was quiet, full of anticipation as he waited for her reply.

She fell silent, the words of James Palmer suddenly in her mind. Surely he had not been right after all? This gentle man beside her who had loved her mother so dearly, how could he ask this? She recoiled, shocked by his words. There was turmoil in her thoughts, as she strove to find an adequate response. At last, with a deep sadness in her voice, she asked, 'Oh Adam! How could you ask this of me?' Then, with a growing realisation and bitterness, 'How could you? I have heard rumours which up to now I have ignored, but I realise that you have mistaken my friendship for something else. I could never be a man's mistress!' She lifted the hem of her skirt from the snow and hurried away, tears running down her face, striving to control her bitter disappointment in Adam and in the disintegration of all her dreams.

Her words stung Adam as deeply as if she had slapped him across the face! 'No! No! You misunderstand me!' He called out in bewilderment, endeavouring to stop her. 'I offer you a home out of friendship…' But she was almost amongst the group now, leaving him no opportunity to correct her misunderstanding. How could she have misinterpreted his words so badly? He could remember no word, no deed of his that would have conveyed such devastating ideas. Everything he had tried to achieve had come to naught before his eyes, and his efforts to build a lasting friendship with his daughter without causing pain had failed. How could she believe he wanted her for a second wife—or even worse, a mistress? He was not of that mould—nor ever could be. Was he always destined to be misunderstood? What could he do now, how could he explain his meaning? He dreaded leaving her with this terrible impression of him, but knew he must, or disclose his secret to her.

Each time he headed towards her she backed away, mingling with the others, avoiding him, and he knew that tonight was not the time nor the place to explain. It was also important now, to consider how he was to do it without causing further grief.

By this time the youngsters had reached the dam and were busily constructing a fire in a clearing where a previous fire had been. Adam tried to keep his mind on helping them but his eyes constantly strayed to where Becky stood, and he watched for an opportunity to catch her alone.

Seeing Adam occupied, and in no mood to join the fun, she turned to escape, only to find herself confronted by Elizabeth Palmer and her brother James! It had not been Elizabeth's idea to come skating but James had insisted that an evening out would do them both good, had gathered his skates and dragged her along.

Becky acknowledged them politely for Elizabeth's sake. She was trapped between both men and knew that before long one would manage to engage her in conversation. At the first possible moment she edged away from the group, donned her skates and joined the other skaters on the ice, and was grateful that no-one took much notice of her. It was not quite dark and the snowy banks of the pond reflected the lights of the skaters' lanterns, but it was dark enough to conceal her. Yet, there was no pleasure for her in being swept along with the crowd, for her action only served to add to the feeling of isolation as she wrestled with her problems.

Once her confidence in her ability to skate returned she sped across the ice, but she was near to tears. Had she misjudged James Palmer after all and fallen prey to Adam's silken tongue, or were they both as bad as each other? It pained her to think of them and of her future. She headed towards the brightly-lit booths on the opposite bank, where hungry skaters were buying hot refreshments, seeking refuge. She had not been aware, however, of the figure gliding strongly and purposefully behind her, until the sound of his voice cut into her thoughts.

'You are avoiding me, Miss Webster!' James Palmer called out as he caught up with her, 'Can we not be friends?'

'Oh!' she cried out, plainly disappointed. 'I had thought to escape you but I fear I am unlucky?' She knew that she was being rude but couldn't help it.

'You offend me', he mocked, laughing at her, 'and I have come especially to make amends!' He drew his feet together deftly, blocking her path and stood facing her. She almost stumbled into his arms. 'You did not read my letter then?' he asked, challenging her.

'No, I did not!' she snapped back. 'Please, go away!' But he was not to be rejected, and holding up his hand tried to prevent her from moving off.

'I have no wish to fight you,' he persisted. 'I simply wrote to apologise for my bad behaviour. Please!' he begged. 'Take your hand from your muff and hold my arm so that we can skate together. Allow me to explain my feelings.' She tried to move away. 'Look! People are beginning to watch; it would be less conspicuous to accept me than make a scene by saying no!' He took her arm and she was powerless to do anything but follow lest she fell on the ice. 'You see, many people are in pairs, and it means nothing Miss Webster, I can hardly molest you on the ice, can I?'

Was there no escaping the man? She placed her hand on his arm, but with every intention of escaping at the first possible opportunity. He skated well, with a rhythm that was almost pleasing, and she could not help but notice that several people turned to watch admiringly as they wove in and out of the other skaters.

'You have skated before, I think?'

She did not reply.

'You are as frosty with me as the pond is icy, Miss Webster. Are you afraid that you might fall in love with me?' He was laughing at her now, deliberately goading her. What had he to lose? He felt the grip of her hand slacken in response and heard her sharp, angry intake of breath. She would have fallen if he had not placed his arm about her. 'Keep going, you are doing well,' he said softly, covering her hand with his own. He lowered his head dangerously near. 'You are very appealing when you are angry. Put on a brave face, Miss Webster. If I let go of you now you may take a tumble.' There was a mischievous note in his chuckle.

He was controlling and manipulating her, and there was nothing she could do about it. He was also making fun of her! She could not avoid the warm touch of his hand without losing balance. His firm, possessive fingers cupped hers gently, holding them as a lover would and she was surprised by the pleasure it gave. He squeezed her waist gently as they cornered, sending tiny thrills of excitement through her. She tried to resist but was trapped on the ice, trapped with one man and afraid to leave him to face another!

There seemed to be many more torches sweeping to and fro in the darkness now, casting shadows and strange lights over the skaters on the ice and emphasising the tallness of the figure beside her. Becky glanced sideways at his face. His features seemed mysterious and stern in the flickering lights and, as if feeling her gaze, he looked down questioningly at her. Only then did she realise that he had removed his spectacles before coming on the ice. His eyes were soft, even kind, and she was unaware that they had slowed down until, pivoting her round to face him, he searched her face earnestly. She softened under his gaze, responding to his warmth, and he knew it. He could sense also the softening of her body and could have kissed her then, pouring out his soul and his love for her, but he wanted no mistakes this time. He lifted her chin gently with his fingers, sensing that she would not refuse him. Quietly he whispered, 'I will not make the same mistake again, Miss Webster. You will not scorn me a second time!'

Her hand was trembling and she lowered her eyes to avoid his gaze, ashamed of the way she had blatantly offered her mouth to him. He took her hand tenderly and led her to the bank, where he left her by the fire as though nothing had happened. Joining Elizabeth on the opposite side of the fire he gave his skates to one of the youths and looked at Becky as if she were not there. There was no laughter now in his eyes, no vengeance, no recognition even, and she knew then how much she had hurt him the evening she had spurned him.

With a start she became aware that Adam was also watching her across the hot embers of the fire. She lowered her eyes, not wanting to face either man yet not daring to move for fear of being followed by one, or both. Then, sensing someone moving, she waited before raising her head to see if either had gone, only to find Adam by her side. His face was sombre and his gaze showed nothing of the lustful, wicked man that James Palmer had insinuated. Perhaps she could no longer trust her own judgement and certainly she could hate neither of them anymore. Glancing over towards where James and his sister had been she saw to her relief that they were walking away.

It was only then that she realised Sarah was also nearby and was not her usual happy self, her previous gaiety having quite disappeared. 'Aren't you enjoying yourself?' she asked, and moved to her side.

Sarah made no reply, and Becky looked more keenly at her bent head. 'There is something wrong—what is it?' She drew Sarah from the fire to a quieter spot.

'Oh, I can't bear it!' Sarah sobbed quietly. 'Luke is to leave in four days time and I shall not see him again!'

'Four days!' Becky started, looking across at Adam. Why had he not told her that before? 'Why so soon?' she asked.

'They are needed elsewhere and I don't know what I shall do without him!'

Placing an arm around her sister's shoulder, Becky was disturbed by the depth of misery in Sarah's voice. 'Hush, Sarah! We'll sort something out. Did Luke tell you of this?'

Wiping away the tears with the edge of her muff, like a child, Sarah nodded. 'He doesn't want to leave me but he has to. He says he will come back for me before he goes home, but will he?' she sobbed.

There was something in Sarah's heartfelt cry that matched Becky's own sense of despair. She acknowledged too that in the end, Sarah would either be deeply hurt by the separation or join Luke and go out of her life forever. Had Adam realised this?

Perhaps he had been genuine in his offer and James Palmer had poisoned her mind against him. She tried to recall Adam's exact words but they had gone completely, all she could remember was the look of horror on his face and the pain in his eyes at her outburst. She groaned inwardly, not knowing what to think except that she could have been wrong, and that she had now been seen apparently encouraging James Palmer.

'Let's go home!' Sarah pleaded, 'before everyone sees my tears.'

'Hush!' Becky consoled her. 'We'll tell one of the girls that you are unwell and that we are leaving, then we'll slip quickly away and go home. I too have troubles of my own, not least being that wretched man James Palmer.'

After reassuring themselves that their departure would not be observed, they quietly left the group and hurried away from the dam. At first their path on compacted snow was easy, but as they reached the road leading to town they found it a churned mass of icy ruts. The lantern which Becky carried swung precariously as she slipped and slithered in the ruts made by countless horses and wagon wheels. 'Does Luke know how upset you are?' she asked, leading the way carefully towards the path which seemed to be an easier route.

'I think so,' Sarah replied wretchedly, 'but that doesn't help. He is homesick and wants to return home. Oh, what shall I do?' she cried miserably. 'Adam will be very angry if he finds out that Luke and I love each other.'

'I think Adam already suspects something of the kind. You knew at the beginning that Luke would have to leave one day—I told you myself.'

Shaking her head, Sarah cried, 'I didn't want to love him, it just happened you know!' She fell silent as someone approached out of the gloom ahead.

The burly figure of a man began to move quickly towards them, leaving them with no other alternative but to separate and let him pass between them. Because she was preoccupied with their problems, Becky thought nothing of the incident apart from the fact that the man had few manners. Then, suddenly, after he had passed she felt a blow to the head and fell headlong into the snow at the side of the path. Sarah screamed with fright as the lantern fell from Becky's hand and the dark figure lunged at her, seizing her arm roughly. He carried a stout stick which he held menacingly in the air, poised to strike.

'Gimme wot yer've got else yer'l regret it!' he threatened.

Petrified, Sarah held out her other hand and watched helplessly as he tore the ring from her shaking finger before thrusting her violently backwards to the ground. Then in a flash he was gone, leaving her in the gloom!

The attack took only seconds but to Sarah it had seemed a life-time during which Becky had lain stunned by the blow. Picking herself up she peered at Becky who had not stirred. 'Are you alright?' she called out frantically, bending down to touch her shoulder.

Only now as Sarah's anxious voice cut through her dizziness did Becky begin to stir and try to move. She pushed against the snow in an effort to rise, but her foot slipped sending a stab of pain through her leg. She groaned out loud.

Still shaken by her own unpleasant experience, Sarah stood looking helplessly around for help, half afraid that the footpad would return to see what other items of value he had missed.

'Help me, Sarah!' Becky cried out weakly, renewing her efforts to stand. 'Did he attack you as well?'

Sarah shuddered. 'It was horrible. He tore the ring off my finger and flung me into the snow. But he hit you!' she cried softly, struggling to help Becky.

'If only I could get up. I feel so strange and I fear that I cannot walk.' Repeatedly she attempted to rise only to find her head spinning and the pain in her leg growing worse. She began to feel frightened. 'Go back to the dam and fetch someone to help me,' she begged. 'I will never be able to manage.'

'But I can't leave you here, Becky, It isn't safe!'

'There is no other way, you are not strong enough to support me. Now hurry! I am beginning to feel so cold.' She fought off the nausea caused by the spinning in her head and kept her voice calm so that she would not further alarm Sarah.

Reluctantly Sarah agreed to go. The lantern had gone out in the fall and Sarah was afraid, expecting hidden danger in every shadow. She knew Becky was in pain but she must go and get help.

'Fetch Adam. Quickly!' Becky called out as Sarah disappeared into the night, leaving her with only the brightness of the snow for company. Had she done right in sending such a young girl back to the dam alone? Perhaps it would have been wiser to remain together? It was too late now, for Sarah had disappeared. Alone and no longer caring for her own safety she tried again and again to stand but in the end she knew it was hopeless.

Fear drove Sarah on, her imagination playing havoc with her nerves. Twice she stumbled and fell in her panic. It was further than she remembered and if it had not been for the sudden sound of excited voices up ahead she would have thought herself to be lost. To her great relief the dam finally came into view.

Gasping for breath, she rushed to the fire, but Adam was nowhere to be seen, neither was Luke. Only James Palmer stood there, his lean body blocking out the fire as he held his hands against the flames. He seemed not to notice Sarah.

'Where is Adam?' she cried out breathlessly. 'I must find him. Becky is hurt and alone!'

'What do you mean, hurt?' James Palmer demanded, springing to life and spinning round to face the dishevelled and distressed Sarah.

'We were attacked on the way home and Becky was hit by a man with a stick. She can't walk. Where is Adam?' She looked round wildly.

'Never mind Adam, where is she? What in Heaven's name possessed the pair of you to go off alone?' He was angry now, almost beside himself. 'The others are on the ice. Come on, hurry, take me to her!' He hesitated for a moment, 'Let me tell Elizabeth to alert the others!' He snatched a lantern from the pole by the fire and ran to inform Elizabeth.

Returning quickly he strode with long impatient strides which left Sarah struggling to keep up. She was well aware that she was holding him back but no matter how hard she tried her legs would not go any faster. 'I can't walk any quicker,' she called out apologetically, and near to tears. He slowed down and waited anxiously for her to catch up. 'It can't be far now?' she said, a question in her voice for she was puzzled. They were approaching the bridge yet she and Becky had not walked that far. She bit her lip in dismay. 'She's not here, we didn't come this far. Where is she?'

'Oh, God!' James Palmer cried out in anguish. 'Is that woman never to give me a moment's peace? Where can she be, are you sure you came along this way—why didn't you stick to the road?' His questions were fast and urgent and his eyes roamed over the area as far as it was possible to see. 'Miss Webster! Where are you?' He called out several times, but there was no reply.

'It was easier to walk on the path than in the ruts on the road,' Sarah explained, lamely.

'No matter now,' he said comfortingly. 'Let's go back a bit, perhaps we have come too far.'

'Look!' Sarah cried out suddenly. 'This is the spot, here's the lantern! What can have happened to her?' There was a quiver in her voice which alarmed him.

Taking her arm he tried to calm her. 'Shush!' His voice was gentle. 'We will find her.' In spite of the confidence in his voice, he too was succumbing to fears for Becky's safety and he called out again and again but there was no reply. He peered searchingly into the night but to no avail. 'Sarah, we need help, we must hurry back to the others. They can search as well.' Where could she be? His mind was in turmoil and he blamed himself for playing childish games with her.

Hurrying Sarah along, he remembered that she too had had a terrible experience. 'You must think me very hard and unfeeling Sarah. Please tell me if you are alright? I was overwhelmed with fear when you told me that your sister was hurt, yet it must have been a dreadful ordeal for you too.' She could hear the remorse in his voice. 'Are you hurt in anyway?' They were walking briskly now and nearing the dam.

'He took my ring and pushed me back into the snow. My fingers are quite sore but I have not thought about myself until now. I am terribly afraid for Becky.' A chill passed over her and she shuddered. 'Something has happened to her, I know it has!'

'Oh, God! I hope not!' he cried passionately. Then, to reassure them both, he reasoned with Sarah. 'At least we have not found a body and there is no sign of anyone being dragged through the snow. She can't have just disappeared!'

'A body?' Sarah cried out in horror. 'You don't think she's dead do you?'

'I didn't mean that, it was a slip of the tongue!' he hastened to reassure her, wishing he hadn't spoken at all. He didn't dare to let his mind dwell upon the dangers that could befall a girl alone in the darkness of the night.

Sombre, anxious faces greeted them on their arrival back at the dam. 'Where is she?' demanded Adam, his eyes peering into the dark beyond them. 'Isn't she with you?'

'She's gone without trace and although I thoroughly searched the spot where Sarah left her, only this lantern remains. There is no sign of her! I called out—there was nothing. We must go back and spread out until we do find her!' He had to be calm, and organise the search carefully if they were to be successful. 'Come! We've no time to lose, we know she's hurt! Get all the lanterns and follow me!'

Sarah found herself wearily retracing her steps along the path away from the dam, but she was on the verge of collapse and felt physically sick with fear. The journey was becoming a nightmare and the more she stumbled the more she despaired. Reality was fast disappearing, and she would have fallen if Adam had not caught her in time.

'Take her back to the fire, Luke!' he ordered. 'Stay with her—we'll come back the moment we have any news.'

The crowd pressed on. 'Why on earth didn't they stay on the old London Road?' Adam asked James as they proceeded. 'Fancy using this lonely path, and in these conditions too. They should never have left the dam in the first place!'

They were now at the spot where Sarah had found the lantern. 'Now spread out, everyone,' James called out, 'and search thoroughly as you go!'

'Hey!' The voice of a man could be heard. 'Are you looking for a woman, a Miss Webster?'

Adam hurried towards him, 'Thank goodness, where is she? Is she hurt?'

'She's in the Heeley Toll House, up the road. Me and my lad were returning from rabbiting when we found her. This is no place for a woman, alone at night!' he reproached Adam. 'We carried her to the toll house up by the 'Red Lion' and she asked me to find you lot. Said her sister had gone to fetch you, so I knew someone would come back.' He paused for breath. 'I don't know, you townsfolk wander all over, you've no idea what you're about! A woman of her sort is asking for trouble out here at night, and alone!'

'We're very grateful to you both,' James conceded, ignoring the criticism with which he was in full agreement. 'She is obviously safe, but is she hurt?'

'Best see for yourselves. She's bruised about the head, and has badly sprained an ankle but I think it is more shock that's affecting her now.' He turned to Adam, 'Your daughter is she? You shouldn't have allowed her out in these conditions. She's lucky we came along when we did. I'd have strong words with her if I was you!'

The words stung Adam, who was too shocked to reply. He chose to ignore the man's comment and avoided James Palmer's penetrating glance. Had the stranger noticed a resemblance in the lantern light or just presumed that because he was older that he was her father? Either way he had seen in Palmer's eyes a thoughtful look which worried him. Perhaps it was providential that his departure was due four days hence. He spoke tersely to James, 'I'll go to the Toll House if you go back for Sarah and Luke, and take them there'. Then, turning to the stranger, 'Will you show me the way, Sir?' James fumed at his cursory dismissal, but had no choice but to agree.

The Toll House was no great distance away and it wasn't long before Adam faced Becky once more. Her face was very pale and this emphasised the rich colouring of her hair. She was as much like him as she was Fanny, he thought. She looked away as he approached, leaving him unsure whether this was due to the attack, or their earlier confrontation. Nevertheless he drew up a chair near to her side.

How he ached to acknowledge that she was his daughter. He couldn't let her think evil of him or, for that matter, disguise his obvious concern for her. 'Listen,' he begged, 'I care for you like a father, and fear you have misconstrued my intentions. I blame myself for allowing this situation to arise'. His voice became husky, 'I love my wife—even if I don't tell her that often enough'. Taking Becky's hand, he continued, 'You shouldn't listen to gossip. There are valid and special reasons why some men have taken another wife, but that is a story for when you are better. I want you to know that I care about your happiness, as a friend, as a daughter even.' The sincere expression on his face and the honesty in his eyes made it hard for her to disbelieve him.

Becky nodded in acceptance of this, and said miserably, 'I don't understand why people are so hateful—but I ran away from James Palmer too!'

His understanding smile comforted her. She searched quickly for her handkerchief as tears started down her face, and before she realised it she was sobbing like a child on his shoulder. He held her close and protectively until she grew calm.

'You must think me very foolish,' she murmured, 'I am quite beside myself!' Drawing back, she smiled woefully at him as she wiped her eyes. 'I am sorry I misjudged you but there are so many rumours and so much hatred against you that I wasn't sure what to believe.'

Adam nodded, 'It's the devil's work, and we've got to be strong!'

Sensing that they were not alone, Becky raised her head and found herself staring into the anxious eyes of James Palmer. How long he had been there she could not guess, nor from his face tell if he had heard all that had been said. She blushed, lowering her eyes and wondered why he stared so inquisitively at Adam and herself.

Hesitatingly James moved forward, saying quietly, 'Miss Webster, I am at your disposal'. His voice was pleasant and without arrogance, as he continued, 'Anything I can do will cheerfully be done. Shall I go to your brother's house and fetch the carriage?'

He now looked more like the man who had so charmingly shared the marshmallows with her, and had gently woken her when she had slept by his fire. Then she remembered what followed, and as their eyes met she saw that same affection which had been there before she had scorned him.

'I would think it a very kind thing to do,' she said softly, trying to undo the hurt she had done him. 'Please stay on the road, I would not like anyone to harm you!'

In spite of Adam's presence he took her hand and pressed his lips to her fingers, 'Your concern will make me watchful,' he said, then left abruptly, with a nod at Adam. His departure was so brisk that it left her with a feeling of disappointment. Why she had ever thought him obnoxious was a question she found difficult to answer. The room seemed empty without his tall, elegant figure, but then she recalled the reasons for her flight from the dam. She turned to Adam, who had been quietly observing the flickering emotions on her face. 'It was not only your fault that we left the dam' she said. 'I had been trying to avoid Mr Palmer as well!'

'I think he is an admirer of yours,' Adam stated, 'and if you wish to discourage him without hurt then you will need to be firm with him.'

'You are right, and it would be wrong of me to encourage him in any way. But there is something else—Sarah told me that you were to leave in four days time.' Her tone admonished him. 'You didn't say that you were going away quite so soon.'

'Nor did you give me much opportunity to explain anything, if you remember. Will you both be very unhappy when we go?'

'We will be sad to lose such dear friends, for that is what you have become to us, but I'm afraid Sarah has become more than fond of Luke!'

'Not too much I hope. Luke has work to do and his mind must not be distracted by emotional ties. Once we are gone she will probably forget him.' Adam seemed to dismiss the talk of Sarah's affections rather brusquely, and Becky might have discussed this with him, had not sounds of merriment reached their ears.

From the cobbled yard outside came the clatter of feet, and excited voices of the young people who had followed James from the dam. Sarah entered, and, seeing Becky sitting calmly in the chair she ran forward, throwing her arms around her sister. She cried in little gasps of breath, 'I thought...you had gone...for ever!'

'No, I am here, where it is warm and comfortable, but did that man harm you?'

Sarah shook her head, 'No! But I am tired of all the walking I've done tonight!'

'Well, perhaps you had better all go back now and enjoy yourselves, you can do me no good by being here. Mr Palmer has gone home to fetch Henry, and that could take a while. Go on, enjoy yourselves, I have a headache,' Becky feigned, putting her hand to her forehead. By this time, Adam was in close conversation with Elizabeth, who said that she was too old to go back with the youngsters and preferred to sit for a while. Becky was indeed tired and her head sore, so she closed her eyes as if sleeping and let them talk.

A hand shook her gently on the shoulder and a voice called to her, interrupting her dreams. 'Come on, Sis, let's get you home!'

She woke with a start and, looking quickly at the long-case clock on the wall opposite, she saw she had been asleep for well over an hour and a half! She made to stand but her ankle could not take her weight. 'I'm afraid I can't walk!' she said weakly and sank back on the chair.

George bent and swept her up in his arms as if she were a mere slip of a girl. 'We had better take Elizabeth with us, and pick Sarah up as arranged with James Palmer.' He turned to Adam, 'I'm very grateful for the care you have taken of Becky, but I'm afraid there is no room in the carriage to give you a lift. Under the circumstances I think it would be best if you escorted the young people back to town. It is rather late now and who knows what ruffians may still lurk out there. George held out his hand in thanks, 'I am grateful', he repeated sincerely.

They took their leave of the Toll-keeper and the carriage left the yard, rumbling and jolting its way along the ice-rutted road to Heeley Bridge where Sarah waited with James Palmer.

By the time they reached Bank House, George considered that it was too late to send Miss Palmer home and he offered, 'Why don't you stay the night with us, Miss Palmer? It is rather late and we have ample accommodation, haven't we, Sis?'

'Of course,' Becky replied, 'and it would please me too. You really will be most welcome. I have never repaid you for your kindness in looking after me, but I'm afraid I may not be very good company. My head throbs even more than my ankle now, but if I am well tomorrow I shall enjoy sitting with you!'

'I would like that very much,' agreed Elizabeth. 'James has told me that you have a lovely garden. What a pity the weather will prevent me from seeing it.'

Sarah joined in proudly, 'You must come and see it in the spring! However, it is the views from the house which give me greatest pleasure, and you will see those for yourself tomorrow!'

'But James will not know where I am,' Elizabeth exclaimed with disappointment. 'I really must go home.'

George came to her rescue, 'I intimated to your brother that I would entreat you to stay, for Becky's sake, but that if you preferred then I would get Henry to run you home, so you have nothing to worry about'.

'Oh, please stay,' Sarah implored eagerly. 'I will have to go and take care of the shop for Becky, and that will leave her alone and unable to walk about!'

'Then I am outvoted and have no choice—I will be happy to stay.'

Standing in the chilly morning air before the window, Elizabeth gazed in fascination towards the town. 'The views alone make my stay rewarding,' she exclaimed to Becky, who could not join her. 'I am not a good walker, so I have not seen the town from this angle before, although it is a pity that so much of the view is obscured by smoke. The view to the south must be wonderful when the snow has gone.'

'Yes, and in late summer the horizon is a haze of purple heather, which on damp evenings allows the winds to fill our nostrils with a musky perfume. I love it here, but I fear that we don't have many friends who are willing to walk out this far to call on us.'

'That is a pity,' Elizabeth agreed, 'without your carriage you too would feel a little cut off.'

'Henry will take you home of course, when you wish to leave, but I beg of you to stay a while longer. Tell me,' Becky asked, trying to be as casual as possible, 'How did you manage to get your brother to join us at the dam last night?'

'That was a puzzle to me too. He practically dragged me there. But I don't think it was a change of heart, rather I fancy it was his idea of appeasing me, and in order to prevent my conversion to the Church. He has become strangely affected these past months and I suspect that he is not completely at one with himself.'

'Why has he never married, Elizabeth? He is handsome enough, and personable, in spite of his over-strong opinions.

'Who knows? He's had opportunity enough but seems to lack the desire to part with his independence. Perhaps if I were not there to wait upon him hand and foot he would be more inclined to do so.' She moved closer to the window, 'Well I never, here he comes now. Let me go and greet him at the door and save Henry the trouble.'

Before Becky could protest Elizabeth had gone, nor did she return. A tap on the door was the only warning she had of his approach, and in the strong light of day he appeared to be even taller against the oak panelling of the room. He had entered with an air of confidence, assuming that he would be welcome and his tone was light and friendly. 'Good morning, Miss Webster. I trust you are on the road to recovery?'

Once more she felt at a disadvantage in his company, confined as she was to the sofa, her legs raised on two cushions. However, he had taken a lot of trouble on her behalf and she was in his debt. 'I cannot thank you enough for your trouble last night', she said calmly. But for you I would have remained there in most uncomfortable circumstances.' Her voice revealed none of the strange pleasure she felt at his presence, and she was annoyed with herself for the rising desire within her to call him James.

He was not sure whether her warm response was out of gratitude or genuine pleasure at seeing him, but he suspected the former to be the case. 'The pleasure was all mine; in fact the long walk was invigorating and not without its rewards. The stillness of the night allowed me to ponder on many things which I had pushed to the back of my mind for many months.' She still avoided facing him for more than one fleeting moment at a time, which led him to suppose that she was still displeased with him.

'Are you still angry with me?' he asked. 'For the life of me I cannot understand why we fight every time we meet. I almost believe that you receive some satisfaction from our provocative discussions?'

Raising her eyes sharply, she answered heatedly, 'I don't see them as provocative, and it is possibly your great arrogance that makes you see them so. Battles of principles they may be, together with your insistence that we all agree with your opinions, but where is the provocation in that?'

The challenge on his face became a wry smile. 'You are being provocative in your reply. If you did not care something for my opinions you would dismiss my argument and humour me until I took the hint and retired from the field. It is your fiery spirit that draws me back time and time again for further discussion.'

'There is your conceit again, Sir!' she rebuked. 'I care not for argument for argument's sake, or your opinions. I care for my belief in truth and a sincere obedience to that truth. I am learning to question that which has been fostered for generations and which has been distorted to suit mankind. It is my duty as a convert to correct misunderstandings.' She raised her head proudly.

He laughed out loud. 'And you say that it is I who am arrogant! Do you not see that to defy every accepted religious principle with your new-found beliefs is arrogance in itself?' He shook his head in rueful tolerance rather than anger, amused by her haughty display of self-confidence. 'If I did not admire your spirit so much I would think you self-willed, or a handmaid of the devil.' She was arousing in him again desires which he hoped he had conquered, yet in spite of this he felt the need to make her abandon her defiant stand.

He stepped closer, involuntarily, the look in his eye disarming her, and she knew that if he advanced further towards her she was in no position to escape him. She just wished that he would leave, and as he towered above her his voice, when he did speak, was soft and almost sensual. 'Why fight me—I could love you as passionately as you fight against me, given half the chance!'

She froze, clutching tightly with trembling hands the book on her lap, unable to speak.

His head came suddenly closer, descending with a magnetism which forbade withdrawal. There was no escape! She could not move or bring herself to spurn his lips which touched hers briefly, lips soft and tantalisingly warm. She stirred and murmured in protest but his simple lingering touch became a vehicle for his mounting passion and aroused in her a primitive hunger which she could not deny. It was as if her very spirit was departing, blending with his in a sweetness which stole all sense of reality. The intensity of their union shocked him and he drew back, half afraid that he might again have angered her. Instead her puzzled eyes gazed back at him. They were not filled with fear but instead with a soft bewilderment that matched his own. Then, as if the ecstasy were too great, her eyes closed demurely.

He would have spoken then, but the sound of people approaching down the hall startled him, and caused him to draw back from his undignified position. He quickly crossed to the window and stared out, fighting to regain his composure, unable to comprehend why he felt as guilty as a callow youth. He had not, after all, compelled her to respond to his kisses, and although he had surprised her, there was no need to feel like a thief of the night! He did not turn as his sister entered the room and felt like a coward, leaving Becky to face Elizabeth alone.

'Becky!' Elizabeth cried out. 'You do look flushed. You should be in bed!' She turned to her brother accusingly. 'James Palmer, have you been arguing again? Have you no sense at all, tiring Becky out like this? She is in no state to receive visitors!"

'Don't scold him,' Becky said softly. 'It's not entirely his fault!'

'What do you mean, not his fault! There he stands admiring the view, completely unaware that he is only adding to your discomfort.' She crossed the room to the window and clapped her hands, 'Shoo! Shoo! Out of this room, James Palmer, and I shall not be returning to cook you a meal today, I'm needed more here! With that she took his arm, half expecting him to protest but was completely taken aback by his easy compliance with her order, and as she led him towards the door, said, 'You look as though you have been quarrelling with Becky again!'

'No, I have not!' he protested, as she ushered him out of the room.

'There, that's better,' Elizabeth declared as she rearranged the cushion behind Becky's head. 'You're looking better already, but I do hope my brother's visit was not too tiring for you? He is quite stuffy at times and I do wish he would learn to unbend a little.'

'No, you need not worry, Elizabeth, he was...' she hesitated, 'very concerned for my welfare.'

The incident left Becky drained and more than a little disappointed that James had gone so quickly. She felt slightly shocked at the memory of what had given her so much pleasure and wanted to know if he had felt the same joy that she had, or had it merely been a game to him?

Trying to discover more about him without betraying her true feelings, she asked Elizabeth, 'What was your brother like as a boy?'

'Well, he was quite a serious little chap, always reading, except when teasing me. He was always shy and still hides his inner feelings from the world, but he has a heart of gold.' Elizabeth shook her head. 'He really has been behaving peculiarly of late. Now you rest—I will go and make sure that he has gone.'

Becky was afraid to question Elizabeth further, lest she should arouse her suspicions, so she lapsed into silence.

Chapter 15

*W*ith only three days left before his departure, Adam was keen to leave and be on his way to seek peace elsewhere, yet he felt far from well. He was weary, more so than he had ever been before. The long, arduous evening previous had strained and disturbed him greatly, and now he was confronted by another problem. It had become obvious that Luke's growing affection for Sarah could only be resolved by their separation, and now that he had made peace with Becky, their departure for pastures new could not have been better timed. Luke had lately become so pre-occupied and withdrawn that Adam feared the boy could easily be persuaded to do something rash. If they could just manage to get through the next few days without further upset, then he felt all would be well. He had, however, underestimated the tenacity which lay beneath Luke's quiet exterior, and was dismayed when over breakfast he said, 'Father, I have decided to return to Sheffield as soon as I can, and marry Sarah Webster!'

Adam was temporarily at a loss to know how to reply without hardening Luke's resolve, and so tactfully remarked, 'But Luke, you can't expect a gently-bred girl like her to uproot and leave her family to settle in a strange country!' His argument was weak he knew, but it was all he could think of at that moment, he was so taken aback, and unable to concentrate.

Luke then bemused him further by the very truth of his quite forceful reply, 'But isn't that just what we're here for, to encourage our converts to build Zion in America? Sarah would be an ideal wife for me!'

She probably would, thought Adam, and he sighed inwardly—feeling the pressure of events crowding his mind. He didn't want another quarrel, and his feeling of lassitude and depression increased as he struggled with his conscience. Even his breathing seemed difficult! It had, after all, been his own intention to take Becky back with them, so why not Sarah? Without Becky the past could fade, but with her sister there he would have a constant reminder and he would never be allowed to forget. Suddenly he felt beaten, saying weakly, 'There will only be trouble with George Webster again, and the adverse publicity must spoil our cause. You'll find someone else, son, wait until we get back'. His voice was faint, and sounded as if it was coming from a distance.

'You won't dissuade me!' Luke declared adamantly. 'I have committed myself to Sarah and I intend to keep that promise.'

Adam wanted no trouble with Luke. 'Don't take on so, my boy.' Adam pleaded. Always there was a battle! Somehow he had survived incarceration and deprivation in the past, but with the search last night for Becky and now this discord with Luke, he seemed unable to cope.

Now he felt a pain in his chest, almost like heartburn, a slight giddiness beset him, and he realised that there was something very wrong. 'I don't feel well!' he muttered, tears running down his cheeks. 'Luke—help me!' he gasped gripping the table as he slumped back in his chair. Every breath hurt now, and he could only see Luke and the room around him as if through a grey veil. A face familiar and fresh seemed to come out of the mist and a hand beckoned him, reaching out to help him. Then his head was no longer resting on the back of his chair, but gently and peacefully on the breast of a woman whose face he recognised—she smiled lovingly, at him—it was Fanny.

His eyes were closed as if he were sleeping but he breathed no more. No longer would the winds of fate drive him, or the seas of adversity torture his soul. The tears which he had shed so often over his memories had ceased in Fanny's arms.

Luke stared! He was suddenly bereft of his senses, numbed by shock. He had never experienced death at first hand, and at the realisation that his dear father was dead, he could think of only one place to go.

Fortunately, George was in his office when Luke arrived shortly after midday, and he realised immediately that something dreadful had occurred. Luke had stared helplessly at him, and gasped, 'May I come in Sir? I am alone, completely alone, and I don't know what to do!' George opened the door wider and drew the young man inside, as Luke continued, 'It's my father—he's dead!' and tears started in his eyes, as he slumped down on a convenient stool.

In spite of his misgivings about Adam, George was stunned by the news. 'In Heaven's name, how? When?' The words tumbled out in his confusion.

'This morning!' Luke sounded as though he didn't believe it himself, 'he just simply died!' He fell silent for a moment, then continued as if talking to himself, wondering, 'It was as if he had fought a great battle and then, suddenly, gave up. I came here because he considered you all to be part of his family, in spite of your differences. I know he would have wanted me to tell you myself, but I can't bring myself to tell Becky and Sarah.'

George was at a loss for words. He remembered his own bereavement such a short while before. 'What will you do now?' he finally asked.

'I suppose I will have to raise some money from friends. It will take too long for finance to come from home. After the funeral I presume I will move on as instructed, but I don't have the same heart for it as father did.'

He paused. 'This is not your problem I know, and I'm sorry to have burdened you with it. I suppose I had better leave; there are many things to arrange, and I must write to my mother!'

George stayed him with a hand on his shoulder, 'Look, financially we have some responsibility for your father's affairs and there will be business matters to discuss. I have no quarrel with you, or the dead. Go back and fetch your belongings here, you can't be alone at this time. Henry will take you back to your lodgings and you must stay at Bank House with us. Have you seen the Doctor and undertaker yet?'

Luke nodded slowly. 'Yes, but 'Ratcliffes' say the ground is frozen solid and it may be days before they can dig a grave. I don't think they really want him at the lodging house, either!'

'You can't leave your father there; my parents would not have liked that. I'll have him taken to the house.' He left the office and called out, 'Find Henry, somebody, and send him here immediately!' He returned to find Luke still in an agitated state. 'Is there anything else I can do for you, Luke? I am genuinely sorry about your father. This is something I would not have wished under any circumstances.'

'No, thank you—I'm grateful for all you are doing. Would you tell Sarah and Becky though? I don't feel I can face them at this time.'

George agreed immediately, and had just done so when there was a polite tap at the door, and Henry entered. 'Ah, there you are—come in and close the door.' George glanced at Luke, who had now regained his composure and then gave his attention to his coachman. 'We have had some bad news I'm afraid. Mr Johnson's father has died suddenly and I will be assisting him with the funeral arrangements. So far, my sisters know nothing about this and I don't want you to tell anyone until they've been informed. Later on the coffin will go to Bank House, but in the meantime, take Mr Johnson back to his lodgings for his belongings, and on the way, take a note to Ratcliffe & Co., regarding the funeral arrangements.' Henry turned and went to prepare the gig, and George sat at his desk to pen a note to the undertakers. Sealing it he said, 'That will do, Luke. I will walk to the shop and tell Sarah the bad news, and you can pick me up on your way back to the house. I'll tell Becky as soon as we get back.'

'Thank you', Luke exclaimed. 'This is more than generous of you. I must confess that I am bewildered by it all, and perhaps should not have come here but gone straight to the members of my Church, but they probably wouldn't have the finance to help me, or room to take me in. It was Mrs Sanderson at the lodging house who went for the Doctor and undertaker whilst I watched over my father.' His drawn face reflected the misery he felt.

'There is no need for you to worry on any account,' George reassured him. 'I could not turn my back on you in these circumstances. Just give me a few moments and I'll see you to the gig.'

The black-draped, horse-drawn hearse made its way sombrely down from Bank House and crossed the edge of town before winding along Ecclesall Road to the gates of the General Cemetery. Henry reined in the horses drawing the Webster's carriage which followed behind, and passed through the tall, imposing Doric arch of the lodge gates. Becky stared out over the cold, bleak graveyard, its terraced slopes ascending from the river over which they had just crossed. The catacombs lodged in the terraces stood cold and forbidding.

This was the second time in a year that she had followed such a coffin, twice she had parted with a loved one. She reflected on her mother's recent demise. It was the cruellest thing for Adam to have come so far after so many years to find her dead, crueller too that they should end up barely a mile apart in the cold hard earth.

Slowly the carriages climbed the steep hillside ignoring the Egyptian-style Chapel, for the Latter-day Saints held their Memorial Service earlier in private, leaving only the final farewell and committal for the graveside. George had been prepared to arrange an elaborate cortege, black-plumed horses and all, but the request for sombre simplicity did not offend him.

Climbing down and holding back her tears, Becky placed a hand gently on Luke's arm, and walked with him up to the gaping hole in the ground. There were more mourners than even she had expected for this stranger in a foreign land, but she knew that Adam had been greatly respected amongst his own kind.

It was only after the coffin had been lowered into the cold, unwelcoming earth that she let the tears flow. She had known this man for only a short time, yet so much had transpired since his arrival to bring them close that his death left a strange void in her life.

James Palmer stood back behind the mourners, unnoticed by the party from Bank House, and wondered about this stranger who had possessed the power to disrupt his life so completely. He was unable to suppress the deep feeling of guilt at the animosity he had felt towards the dead man. It had sprung not from their religious discord but from his own suspicions and jealousy.

In freely admitting these faults, James Palmer was forced also to acknowledge his other weaknesses. He was not normally a man to bear a grudge, and for this reason he had forced himself to come today to make peace with the dead. But it was not easy with Becky standing in sorrow beside the grave. He wanted desperately for her to forget the man in the grave and think only of him, and so great was his anguish that he turned and left the graveyard. Although invited, he could no more go back with Elizabeth to Bank House than he could stand the thought of remaining in the town. He was ready to renounce his faith, women and the town forever. The time had come to change his lifestyle completely, and it would be best if this was done in another town far from all who knew him.

His unexpected movement did not go unnoticed by Becky, and although she did not know the reason for his departure she sensed a finality in the gesture.

Several days after the burial, when his grief was beginning to ease, Luke was forced to think long and hard about his immediate future, and set about disposing of those belongings of Adam's which he either did not want or could not carry. He had no idea what mementoes his father carried, and it was with some trepidation that he removed items from his father's carpet bag and placed them on the bed. Other than clothes, most of which were of no use to him, there were a few other items to dispose of. There was a bundle of letters in his mother's handwriting which he destroyed without reading, having no desire to pry into their intimacy. There was, however, another letter in unfamiliar script, the contents of which might have been of some importance, and this he opened.

It was not addressed to his father at all and so he scanned it quickly, gathering that it was from a dying woman. Suddenly he saw names which were familiar to him, and the letter began to take a disturbing twist as he remembered with a start that his father had not always been called Adam Johnson. He read the letter again, this time slowly. The writing wavered before his eyes and all sense of understanding left him. This was yet another of his father's well-kept secrets! He'd had a lover and a bastard child, and that lover had been Sarah's mother, Fanny!

He sat rigid on the bed. The letter was dated six months before he and his father had left America, and it was the letter Becky had brought the day his father had disappeared for hours on end. The truth began to dawn. Rebecca—Becky! She was his half-sister! How did his father dare to have preached with such fervour when his own sins were of such magnitude? Luke struggled with his feeling of incredulous amazement at the whole affair. Chief amongst these was the knowledge that his father had caused so much upheaval and that Sarah might be a blood relation! But, no! She couldn't be another half-sister, his father hadn't returned after Becky's birth.

Why had his father kept such a damning letter, when one day someone would surely discover it? Did Becky know the truth? He must burn it, destroy forever the evidence that could spoil all their lives. There were so many unanswered questions that the pressure of it all made him dizzy.

He was so deeply engrossed in his thoughts that he did not hear Becky approach and it was only when she tapped on the door and entered that he remembered that he had asked her to come up. He started, endeavouring to collect his thoughts and conceal the letter at the same time.

He was ashen-faced and obviously disturbed. 'What on earth is the matter, Luke? You look as though you have seen a ghost!' She was deeply concerned for him, and puzzled by his frantic effort to hide the paper in his hand.

He seemed incapable of answering and without thinking she limped forward, reaching out as she did so. He pulled back but not before she recognised the handwriting. 'Is that Mother's letter?' she demanded. 'The one which I gave Adam in the summer?'

Luke made to fold the sheets of paper, answering sheepishly as he did so. 'Yes! I wasn't sure whether to throw it away or not!' He indicated the mound of ashes in the grate. 'I burned mother's without reading them but I didn't know who this was from!' His face was red and his eyes were evasive. Even as a child he had never been able to lie without looking guilty.

'You read it?' Becky asked, cautiously. 'Then within those pages you will have discovered something which surprised you?' She did not want to put words in his mouth that were not in the letter.

'Yes!' he confessed.

'That mother and Adam had been in love!'

'No! I mean, yes!' The confusion in his face puzzled her and she made to take the letter from his hand. 'No!' he protested, but in vain.

'You should not have read it! I never asked your father what was in it, although I know the sad story of him and mother, but I considered it to be private.'

Stammering, Luke endeavoured to explain. 'It wasn't addressed to my father, and before destroying it I thought it best to check on its importance. It was addressed to John Andrews, a name I have only heard twice before and its significance was lost on me until I read it.' He was endeavouring to cover his tracks and prevent her from reading the letter too. 'Yes, I gather they were in love. Now, may I have the letter back, please. I will destroy it!'

'I'm not sure Luke, whether I can trust you to do that. The letter is half mine anyway so why should you have it?' She handled the letter fondly, remembering Adam's story. Poor Adam! 'I would like to keep it rather than let it be destroyed, and you mustn't take it home with you in case your mother finds it!'

Confusion reigned in Luke's mind. Should he tell her the truth, or hope that she would never read it? He took too long in deciding and Becky took his hesitation as a sign of consent. She took and replaced the letter in the envelope. 'I will keep it safe, Luke, you can rest assured of that! Now, have you sorted out everything that you can't wear? The things which don't fit will be a blessing to someone in need.'

There was no way he could demand the letter back without arousing suspicions. However, he knew that if ever Becky read it there would be an almighty uproar. His father's name would be sullied and he would probably lose Sarah. Somehow he had to get it back and burn it! Without further protest he gave Becky the clothes and resolved to retrieve the letter and destroy it before he left the house. Any day now he would have to leave; his transfer could not be postponed indefinitely, and he could not work knowing that on his return he might be barred from seeing Sarah. He had to work quickly.

Opportunities were few and far between, for he was never left completely alone in the house. Servants came and went constantly, and in the end he despaired of ever being able to slip into Becky's room unobserved. He was convinced that she had not yet read the letter, nevertheless he was becoming very anxious. It was only when she returned to the shop, the day before he was due to leave, that an opportunity occurred.

He stood behind his bedroom door, watching and waiting. There was no sound from below except the clatter of kitchen utensils, so he made his way along the landing, all his senses constantly alert, until he reached her door. Taking care to make no sound he turned the knob and breathed a sigh of relief as the door opened freely at his touch. Where was he to start? There were so many places in the well-furnished room where a letter could be concealed and although he had to do it he had no heart to pry. He tried the obvious writing desk, to no avail, before opening the small drawers of the side-table, with similar results.

Taking care to be as quiet as possible he pulled open the top drawer of the heavy commode, and found amongst the silks and laces a small rosewood box, large enough to hold that which he sought. There was no lock on the box and to his relief, there the letter sat. He took it quickly and replaced the box in the drawer.

'I'll take that! If you don't mind!'

Luke spun round to face the door.

'What the devil of a cheek!' George fumed. 'I never had you down for a thief, Luke! A fool maybe, but never a thief!' He moved forward and motioned to Luke's hand. 'I'll have that, now!'

In spite of Luke's gentleness of spirit he was in no mood to be beaten. He stood firm, so much depended on it! 'This is between Becky and me and I will not return it, least of all to you!'

'The devil you will!' George was furious now. 'I'll take it from you by force if I have to!'

They faced each other with angry determination and it was only when Luke made a sudden bolt for the door that George sprang to life with equal speed, grabbing Luke's coat in an effort to stop him. As the two men stumbled to the floor, Luke knew that he had to win. He needed a chance to get away and hide the letter, he was not concerned for his own safety. Becky would confirm that the letter was his father's anyway, and once destroyed would harm no-one.

He had, however, reckoned without George's agility, and struggle as he might he could not better his opponent as they twisted and writhed on the bedroom floor. One moment it would seem that he had George pinned down flat and in the next he found himself trapped in similar fashion. Luke once scrambled free, only to find his legs gripped again by iron strong hands. Together they smashed themselves with an almighty thud against the wash stand, knocking it over with a deafening crash which echoed through the house, its jug and bowl shattered. Luke lashed out with his fist but George out-manoeuvred him, catching his opponent's wrist in mid-flight.

Two strong arms seized Luke firmly from behind as Henry came to the aid of his young master, and the fight ceased immediately.

'Thanks, Henry!' George panted, 'What took you so long? I should have thought you could have heard the row for miles!'

'I couldn't believe my ears at first, Sir! It's not something you'd expect in this house, if I might say so.' Luke had now ceased to struggle. 'Shall I fetch the constable, Sir?' Henry asked.

Recovering the letter from the floor and endeavouring to tidy up his apparel, George shook his head. 'That won't be necessary, Henry, he's leaving in the morning, and besides, I have what I want! Lock him in here until I decide what to do!' George strode from the room followed in quick succession by Henry who quickly turned the key in the lock and followed his employer down the stairs. 'It's time for you to fetch my sister back from the shops, Henry!' George reminded him before entering the study.

Once left alone, Luke had to admit defeat. There was little point in trying to escape now, the damage was done. He looked around Becky's devastated room and set about trying to put to rights the damage, but the shattered water jug and bowl could not be restored.

The silver-handled paper knife lay balanced between the fingers of George's right hand, poised to break open the seal which Becky had placed on the letter after retrieving it from Luke. He hesitated, loathing himself for the humiliating way he had been forced to writhe and wrestle like a ruffian on the floor of his own home. Now he was about to pry into someone else's letter! Had it not been sealed he would have already done so, but this had made him pause long enough to weigh his action against his conscience.

The letter was as much a puzzle to him as was his own and Luke's behaviour, being addressed as it was to 'John Andrews'. It hadn't even been sent to either Becky or Luke, yet the handwriting was somehow familiar and although rather indistinct, it could almost have been that of his mother. What had prompted Luke to protect the letter so valiantly from seizure, George wondered? He did not appear to have taken anything else from the room, and for that matter, why was the letter in Becky's room in the first place?

George fidgeted irritably with the letter for some time while he wrestled with his thoughts. He was after all only human, and beset by curiosity.

Concluding that it would do no harm to allow Luke to brood and worry in the locked bedroom for a while longer, he left him there, and placed the letter unopened in a book.

Henry was both silent and broody as he drove Becky back to the house. His reluctance to chat or be drawn into conversation quite amused her as previously she had only seen him in this mood when he had been involved in a dispute with George. However, she sensed by his erratic driving that whatever it was must be of great moment. Perhaps he was afraid to speak out for fear of saying too much?

George met her in the hallway, took her cloak and led her into the study. 'Something has happened,' he began seriously.

'I'm not at all surprised,' Becky broke in, 'Henry's odd behaviour on the way back was rather obvious. What on earth is wrong?' Nothing would surprise her any more, she mused.

'I slipped back this afternoon to fetch something, and found Luke in your bedroom...'

'What!' Becky cried in astonishment.

'I found him there, stealing from your top drawer!' He paused, observing her closely. 'He took a letter and refused to hand it back. To cut a long story short, Sis, we had a fight. He's still locked up in there!'

'Locked up?' Becky couldn't believe what she was hearing! Everything was happening so quickly that she was not entirely sure that she understood it. 'But why, if the letter was so important to him didn't he just ask for it? He said that he was going to throw it away and I couldn't bear to see him do that...' Immediately, she realised her error in saying this; she had put too much importance on its existence.

A look of annoyance crossed George's face, 'Why? Why is it so important? It looks almost like mother's writing!'

'It is!' Her voice was hesitant, 'Mother wrote it before she died and asked that if ever John Andrews returned, I was to give it to him, if he did not, then I was to burn it. It was in Adam's possession and Luke was going to get rid of it!'

'Do you know what's in it?'

She hesitated before answering, but could tell that half-truths would not do. There was no point in lying any more and as gently as she knew how, she told him. 'Perhaps you should know, Adam and mother were once in love, when they were young. They were wrenched apart when he was transported to New South Wales. Father was their friend and he took care of mother.'

George stood, staring at her as if in a dream, his features disturbed with changing and conflicting emotions which left him speechless.

'He never did anyone any harm!' Becky cried. 'If you had heard his story you would not have been so antagonistic towards him. He did not come back for mother, he was sent here by the Elders of his Church to do a job of work. He could hardly refuse on the grounds that he once had a girl-friend here. He knew she had married, but not to whom. Had he not returned, then I would have eventually destroyed the letter. Yesterday I found Luke burning Adam's letters from his wife, but he had found our mother's amongst other papers. He had no idea who it was from and it could have been important, so he read it!' George remained silent. 'He did look rather sheepish at the time but I put it down to the fact that I had surprised him. He probably felt guilty at reading it, and its contents must have been a shock for him too. I told him that I already knew that they had been in love.'

Suddenly, George came to life. 'Perhaps there was something in it about the money and he didn't want us to know. It may even nullify the will. I think we should read it.'

Becky could see her mother now, sick and pleading with her to keep the letter a secret! 'Mother didn't want anyone else to see it.'

'Well, if Luke has read it and it is so important, then I think we have a right to see it as well.' He lifted the paper knife once more and prised the seal from the envelope. Having done so he proceeded to extract the letter and attempted to read it.

'No!' Becky protested, but it was too late. In any case George wasn't even listening. She followed the movement of his eyes as they swept from line to line, and again as he re-read the letter. He seemed to forget her presence and when, finally, he lifted his eyes to hers his face was pale and drawn with pain, whilst his mouth formed words which he could not utter.

Finally he cleared his throat and muttered, 'I think, Sis, that you had better read this!'

Whatever he had seen had both shocked and humbled him. He was neither angry nor reproachful, but somehow resigned, and Becky thought she saw tears in his eyes.

Her hand trembled as she took the letter, aware that he was embarrassed as he turned away and rested his hands firmly on the back of the chair.

What more was there to know? The trembling of her hand increased the more she read, until in the end her vision was obscured by her tears. Still no word came from George as he stood, statue-like, looking straight ahead at books which he did not see.

Stumbling towards the nearest chair, Becky sank onto it with a heavy heart and deep distress in her mind. Adam had known all along that he was her father, yet he had never given her the slightest hint. There had been such pain in his eyes when he spoke of her mother, that she had wanted to hold him, and comfort him. It had been a strange love that she had felt for him, and she had felt guilty, as though it were wrong, but there had been a bond drawing them together all this time, though she had not known what it was. Her heart beat faster, he had not told her when he could so easily have defended himself by telling her the truth. She raised her eyes helplessly to George, 'What shall I do, George?' she pleaded sadly.

He turned. 'I can't believe it either, Sis. If it wasn't in mother's handwriting I would say it was all abominable lies, but it is as if she was telling us herself. Did Adam, did he never hint at this at all?'

Her head was heavy, her eyes misty, and in a voice hardly louder than a whisper she cried, 'Never once! Oh, why didn't he tell us before it was too late?'

'Perhaps he had no intentions of doing so. Weren't they leaving last week?'

'Yes, they were!' For a time they both fell silent, deeply engrossed in private thought, stunned by the revelation.

Finally, George broke the silence, his face calm and his voice under control. 'Don't you mind? What about our father?'

'He will always be my father too! I knew the whole sad story, except my part in it, and had begun to see the tragedy like a romantic tragedy. They all loved each other, all three of them, and father obviously knew about me, yet he loved me very much. I would rather have two fathers than none as it is now.'

'So that's why you were born at Pilling, and not here in town!' George conceded. 'There always did seem to be a mystery about it all.'

The slow light of understanding flickered across her face. 'There is yet more to it than you know. When I went to Pilling before Christmas there was a child in the grave with aunt Meg. It seems I had a twin who died when he was only a day old, they called him John Andrews Webster. I thought it was a mistake on the part of the stonemason, adding an 's' to Andrew, but when I checked the register there was an 's' there too. It puzzled me until now—they must have called him after Adam and father must not have minded!'

'God, what a mess! And Luke. Oh, no! He's still locked up in your bedroom.'

Becky broke in, 'Whatever shall we tell Sarah, George?'

He smiled sympathetically, 'Nothing of course!' He sighed, 'but it does make you wonder what life is all about—with all this trouble and sorrow. I suppose I had better go and fetch Luke and apologise to him. I think I misjudged him, he may only have been trying to stop you seeing the contents of the letter'.

The letter was still in her hand when he left. She re-read it slowly, wondering just how different things would have been but for the misfortune in Adam's life. Poor Adam! She would always think of him as that, he had remained so loyal. Perhaps it was a blessing that he had returned at the end, when mother was dead. And Luke, who was a pawn in someone else's game, he was her half-brother and no doubt as staggered as they were. Her heart was big enough to accept him and Adam, but Gervase would remain the loving father he had always been in her eyes. It had been he who had played for hours with her, taught her to read, and told her the names of all the flowers which she still picked on her walks. He had been so big and yet so gentle, and obviously deeply in love with mother and she with him. They had been happy, so complete as a family and now, sadly, they were gone. She fought back tears of sorrow as she heard movement and voices coming from the hall.

They were the quiet, orderly sounds of men in earnest conversation, and this gave her comfort. Luke entered the room first, and looked nervous and subdued as he sought her eyes. 'I would have avoided this mess if I had been able to destroy the letter,' he said, and was full of apology. 'I knew nothing about this, I swear.'

As Becky looked at the troubled young man who was now her half-brother she could only pity him. He stood awkwardly as though out of place. 'Oh, Luke!' she cried, 'I should have guessed it. It is not your fault, and after all it is perhaps as well that your father didn't tell us. Have you told anyone else?'

'No, I couldn't do that. In fact my dearest wish is that my mother never finds out.'

'I wonder,' George observed, 'do we need to let it go beyond these four walls? You, Luke, inherit your father's share in our firm, so what is to be gained from dragging up the past and giving the ears of this town a field day? Let it be our secret, what do you both say, shall we burn the letter?'

Luke's face brightened with relief and surprise. 'I would appreciate that more than anything. But Sarah—what about her?'

It was Becky who spoke up; she had been immersed in her own thoughts. 'She is happy enough as she is, so don't spoil her innocence, it will achieve nothing. Leave her with her memories intact, and then there will be less chance of an accidental disclosure of this affair later on.' Perhaps she ought to do Luke a favour and save him more embarrassment. 'There is something, George, about Sarah which I think you ought to know!'

'That she wants to marry Luke and go away!' George interrupted. 'Do you think I haven't guessed as much already? For months now I have seen my family disintegrate before my eyes and I knew this was likely. I feared that you would go too.'

She took the letter and crossed to the fire, placed the letter into its flames and said, 'It is best this way'. They watched the greedy flames devour the only evidence of her mother's secret. 'Where is Sarah, anyway?' Becky asked.

'She has gone home with Elizabeth Palmer,' George recalled casually, remembering the news. 'I forgot to tell you. Elizabeth came to tell us that they are moving. James Palmer has taken a job back in Lincolnshire.'

Had she heard correctly? She stood still, astounded by his words. Her hand clasped the brooch at her neck and she fought to control its shaking, as this would expose her true feelings, and she hurried from the room to escape prying eyes. She lay on her bed, incapable of clear thought, her mind and body exhausted by the speed of events which the day had thrust upon her.

How long she remained there she did not know, and it was only the sound of distant church bells which finally awoke her. Had she slept all night, fully clothed? Yet someone had covered her against the chilly night, and pulled the heavy curtains too.

The day ahead held no joy for her. Adam was gone! She had been denied the chance to tell him that she cared for him, he who was her father. But it was the face of James Palmer which haunted her most, for with his departure she was bereft of all comfort. It was true, she knew it now! She had come to enjoy challenging him because he saw her as an equal, worth having a discussion with. She had given him a hard time, that much she acknowledged. So much had transpired since Elizabeth had shooed him from her sick-room and she had waited, half expecting him to call again. There had been, in those few moments with him, a realisation of all her longings, but he had not returned, made no effort to communicate, and now he was going away. She did not want him to go, and that fleeting glimpse of him at the graveside had given her no clue as to his present feelings for her. What right had she to stop him? She had spurned him enough! She would never know if Elizabeth's assessment of his true personality were correct; she had never really given him a chance to show it.

Rising from the bed she caught a glimpse of herself in the mirror, and was further dismayed. She was dishevelled, her hair a mess, but she had no heart to improve the image. As she sat back on the edge of the bed she closed her eyes. He had kissed the pale lips which she had just seen in the glass, and done it so tenderly before Elizabeth's arrival had sent him scurrying to the window. Now more than ever she needed his touch, his gentleness and protection, and knew that only she could make the effort to make him stay. She would have to go to him. If he rejected her then he condemned her to a life of loneliness, for what she felt for him she could never hope to feel for someone else. A barren existence stretched out before her, empty and useless, and that she could not bear. If she could not have him then she would go with Sarah and Luke, to help them build Zion in that far-away land.

She rose again. The water jug and bowl were not hers but were neatly prepared for her. It was only a small change but then everything around her was changing with such speed that she was in danger of becoming lost forever. She needed James Palmer far more than she dared admit, and for once in her life she would have to beg for what she wanted.

On the pretext of a visit to Elizabeth, Becky approached her house with more than a little trepidation. There was no reason to suppose that James Palmer was at home but she had to find out from his sister what was happening.

The echo from the heavy brass knocker rang through the house and she knew that it was impossible for anyone inside not to hear it. She knocked again, with less enthusiasm this time, her heart sinking with disappointment. She had no knowledge of where he worked, other than the fact he was an assistant master at some school or other, his office of Minister being only a part time post.

Having left home after George had gone out, and after Sarah and Luke had happily volunteered to mind the shop, Becky had no opportunity to talk to anyone about her problems. As it was only a five minute walk back to the firm from the Palmer's house she retraced her steps and entered the yard.

'Mawnin, Miss! Mesta George's int' office,' a voice called out from behind a dray.

His welcoming, 'Come in, Sis,' gladdened her, for he was more like the old George again. 'Any better now?'

She smiled weakly, 'Am I still a sister to you, George?'

Sensing her insecurity he closed the door. 'Little pigs and all that!' he winked. 'Of course you are! We are all linked together and I've been thinking how proud I am to have had a father with such broadness of mind and strength of character. How can I want to change that which he found so easy to accept? We've seen a side of him which most of the world did not, and I love him the more because of it.'

'Thank you,' she murmured.

'What are you doing here anyway? I left instructions that you were not to be disturbed.'

'I went to see Elizabeth Palmer.' Her voice trembled at the lie.

It was George who smiled this time. 'And not, I suppose, to see that brother of hers!' He chuckled at her surprised reaction. 'Give me credit, Becky! You must think I'm blind. Isn't it time you both came to your senses and stopped fighting each other? I gathered by the look on your face last night when I told you he was leaving that something was afoot.'

'You don't think he's left already, do you?'

'No! You don't get another teaching post that quickly, unless you are desperate. Is he that unsettled do you think?' There was a challenge in George's question.

She refused to be drawn, however, and asked, 'Where does he work? I've never asked, I only know that he teaches'.

'Huh! Nowhere marvellous, he dedicates himself to that dreadful charity school up on Peacroft. He could do better, but he's devoted to the poor wretches!' Then he admonished her, 'You've got him all wrong you know!'

Ignoring this last remark, Becky picked up her purse and muff, then turned to leave, 'I suppose I had better try again later. Thank you for taking care of me last night, and for understanding Luke's actions. People do not always know what to do for the best when they've had an experience such as he had. I'm pleased that he has decided not to leave just yet. Maybe now, things will settle down again'.

It was not really acceptable behaviour to call at his school, yet she had a strange desire to see what kind of place it was that could persuade a man such as he, to devote his life to its cause. Her curiosity was too powerful to be restrained, so Becky made a diversion from her usual route to the shop, where Sarah was waiting to be relieved. Twenty minutes delay would hardly be considered excessive after the turmoil of the past ten days.

Peacroft stood high on the hill overlooking the broad valley of the River Don, and was surrounded on all sides by a rabbit warren of tiny, crumbling houses, rented by only the poorest inhabitants of the town. Never before had she walked along these drab, dirty streets where so many Irish immigrants fought to survive their poverty and the cold. It was a far cry from the glorious and proud setting of Bank House, and Becky was relieved that her subdued mourning clothes concealed, to some degree, the evidence of her own comfortable existence. She felt disturbed and anxious in the midst of such deprivation.

It took longer to reach the school than she had calculated, so that by the time she reached the top of the narrow street ten minutes had elapsed and she was quite out of breath. She was also beginning to wonder at the wisdom of her action, for such impulses on her part had been rare until recently, which led her to suspect that she may previously have been a rather dull creature.

On seeing the low ancient structure which housed the school, she was dismayed and saddened by its obvious decay. It had once been a proud building, but the cracked and broken masonry led her to think that it would not withstand the battering of many more harsh winters, nor would the many boarded-up windows succeed in keeping out the cold. There were several holes in the roof where the heavy stone tiles had fallen and slipped down to the moss and weeds in the guttering below.

Not a place to encourage great learning she thought, but its merit was in its provision of an opportunity for poor children to receive hope and encouragement in the depths of their poverty. She had thought James Palmer a proud and arrogant man, but what vain scholar would condescend to work under these conditions for small reward?

She could hear from within the building the murmur of children's voices, and found it impossible to stay outside; she was compelled to enter and discover what drew him through those shabby, battered portals.

The doors were not locked, and opened readily to her touch to reveal, not as she had expected a vestibule with rooms leading off, but a large lofty room which was crammed to overflowing with a multitude of grubby children. She recoiled at the stench of so many unwashed bodies, and coughed helplessly as it caught the back of her throat.

She had not anticipated being directly confronted by a mass of faces either, but it was too late now to withdraw, for they had seen her enter. It seemed that from every corner of the room heads were turning in her direction, glad of the chance to break from routine. They were in groups and circles, some on benches, some on the floor, their faces ranging from the mischievous to the streetwise and cautious. James was nowhere to be seen! She felt a little foolish, an interloper in their midst.

As if resentful of the strangers intrusion, a woman of matronly proportions stood up briskly, warned her group of children to be on their best behaviour and marched towards Becky. James Palmer she said, had

237

gone off to Lincolnshire in rather a hurry and would be back heaven knows when! He had left them short-staffed at a most inconvenient time. 'What!' she declared, 'has come over him of late, I just do not know?'

After apologising profusely for her untimely interruption Becky left, grateful to be out in the fresh air once more, yet she was haunted by the memory of those ragged children with their pale, thin, little faces. Faces and bodies which reflected the appalling and sad conditions of the area in which they lived.

Once again she pondered on the character of James Palmer. What must he have thought of her high-handed and oft-times lofty opinions? She must have appeared as a spoilt child, arrogant in her vantaged position in her peaceful hillside home. Perhaps there had been revenge in his flirtation; a mere act, with which to humble her? How dreadful if that was all it had been to him! Until yesterday she had thought herself to be master of the situation, now she was riddled with doubt. If only Adam were still alive, he would have guided her with his wisdom. Her steps were slow now, having lost their youthful spring, and with despondency she thought of her shameful behaviour towards him.

So much had changed, even the routine of everyday life, for her world no longer ended at the boundary wall of Bank House. Her new religious beliefs and liaisons had broken the insular path that in the past had provided contentment, leaving her restless and disturbed. The daily running of the shop did no more than keep her mind busy, and her evenings and nights were full of loneliness. Had she known that Adam was her father, would she have gone to Zion anyway? She would, of course, never know the true answer. Yet her memory was short, for hadn't her steps been light and springy with optimism only an hour before, when she had sought to dissuade James Palmer from leaving? What a turmoil her mind was in!

What right had she to hold him back? Her beliefs were so very different from his and she could never compromise on hers, for she believed in them entirely. Having reached the Haymarket she had no real desire to enter the shop at all, but she did, and as the hours passed so increased the feeling of despair at the thought of a home without Sarah in the future.

Later, through the long evening which followed, an eerie silence fell over the occupants of Bank House. Sarah and Luke were immersed in a private world of their own, for Luke was going home ahead of Sarah. His passage had already been booked by the Elders and, on hearing the news, Sarah became nearly hysterical. Such was her determined intention to go with him that she threatened to drown herself in the Sheaf if he went alone. Becky doubted if this threat was even possible, for the highest she had ever seen the river rise, in the very worst conditions, was six feet, and normally it was never more than a foot deep. Sarah also feigned the onset of a decline at the thought of being abandoned, but the pretty bloom in her cheeks and the twinkle in her eyes fooled no-one.

'I shall follow the minute you leave!' she finally stated, with such fervour that this was immediately believed by her brother, who had no illusions about the capabilities of his lively sister. George reluctantly ended his protestations; Sarah was to leave with Luke!

Only three days more and she would be left alone in the house with George forever! Becky felt she would be like Elizabeth Palmer, handmaid to a masterful brother. Unable to bear Sarah's triumphant excitement any longer, and having no appetite for the book on which she had tried to concentrate, Becky went to bed. But sleep did not come easily, her thoughts skipped from one problem to another, allowing her no peace. What was she to do without Sarah? George was a handsome devil, maturing with each problem he tackled and it was obvious that he was not going to remain single forever.

She lay tossing and turning, half asleep yet awake, unable to separate dreams from reality, until without realising it, sleep overtook her. It was a fitful sleep where all around was gloomy, and where unknown figures remained beyond her reach. She was plummeting down a steep spiral of unhappiness which deepened the longer she slept. The spiralling ceased and then she was sitting at a large table around which were familiar, loving faces. Amongst them sat old grandmother Sarah, only she didn't seem to be as old as Becky remembered, and her face was wreathed in smiles. There were unfamiliar faces too, and then more prominently, Adam's.

She appeared to be pleading with the figures around the table. 'Please, can I join you?'

One by one they shook their heads. One familiar voice seemed to speak for them all, 'It is not time yet, you have work to do there first!' All heads nodded in unison.

She was being dragged slowly back from them through a mist, but still whispered voices reached her ears from that same table. 'Not humble enough!'

'Too much pride', from another.

'Not been tried and tested', yet another.

Protesting, she was finally surrounded by the damp clammy mist, and the voices receded, to be heard no more.

Waking with a start, Becky shivered. Not from the cold but from the damp sweat which clung to her body and the deep feeling of panic which the dream had caused. The thudding, quickened beat of her heart frightened her, and in spite of the friendly sunshine which poured in through a chink in the curtain, nothing could allay her fears. It was only a dream, but in those dark, vivid moments between sleep and consciousness she had endured terror, the like of which she had not experienced before. In waking she had regained her grip on reality, only to be disappointed by the bleakness of it.

There was no choice, life would continue its wearisome course and she would spend it like so many other women, in a position of servitude. She had been wrong to promise George that she would stay in England. She must go with Sarah and face new challenges, a new way of life. See things about which she had only heard. It was an idea germinated by her panic awakening, but the more she thought about it the better sense it made. It was what Adam would have wanted and she would at least be there to take care of Sarah when she needed love most, in motherhood. There were also half-brothers and sisters to meet, although that secret must always remain her own. With this in mind she rose wearily from the bed, feeling cold now that the feverish dream had subsided, knowing that only the new plan gave her the desire to rise at all.

No one could accuse her of running away, for only she was aware of the accumulation of sorrows which had brought about this momentous decision. Even George must see that things would never be the same again. She was not without means of support and, unlike most of her fellow converts, could return with the certain knowledge that a home and security awaited, even if she was a failure.

As for James Palmer, he had not been back since her convalescence; poor constancy for a would-be suitor which was confirmed by his intention to leave the district.

The suddenness of her decision to leave was a blow to George, but he reluctantly accepted that Becky was far from happy, and recognised the finality in her voice. He agreed not to interfere this time and was, to some degree, relieved by the fact that Sarah would be chaperoned until her marriage to Luke. He would have preferred that she married before leaving but this compromise was at least a little consolation in his disappointment. He agreed to manage and oversee the running of the shop by hiring an assistant for a year, after which time, if Becky did not return, he would dispose of it all and forward the proceeds to America.

Knowing that she would probably never return, Becky spent the next three days in hectic preparation, sorting out her affairs, packing and saying farewell to friends. She deliberately avoided calling upon Elizabeth Palmer in her fear of bumping into James; instead she would write to Elizabeth from Liverpool before the vessel sailed. There were moments of sheer excitement as the two sisters selected suitable items and attire to pack in the two trunks which Becky had purchased for the journey, including a length of beautiful silk from which to make Sarah's wedding dress.

There was an almost frenetic purpose to the physical effort which Becky put into her packing and preparations, aimed at leaving no time for reflection or regrets. It was only in the quiet of her own bedroom that niggling doubts assailed her, and if it were not for the unknown prospects ahead she would have sunk to the depths of despair.

On the day prior to her departure Elizabeth Palmer arrived to inform them that she had heard from her brother, telling her that he thought he might take up an appointment at a school for young gentlemen in the town of Lincoln, and she was to start preparing to move. 'But I don't want to go!' she cried in exasperation.

'I have heard that Lincoln is a beautiful place,' Becky offered consolingly, 'you will find it much more inspiring than Sheffield. Have you heard, I am going with Sarah and Luke to America? We leave for Liverpool at first light tomorrow and sail three days from now!'

'America?' Elizabeth stammered. 'And so soon? She was stunned.

'I am not going to my doom,' Becky laughed at the look on her friend's face. 'And you're going to Lincoln with James, aren't you?'

Elizabeth did not smile in return, but said despondently, 'I had not heard of your decision, I have been so busy. What can I say, other than that I am going to miss you anyway, for you have become my dear friend and I shall be bereft without you. Why have you decided to go?'

'There is nothing left for me here now,' Becky said, 'and I need to go away. I need a challenge in my life and once Sarah goes I will have nothing. Besides, Sarah is so very young and should she become a mother in the new land she would benefit from my being there.' The sad look on Elizabeth's face caused Becky to reflect on her own troubles, and her eyes filled with tears. She opened her arms and the two friends embraced each other in mutual despair. 'I would lose you anyway! We must write to each other of our new experiences,' she said weakly.

Releasing herself and brushing the tears from her eyes, Elizabeth asked, 'But what about the shop? Surely that was a challenge which you still have? It outshines anything I have ever done. I have only looked after and kept house for James. I don't think I could ever leave him entirely—won't you miss your brother?'

'Ah!' Becky thought silently to herself, 'but you are not leaving James, you will have him by your side.' Cautiously she said, 'I think Sarah needs me more than George does. I also feel I am at a cross-roads in my life and need a dramatic change to give me a new sense of purpose!' She sighed deeply. 'I want to get away from all the painful memories, and if Adam had not died I would most likely have gone with him in the end.'

'Becky!' cried Elizabeth, 'He was a married man! That would not have been proper or wise!'

Becky smiled patiently, 'You have been listening to James, and you are both wrong; it was not that kind of love, Elizabeth, but I cannot explain it to you. It was a dream of a future, not here, not now, but forever in eternity. A way of getting closer to the heart of things. Surely you must understand something of the great dream since you met Adam? Sadly, there is little future here for me now!

'Why is it that everyone is so restless these days, always wanting what they cannot have?' Elizabeth complained wistfully.

Becky looked across at her friend fondly. She would have been happy to have had her as a sister, but it was not to be. 'Won't you come to Liverpool with us, Elizabeth?' she begged, 'I should like that. George will bring you back!'

Elizabeth shook her head sadly, 'No, it's not possible. I don't know what James' plans are for moving, but I get the impression that we could move soon, so I must be on hand to pack. Your news is sad enough and going to Liverpool would only prolong the pain of parting. Write to me before you sail, I would think that a true act of friendship, and later once you have settled down. All I can hope is that you find the happiness which eludes you here'. She rose to go, 'James will be disappointed not to have wished you luck, I know that'. Fresh tears rolled unashamedly down her cheeks and she embraced Becky again. 'We shall both miss you!' she cried softly through her tears.

With great restraint Becky controlled her own emotion. 'When does he return?' she asked, aware that she was bitterly disappointed not to have seen James Palmer once more before her departure.

'It should have been yesterday but a letter arrived to say that he would be delayed. I have no idea exactly when he will return, but this will come as a shock to him, I know.'

With a trembling voice Becky whispered, 'Tell him that we never did enjoy that promised game of chess!'

With a heavy heart Becky walked slowly from room to room, savouring for the last time the furnishings which reminded her of her happy girlhood. Each item added a little more pain to the deep well of memory. All was ready, farewells had been said, all that remained was to sleep, for they were to rise at five in order to catch the Liverpool coach. On entering her own room she firmly resolved to think of nothing but the journey ahead and Sarah's obvious happiness.

Chapter 16

By six o'clock next morning the house was ablaze with lights as the feverish activity and preparations for departure drew to a close. Becky watched from a window as the stillness of the dark night gave way to the yellow light of dawn. There was excitement in the air as she watched the world awakening, knowing that beyond, to the west, where sky and earth meet, there was much to see and discover. She could not escape Sarah's lively chirping nor suppress a smile at her sister's childish enthusiasm to be off. As children they had often travelled short distances but never as far as the coast. Now, the thought of seeing at last the great expanse of water upon which they would travel excited even Becky. A small shudder swept over her when she recalled what Adam had said about his prison ship, but things were different in her case and the journey would last a mere twenty-one days at most. He had said that the salty air had cleaned his lungs and the swooping birds been welcome callers on the deck. Her head was filled with eager curiosity to see things about which she had only heard and read, things which she could write about and describe to Elizabeth.

It was chilly in the morning air as Henry stacked the hand luggage in the carriage, their two trunks having been delivered in advance to the coaching inn. 'There is hardly enough room for the ladies and luggage, let alone you men,' he complained, mumbling to himself as he worked. As the last bag was installed he gave up, saying, 'It's no good, you'll never all get in there. Don't you think we had better make two journeys? We could do it if you're quick about it, the coach doesn't leave for another hour yet.'

'Quite right, Henry! We have just time enough to spare. Luke and I will go with the bags and you can return for the ladies.' George strode into the house and called out as he went. 'Luke! Luke! Come on, we're going on ahead, there's not enough room for all of us.' He waited until Luke appeared, 'Henry will come straight back for Sarah and Becky whilst we're loading our bags onto the coach. We'd best make haste or we won't have time. Come on!'

Sarah stood fidgeting excitedly, her cheeks flushed as she watched the carriage rumble from the yard and gather speed along the back lane. Within minutes the carriage had disappeared into the dawn.

Suddenly the stillness was disturbed again by the sound of rumbling wheels coming back along the lane. It was impossible to imagine why

Henry had returned so quickly, and Becky ran to the window and looked out, afraid that something was amiss.

It wasn't Henry at all. 'Who is it?' Sarah called out from behind her.

Shrugging her shoulders, Becky peered out just as the door of the carriage opened. 'It's Elizabeth!' she gasped, 'What on earth is she doing here at this time of the morning?'

'Perhaps to see us off?' Sarah offered.

With Henry absent, Becky hurried to the door to let Elizabeth in. 'You nearly missed us!' she cried, throwing open the door. But Elizabeth was not alone! For a moment Becky stared at the tall figure behind her friend, unable to speak. It was fortunate that Elizabeth chose that moment to explain why she had come.

'I had to come and see you off, and James would not allow me to come alone at this hour.' She clasped Becky to her affectionately. 'I see I have surprised you!'

'No! No! Come in. We don't have much time that is all. Henry is coming back for us. He said he couldn't risk overloading the carriage, so he has taken George and Luke on ahead.' She had now recovered her composure, and stepped to one side to allow Elizabeth to pass through into the hall where Sarah waited impatiently.

This left James Palmer framed within the portals of the door. He made no effort to enter but stood observing her with a quizzical gaze. Becky lowered her eyes. It was their first meeting since the afternoon when he had kissed her, almost three weeks ago, yet he was strangely changed. He did not look well, his features were leaner and his manner most proper. 'Must I remain here in the doorway until you go, Miss Webster?' His voice was quiet and he raised his hat politely.

Something about his tone caught her unawares, 'Oh, please do come in!' It was barely a whisper to hide her embarrassment, 'I didn't think you would be back before we left', she continued weakly.

'Did you hope to leave before I returned, then?' he asked her sadly.

Without realising it, she nodded, admitting more without speaking than she realised. He came forward, forcing her to allow him to pass; she was rooted to the spot, and unable to meet his gaze.

His hand sought hers in a gallant gesture and raised it gently to his lips. 'I shall miss our confrontations, Miss Webster', he murmured, his lips touching her soft skin. She wasn't sure if he was teasing her. He felt her tremble at his touch, whether from fear of him or resentment, he could not tell. He ached to hold her one last time in his arms, but he dare not.

He had left it all too late. On leaving Lincoln he had come to terms with his misery. There had been no solace for him there and he knew that he could not live without her! He had returned, willing to renounce his own beliefs, not for hers, but because he could no longer reconcile them with his own religion. He had been willing to accept her, beliefs and all if she would love him. The bitter blow thrust at him the minute he returned had wiped out all hope. He could not ask her to stay, but he had made an effort for Elizabeth's sake this cold, sad morning to say farewell to his dreams.

Were there tears in those lovely eyes before him? If there were then they would not be for him. Restraining his own misery he let go of her hand and said gravely, 'My dearest wish is for your happiness alone'. With that he moved past her, betraying none of the emotions which were tearing him apart.

She could not bear to follow the tall, proud figure striding across the hall; instead she sat listlessly on the settle and prayed that Henry would hurry back.

James Palmer remained out of sight until Henry returned, then, as the two sisters stood before the carriage, he gently but firmly held Sarah in farewell. He embraced Becky too. Throwing caution to the wind he caught her to him fiercely, brushing her cheek with his lips before drawing back. His face was gaunt, his body trembled, yet he could not speak, for the power to do so had left him. He raised his hand feebly as the carriage rolled down the lane and stood watching, with an aching heart, knowing that no miracle would relieve him of his emptiness.

On reaching Liverpool, and with a day to spare, George hired a carriage to drive out some distance beyond the docks and along towards the dunes. Never in all Becky's wildest imaginings had she thought the sea would be so beautiful, stretching out endlessly to the horizon. In spite of the odd shower of rain, there were moments when shafts of sunlight streamed down onto the water as if pointing down from heaven, forming a backcloth such as she had seen only at the theatre. Ships waiting to enter port moved up and down gently in the quickening breezes and she recalled Adam's words. She could taste the salt for herself, feel the spray on her face, hear the gulls screeching overhead. This feeling of being at one with nature brought her closer than she had ever been to Adam, even when he was alive.

Could they who had gone before into the next world see her now, and know her feelings? Adam had never wanted to cross these oceans yet he had sailed them more times than she ever would. He had sailed away from her mother in despair, without choice, whereas she could decide her own future. She brushed back the strands of hair which had been plucked by the wind from the chignon which she wore. Why? Why was she going?

Suddenly, instinctively, she released the tortoiseshell combs and allowed her soft, rich hair to fly free in the wind. She shook her head.

Could she hear voices, low and sweet in the breeze? She was alive, aware of herself as never before, and yet mingled with the exhilaration was a powerful longing, swelling up from within her breast. She needed to be alone to savour the savagery of the elements. Glancing sideways she became aware that George was watching her closely, his face perplexed and showing signs of disquiet. She smiled at him reassuringly, then squeezed his arm before walking away through the dunes towards the sea.

Once alone she scoured the clouds and waves as if searching for hidden faces. Now, she was running wildly against the wind, free from cares, over the rippled sand and between rivulets of seawater until, breathless, she sat on a tuft of rough seagrass and looked out over the water.

Bending she dug deep into the sand with her fingers; coarse and damp, it clung to her skin, then as it dried she let it trickle back down onto the beach. She sat still, her gaze distant, savouring the peace and solitude. Gone now were the burdens and cares of the past twelve months, for whatever the future held in store for her she would always treasure these moments of pure delight.

'Penny for them, Sis!' George's voice finally broke her reverie. 'No regrets?' he asked, as he approached, helping her to her feet.

She did not answer, but took his arm, her decision was irrevocable. As they strolled back towards Sarah and Luke, she replied, 'I have no regrets at all!' Her voice was lighter and filled with a spirit which had evaded her for so long. Her steps now had a spring in them, almost a gaiety, which stemmed from a deep belief in what lay ahead for her. Gone from her face was the pallor of the past weeks and in its place a delicate, rosy hue touched her cheeks. The sailing ships appeared to have caught her mood and nodded in approval as they danced in the sun, matching the buoyancy of her thoughts.

George coughed self-consciously, aware that she did not see him but some distant dream. 'I'm happy for you, whatever you choose to do!' He placed his arm around her waist playfully. 'Am I forgiven for all the troubles I've caused?' he pleaded earnestly.

With a soft and loving voice she said, 'What troubles, George?' But he could tell by the twinkle in her eye that he was forgiven.

The heavily-laden boat began to pull away from the quayside, and Becky watched Sarah's face as she waved from the comfort of Luke's arms. The happiness she saw there told her that the tears on her cheeks were only a temporary thing. Sarah had that youthful spirit which was invaluable in a changing world.

Slowly the silver stretch of water separating land and boat widened. Becky dried her own eyes and turned. It would be many years, if ever, before they would return to these shores. Drawing her cloak protectively closer she walked away, sure of the wisdom of her decision.

Taking one last look at the horizon Becky walked back to the carriage and climbed in. 'Let's go,' she said calmly, 'they will be happy enough!'

'And you, Sis, what of you? Something must have caused you to change your mind, dare I ask what it was?'

She smiled, a happy, knowing smile. Her hand lay hidden beneath her cloak, tenderly clutching the small piece of paper which James Palmer had thrust into her hand with such desperation, after he had seized her so fiercely on their parting.

'I'm going home to marry James Palmer!' she announced proudly.

The words on the paper were simple, and read, 'If you love me—don't go!'

With those words singing in her heart she lay back and watched as the masts of the vessels anchored in the harbour disappeared from sight. She was content, she was going home.

One day, perhaps, she would tell James all about Adam.